THE GEORGE GUND FOUNDATION
IMPRINT IN AFRICAN AMERICAN STUDIES

The George Gund Foundation has endowed
this imprint to advance understanding of
the history, culture, and current issues
of African Americans.

The publisher gratefully acknowledges the generous support
of the African American Studies Endowment Fund
of the University of California Press Foundation,
which was established by a major gift from the
George Gund Foundation.

THE CHOSEN ONES

GENDER AND JUSTICE

Edited by Claire M. Renzetti

This University of California Press series explores how the experiences of offending, victimization, and justice are profoundly influenced by the intersections of gender with other markers of social location. Cross-cultural and comparative, series volumes publish the best new scholarship that seeks to challenge assumptions, highlight inequalities, and transform practice and policy.

The Chosen Ones

Black Men and the Politics of Redemption

NIKKI JONES

UNIVERSITY OF CALIFORNIA PRESS

University of California Press, one of the most distinguished university presses in the United States, enriches lives around the world by advancing scholarship in the humanities, social sciences, and natural sciences. Its activities are supported by the UC Press Foundation and by philanthropic contributions from individuals and institutions. For more information, visit www.ucpress.edu.

University of California Press
Oakland, California

Library of Congress Cataloging-in-Publication Data

Names: Jones, Nikki, 1975– author.
Title: The chosen ones : black men and the politics of redemption / Nikki Jones.
Description: Oakland, California : University of California Press, [2018] | Includes bibliographical references and index. |
Identifiers: LCCN 2017056077 (print) | LCCN 2017058967 (ebook) | ISBN 978-0-520-96331-3 (epub) | ISBN 978-0-520-28834-8 (cloth : alk. paper) | ISBN 978-0-520-28835-5 (pbk. : alk. paper)
Subjects: LCSH: African American men—California—Fillmore—Social conditions—21st century—Case studies. | Police-community relations—California—Fillmore—History—21st century. | African American men—California—Fillmore—Conduct of life.
Classification: LCC E185.86 (ebook) | LCC E185.86 .J664 2018 (print) | DDC 305.38/896073079492—dc23
LC record available at https://lccn.loc.gov/2017056077

Manufactured in the United States of America

26 25 24 23 22 21 20 19 18
10 9 8 7 6 5 4 3 2 1

*With gratitude for the stories shared
and hope for our future*

Contents

Preface

"Don't pack heat, pack your feet!"

I am standing in a crowd of dozens on a small grassy area adjacent to a community center that was once known to residents of San Francisco's Fillmore neighborhood as the city's "Black City Hall." The Reverend Jesse Jackson stands tall on a raised stage as he calls out to the onlookers gazing up at him from the lawn. In his trademark way, he calls on the audience to repeat his rhyme, and they abide his call.

"Don't pack heat!" he calls out.

The crowd echoes the phrase back to him.

"Pack your feet!" he says in a commanding tone.

"Pack your feet!" the crowd replies in unison.

Jackson is in the Fillmore to talk about gun violence, a topic of concern for all in attendance. He offers this phrase up as a strategy for young men who are the frequent victims of gun violence in the city. He tells the crowd that a young man once told him that he could not walk about freely in his city without "packing heat" for fear that he would be at a loss if trouble erupted. The Reverend shares with the crowd what he shared with the young man: "If there is going to be trouble if you go *that* way—then *go another way!*"

"Don't pack heat," he says, "pack your feet!"

Jackson engages the audience in this call-and-response several times before announcing his campaign to shut down gun shops across the country. He calls for new legislation that would make it more difficult to hide the origins of guns that are involved in killings. He calls for a renewal of the ban on assault weapons that expired under the administration of President George W. Bush. He encourages the crowd to look beyond the local to national politics. He also tells the largely Black crowd to "look beyond race." Gun violence is "not just a San Francisco issue," he says, and "not just a Black issue." Yet the reason for the rally is a recent episode of gun violence that was especially shocking even for those Black San Franciscans who have grown accustomed to reports of shootings and killings in the city.

The anti-violence rally is now a routine response to episodes of gun violence in many cities across the country. Today's rally was organized by one of San Francisco's most prominent Black preachers, the Reverend Amos Brown, pastor of Third Baptist Church and president of the local branch of the National Association for the Advancement of Colored People (NAACP). These rallies typically feature a series of speakers, including the family members of victims of violence and prominent preachers or politicians. This weekend's rally includes a call to the city to do more about gun violence in the city's Black neighborhoods, a call that is especially urgent following four homicides the previous weekend.

As I mill through the crowd, I bump into people who carry these stories of violence with them. One man who looks to be in his fifties tells me about a son he lost to street violence several years ago. He laments young men's lack of freedom and mobility in the city. He tells me that he knows a guy who can't leave his place because people are looking for him. I talk to another person, a twenty-five-year-old woman working as a receptionist in the area, who tells me that a recent shooting took place in the daytime, right outside a church. She grew up in the neighborhood and tells me that the violence is getting worse. It has lost its predictability in some ways. She tells me that, when she was growing up, the shootings often took place at night and in certain places. If you wanted to avoid the threat of violence, "you knew not to go out at night," she says, but now the violence is happening in the daytime, which makes it harder to avoid.

As audience members were waiting for Jesse Jackson to arrive, the Reverend Brown took to the stage to introduce members of a support group for those mourning family members lost to street violence. The group includes mothers, fathers, and family members of young people, mostly young Black men and boys, who have been murdered, most often by other Black men and boys. T-shirts memorialize the murdered young men, typically including their portrait or a collage. Graffiti-style lettering reads "RIP," along with the dates of birth and death. The latter typically indicates short lives. One mother points across the street and says that her son was killed *right there* three years ago, leaving behind two baby boys. As she addresses the group, the woman turns to a refrain that I will hear again and again over my time in the neighborhood. It is a refrain that places the problem of gun violence squarely on the shoulders of Black men who have failed to be real men and Black women who have failed to support them.

"We need the men in this community to stand up," she says. "And the women," she adds, "we need the women to support the men in the community."

A father who lost a son to violence shares a belief that contradicts Jackson's color-blind appeal for enacting tougher gun legislation. If these homicides were happening anywhere else in San Francisco—if they were happening up the hill on Fillmore, which is much Whiter and wealthier than the neighborhood surrounding the community center—then there would be a lot more people concerned about gun violence in the city, he tells the crowd.

As I chat with members of the crowd and listen to each speaker that takes the stage, I am struck by how central young Black men are to each person's story, and yet how few young Black men are actually in attendance at the rally. I notice the presence of Black teenage girls, but I observe no more than a handful of young Black men in their teens or early twenties among the crowd. A newspaper article published the next day draws attention to one young man who attended the rally with his mother. The two live in an outer suburb of the city called the Sunset District, a place that feels like a world apart from the Western Addition. The reporter writes that the young man was "hesitant to attend the rally because violence has become so widespread in the Western Addition." His statement provides some clues to why there are so few young Black men in the crowd: "Now it's like if you stop on the wrong block, you'll die."

The lack of young men in the audience also reflects a series of divisions that are rooted in generational, moral, and class-based divides within the Black community; such divisions influence the Black political scene in the city as well. The men who are in attendance appear to be members of the pastor's cohort: Black men in their sixties or older who may be attending the rally at their pastor's behest. Like other older, longtime residents of the Fillmore, they often recall a neighborhood that had a strong sense of community but was destroyed by urban renewal. Also in attendance is a solid group of seemingly middle-aged, working-class members of the community who are likely concerned, as are working-class families elsewhere, with providing a decent place for themselves and their children to live. Then there are those who are not in attendance: the residents of the housing projects like the one adjacent to the community center. In the minds of many, the young men who live in a handful of such projects in the neighborhood, and their families, are the symptom and source of the seemingly senseless violence that has brought the attendees to the lawn on this weekend day. This group's absence is illustrated by a pastor's loud call from the stage directed at the walls of the nearby housing projects.

"Come out!" he yells into the microphone, as the audience turns toward the housing projects behind them.

It is not entirely clear from the tone of his voice whether this is an invitation or an accusation.

In the decade that has passed since this rally, the politics of inner-city violence and violence prevention have shifted in dramatic ways. Just a few months after this rally, Barack Obama would be elected as the nation's first Black president, ushering in a historic commitment to criminal justice reform. Over the next eight years, efforts to dismantle the infrastructure of mass incarceration would take hold at the federal, state, and local levels. Hand-in-hand with the president's support for reform went an unprecedented commitment, through Obama's My Brother's Keeper initiative, to reach out to the young men and boys whom the pastor seemed to be calling on that day in the Fillmore. In the waning years of his two-term presidency, Obama, along with Attorneys General Eric Holder and Loretta Lynch, would provide leadership in efforts to hold law enforcement accountable for police violence, a concern that was thrust onto the national scene and into national politics via a social media hashtag created following the 2013 acquittal of George Zimmerman for the killing of Trayvon Martin: #BlackLivesMatter.[1]

The Black Lives Matter movement would erupt a year later, after the killing of Michael Brown by police officer Darren Wilson in Ferguson, Missouri.[2] The movement would mobilize Black youth, including youth who came of age in the era of proactive policing and had experienced the heavy hand of law enforcement head-on in cities across the country. This call for an end to the violence directed at Black people, men and boys, women and girls, cisgender, trans, and gender-nonconforming, would be met by enthusiastic support from allies and swift admonishment and denigration from those who thought that "All lives matter" or "Blue lives matter" was an appropriate response to calls for fairness and accountability in the nation's criminal justice systems. Among the most vitriolic of these oppositional responses to the assertion that Black Lives Matter was the common accusation launched from contrarians, pundits, and conservative commentators that Black people should be far more concerned about "Black-on-Black violence," like the gun violence in Chicago that became a frequent reference for the then "law-and-order" candidate and now President Donald Trump, and less concerned with police violence. Here, the accusation was clear: Black people complained about police violence but did little to confront the violence in their own backyards. Such a claim is false and ill-informed, belying an ignorance of the ways that inner-city violence and police violence are intertwined. The violence that erupts in inner-city neighborhoods is shaped by external forces, from the creation of the Black ghetto to the maintenance of racially segregated neighborhoods in the United States to the rise of mass incarceration and the shift to intrusive and expansive forms of surveillance and policing of Black communities in cities across the country.

This claim also demonstrates an ignorance of the various ways that Black activists, politicians, and residents in urban neighborhoods touched by street violence have worked to address the problem of so-called "Black-on-Black violence" throughout recent history. The stop-the-violence rally organized by the pastor and others like it are holdovers from the sorts of rallies organized in the 1980s, as violence began to peak in urban areas. Popular rappers dedicated songs to ending the violence. Loved ones held vigils. Survivors of street violence, including formerly incarcerated men and women, formed groups to help deter young people from the sort of lifestyles that drew them in as children but also led to the loss of their peers and family members. At the same time, some members of these same groups, including Black politicians and pastors, called for an increase in harsh penalties and punishments for young people involved in the violence.[3] Professionals and laypeople outside *and* within the communities most affected by this violence framed Black youth as "superpredators" and "thugs" unworthy of leniency, incapable of change, and undeserving of a second chance. A veritable industry of violence-prevention nonprofits also emerged during this time and continues to employ people who work to address the problem of street violence each day, with varying degrees of success.

Black people care about the violence that confronts their communities. It is also true, as I frequently heard in community meetings I attended, that "Black babies are dying" still as a consequence of the persistence of gun violence in the city. That this violence continues in the face of the wealth of interpersonal and institutional resources directed at ending it suggests that the social organization of these efforts requires some reexamination. *The Chosen Ones* provides one such reexamination. A closer look at the social organization of efforts to combat gun violence in the Fillmore reveals how the various factions of what I describe as the city's "crime-fighting community" engage in "turf wars" that mimic, in some ways, the block-by-block battles that organize street violence in the neighborhood.[4] These tensions take on a heightened significance at a time when violence-intervention efforts rely heavily on an intimate collaboration among law enforcement (federal, state, and local) and a select group of community members, including leaders of youth-based organizations, faith leaders, and street outreach workers, to manage problems associated with public safety, especially the persistent problem of violence. Although outsiders (and some insiders too) may write off battles among members of the crime-fighting community as petty grievances, the ethnographic account provided here reveals the degree to which battles over who is or ought to be chosen to do the work of "saving the neighborhood," as some describe it, are rooted not only in social relations but also in the lingering social history of the Fillmore and its ever-dwindling Black community. Battles over political support and program funding are not merely battles over who gets "a place at the table" when it comes to decision-making in the community—the outcomes of these battles determine who gets a place in the neighborhood at all. *The Chosen Ones* tells a sociological story about the contested terrain upon which these institutional and interpersonal battles take place and the implications of these battles for personal transformation and redemption among the invisible young men that the pastor seemed to be calling on at the rally that day as well as others working to save themselves, young people, and the neighborhood.

Acknowledgments

The research and writing of this book spanned over a decade, from my first visit to the neighborhood while a graduate student at the University of Pennsylvania, to my first year as an assistant professor in the Department of Sociology at the University of California, Santa Barbara, and through the years since I joined the Department of African American and African Diaspora Studies at the University of California, Berkeley, in 2014.

The support, mentorship, and friendship I have received in each department helped to improve my work at each stage in my career.

I remain indebted to those who provided training and mentorship during my graduate years at the University of Pennsylvania. Professor Elijah Anderson remains a steadfast and supportive mentor. Each visit with him is akin to a visit to what I call the "Church of Ethnography." I am grateful for the introduction to the craft that he provided early on as well as the inspiration and motivation that he imparts each time I hear him preach. Our conversations and his writings have influenced so much of my work, and I am grateful to be standing on the shoulders of this particular giant. I still hear the voices of other faculty mentors during that time: Camille Charles, Robin Leidner, Demi Kurz, William Laufer, and Tukufi Zuberi especially. Looking back, I marvel at their tremendous dedication to mentorship and appreciate the training I received from each of them during my time at Penn. My friendships with Scott Brooks and Waverly Duck began in Philly, and it is gratifying to witness their successes and achievements. Most of all, I appreciate those rare moments at conferences or meetings when "the family" is able to spend some quality time together. I thank them especially for their reading and comments on this manuscript as it neared completion.

I began my career as a professor in the Department of Sociology at the University of California, Santa Barbara. While there I benefited especially from the guidance and mentorship and friendship of Sarah Fenstermaker, Denise Segura, and France Winddance Twine. John Mohr, Jack Sutton, Beth Schneider, Victor Rios, and Howie Winant also enriched my time in the department. Dean Melvin Oliver and the department provided important institutional support that allowed me to immerse myself in my field site while also balancing my obligations and responsibilities as a junior faculty member. I am grateful to the entire team research assistants who aided in the transcription of interviews and the thousand-plus pages of fieldnotes on which this book is based. My colleague Geoffrey Raymond remains a key collaborator and friend, and I am grateful for all that I learned from working with him over the years, some of which has certainly made its way into this manuscript.

The first draft of this book was written very shortly after I left the field and with the help of some advice shared by Howard Becker, who, over a lunch meeting near his home in San Francisco, suggested I go home, sit down, and write the book. And don't spend too much time on it, he added. I balked at this initial advice, but, as is often the case when it comes to advice on fieldwork and writing, he was right. I am also grateful to Howie for our early discussion of "the corruption of the indicator," as he described it, which influenced my discussion of the "numbers game" in chapters 2 and 4. Of course, any criticism of the argument falls on my shoulders alone.

I joined the Department of African American Studies at UC Berkeley in 2014, and it has made me a better scholar, teacher, and mentor. I am thankful to Professor Carla Hesse, Dean of Social Sciences, and Peder Sather, Chair in the Department of History, for providing the support and resources necessary to complete this manuscript. I am deeply grateful for the atmosphere of support, collegiality, and brilliance that makes the Sixth Floor an exciting and inspiring place to work. Each of my colleagues in the department deserve a special thanks for the direct and indirect forms of support and encouragement they have provided over the past few years. I am especially grateful to former department chairs Na'ilah Nasir and Leigh Raiford, and current chair Ula Taylor, for providing the space and time needed for me to complete this project. Thanks too to Lindsey Villarreal, Toni Whittle-Ciprazo, Jeannie Imazumi, Perla Pinedo, and Althea Cummings, who help to make the department a warm place to work each day (and who also keep things running smoothly). The questions and feedback shared by students in my graduate and undergraduate courses helped to improve the manuscript greatly. The conclusion to chapter 3 benefited from feedback gathered from students enrolled in 5B: African-American Life and Culture in the United States. Informal conversations with undergraduate and graduate students who share similarities with some of the respondents in this book also helped to refine my analysis. I thank them for the vulnerability they expressed in sharing their stories with me and in the resilience they display on their march toward graduation day.

I thank Maura Roessner, Claire Renzetti, and Sabrina Robleh for their encouragement, patience, and assistance as I prepared the book for completion. My sociological and feminist imagination was inspired early on in the classrooms and office hours of Claire and other faculty at Saint Joseph's University, including Raquel Bergen, George Dowdall, and David Kauzlarich, among others. I owe a special thanks to Andrea Leverentz and the anonymous reviewers at UC Press, who provided encouragement for this book from the outset. Students enrolled in Bill Drummond's journalism course at San Quentin Prison provided helpful feedback on the main arguments in this book. I thank them for their generosity of mind and spirit. I am grateful for the comments provided by Jamie Fader and Shadd Maruna during the final stages of manuscript preparation. The insights they provided helped to refine my analysis of the desistance process (once again, any errors that remain are my own). I am also grateful for the editorial expertise of Adi Hovav, Jane Jones, and Julia Zafferano. I owe special thanks to Cori Pillows for her permission to use her artwork for the cover of this book. Earlier versions of some parts of this work have been published in *The Annals of the American Academy of Political and Social Science* (coauthored with Geoffrey Raymond); *The Ghetto*, edited by Ray Hutchison and Bruce Haynes (coauthored with Christina Jackson); the journal *New Directions in Child and Adolescent Development*; and *Tikkun Magazine*.

It takes some time to write a book (or at least it has for me). During that time, other work must go on. I am grateful to Kenly Brown for facilitating my ability to take on and complete other research projects while also moving forward on this book. Kenly, an advanced graduate student and emerging scholar in the area of race, gender, and justice, managed the team of research assistants who organized and analyzed data that will appear in papers and book projects to come. My relationship with Kenly and our outstanding team of graduate and undergraduate research assistants has helped to make me a better teacher and mentor. I am grateful to have an opportunity to facilitate their success as emerging scholars.

I have shared portions of this work at too many conferences, workshops, and symposia to list here. I am always grateful for the opportunity to share my work with other smart people in settings within and outside of the academy. The feedback I have received has no doubt improved the manuscript. There are several research networks that deserve special mention for their commitment to encouraging not only rigorous scholarship but also the career trajectories of underrepresented scholars in the academy. Elijah Anderson's Yale Urban Ethnography Project gatherings are part research incubator and part family reunion. Perhaps most importantly, the gatherings provide a place for young ethnographers to learn from more seasoned experts in the field in a setting that truly values the contribution of qualitative efforts. The Racial Democracy, Crime, and Justice Network, led initially by Ruth Peterson and Laurie Krivo, with the support of Patricia White and the National Science Foundation, Marjorie Zatz, and Geoffrey Ward, works similarly for young criminologists and others interested in intersections of race, crime, and justice. This work continues under the leadership of Jody Miller and Rod Brunson at Rutgers University School of Criminal Justice in Newark, New Jersey. The investments these senior scholars have made in young scholars of color, women, and other underrepresented minorities will no doubt strengthen each discipline in years to come.

I am indebted to the William T. Grant Foundation for its substantial investment in my development as a researcher, scholar, and mentor. The William T. Grant Award for Early Career Scholars provided important research support for the fieldwork on which this book is based. The annual Scholar meetings allowed me to spend time with an outstanding cohort of scholars interested in using their work to improve the lives of young people. I have a great deal of respect and admiration for Vivian Tseng, the Senior Vice President, Programs, at the foundation. Vivian was an early champion of this research project and provided support, guidance, laughter, and helpful suggestions at key moments during the research and writing process. Special thanks to the 2007–12 Scholar cohort, who helped to make our annual meetings memorable, and the outstanding staff at the foundation, including Irene Williams and Kim DuMont, for their spirit and support of my work, and Amy Yamashita, for her expert advice on how to craft a meaningful and successful career as an academic. I am also grateful for the support of Jeremy Travis, Michael Wald, and Mercer Sullivan, who served as mentors on this project.

I am grateful to my parents and siblings, who have always provided me with love, support, and encouragement over the years, especially during the most difficult periods of my life. My parents instilled a concern for social justice and equality that continues to inspire my teaching, research, and writing. I am grateful to my siblings for lots of things, but especially for my nephews and nieces. Although I do not get to see them nearly enough, thinking of them always brings a smile to my face, and thinking of their futures encourages me to work toward the creation of a more fair and just society. I am grateful to Lydia G., Rod H., Leilah G. and Josh P., and their children for providing much-needed moments of relief, friendship, and laughter over the past decade. I am also grateful for the friends and caregivers who supported my family and me along the way, with special thanks to Callie and Bert W. (and kids), Angela I. and James B., Evelyn F., Bertha R., Gary C. (and his team of angels), Nyota S., and Yvonne M.

Heather Tirado Gilligan has travelled with me from before the beginning of this book through its completion. Our conversations over the years (along with her editorial suggestions) have refined my ideas and analysis in ways that have improved this project greatly. Our partnership has sustained me. I am grateful for her commitment to our conversations, her unwavering love, and her indefatigable spirit. I am also grateful to our daughter Amani, who brings joy and light to our lives each day and connects me to a spirit of love and compassion that makes its way into everything I do.

Finally, I am grateful to members of the Fillmore community, especially the men of Brothers Changing the Hood and Raymond Washington, for their willingness to share their stories and lives (and video recordings) with me from my earliest days in the field. Living in the neighborhood brought me face-to-face with the challenges of inequality and violence, which can be emotionally and physically exhausting, but taking up residence in the Fillmore, even for a relatively short period of time, also brought a good deal of joy and awe as I witnessed the tireless efforts of people trying to better their lives and their community. Although I cannot thank them all by name, I remain grateful to those people for the conversations, the laughter, and, especially, for the opportunity to observe and listen and, ultimately, to learn from you. I hope that you are able to see yourselves in this book, and the respect that I have for you and the work you do.

Introduction

From: Eric Johnson

To: Nicky Jones

Subject: Murder

Date: July 5, 2013, 1:49 PM

Message: Corey was murdered last night

This was not the first message I received from Eric about a murder of someone we both knew. I had received a similar message just six months earlier. This time, it was Corey.[1] I first met Corey in 2008, while he was still in high school. He had an effervescent quality about him that bounded beyond his sturdy, muscular frame. He was known in the neighborhood for his athletic abilities. After graduating from high school, Corey left the neighborhood to attend a state university. He was back in the neighborhood before the end of his freshman year. After his return, one of the young men closest to Corey was shot and killed. Rumors of retaliation and Corey's possible participation in that plan circulated after that man's death. Another homicide followed, and then Corey was killed.

Corey's life, like many of the young men he knew, orbited around a neighborhood known as the Western Addition or the Lower Fillmore, an area of the city that was at the time synonymous with crime and violence.[2] The neighborhood is where men like Corey develop salient social networks; these geographically bound networks in turn form the basis of their deep loyalty to a small slice of the Fillmore.[3] As it was for Eric, Corey's crew was like his family, brothers in spirit if not by blood. To outsiders, these collections of youth may look like gangs, but they often lack the formal organization that has characterized street gangs historically. They are not organized hierarchically;

there are no ritualized jump-ins. Instead, youth claim their space, or it claims them, because their families have lived in the neighborhood for as long as they can remember.[4] Injury or insult to a young man associated with a particular crew can be enough to trigger retaliatory violence.[5]

The email from Eric about Corey's murder made me think of a photograph of Corey and his friends as young boys. Eric referred to the picture regularly over the years I conducted my fieldwork in the neighborhood, usually in the wake of a shooting or another young man's incarceration. The photo hovers, ghost-like, over his life. In Eric's mind the image says it all: his motives and his fears frozen in time on a single piece of celluloid. After years of working alongside Eric, I am now haunted by the picture, too. In the photo, Eric stands with a group of adolescent boys. It is hard to tell from his nondescript outfit of blue jeans, white T-shirt, and dark jacket, but Eric is a pack leader for the Boy Scouts of America. The eight boys that surround him are members of his troop. Corey is in the middle, his light complexion and smile distinguishing him from the tough countenances of the rest of the group. At the time the picture was taken, the organization was trying to increase its presence in urban areas. Instead of following traditional routes to recruit pack leaders, such as churches or schools, the organization came "into the 'hood,'" Eric says. On the day the picture was taken, the boys, residents of one of the most troubled government-subsidized housing projects in San Francisco, were having a bake sale. Four of the boys are seated at a table whereas four others flank Eric, two on each side. Homemade signs are taped to the front of the folding table. Eric remembers this bake sale as an attempt to show "the youngsters," as he often referred to them, how to embrace their entrepreneurial spirit while selling a product different from what was typically sold on the neighborhood's infamous street corners. He wanted them to use the street corner to sell cookies and cakes instead of marijuana or crack.

Eric knew these corners well. He was once one of these boys. By the time he took on the role of troop leader, he had already put in over a decade of work in the local underground economy. He knew from his own experience that, for many young men, selling drugs was about the sociability, stability, and status that come along with making money in a poor neighborhood. He also knew that the path they were headed down was precarious: two years before the picture was taken, a joint task-force drug raid shook the housing complex's residents in the early morning hours. In the wake of flash grenades, kicked-in doors, and shouts from officers to "get on your knees," neighborhood men who had made their names on the neighborhood's street corners were taken away in handcuffs. In contrast to some of his peers and to young men like Corey, Eric was lucky. By his early twenties, he had survived his share of close calls. He walked away from a drive-by shooting without injury and, with the help of an uncle who was also an attorney, had served only brief stints in jail. At the time the photo was taken, Eric was the father of a young daughter. He was looking to break his ties to the underground economy for good.

Years after we first met, Eric and I reviewed the status of the boys in the picture he had referred to so often. Three of the eight young men in the picture were murdered before their twenty-seventh birthdays, including Corey. Two of the murdered boys were cousins. Two other boys in the picture had robbery cases, Eric said. One was, as he put it, "on the run" (had an open warrant for his arrest). These were the very outcomes Eric was hoping to prevent. That he failed to alter their trajectory while successfully changing his own is a regret that is revealed each time he talks about the picture.

Eric's regret is also tinged with anger and frustration when he recalls his encounters with the leaders of the local tenants' association at the time the picture was taken. Eric had yet to learn the powerful role these associations played in providing programming to local residents. These associations and its members, as Eric would come to appreciate, act as gatekeepers. Their approval, whether explicit or tacit, is required to offer programming in the city's housing complexes. Eric expected the tenants' organization to support his efforts to change his life and to work with the young people in the housing complex where he once plied his illegal trade. According to Eric, that is not the sort of response he received: "They told me I shouldn't even be doing the programs up there, I don't even stay [live] on the property. Go take your program somewhere else."

"Who told you?" I asked after he brought this up in an early interview.

"That was some of the residents. The board of directors [composed of housing complex residents], I couldn't get no help from them," Eric said.

I asked Eric if the lack of support was because they thought he was still running with his old crew. Could they tell, I asked, that he was not quite out of the game? Eric admits that at the time he was "still hangin' out a little bit." Still, Eric thought his efforts to change should also be acknowledged and encouraged. He wondered how he would ever find a new place in the neighborhood if local gatekeepers, especially other Black residents with status and credentials, a group he often lumps together when using the term "the community," did not support his efforts to do so. Eric explains, "So it's like I'm trying to change my life and change them [the youngsters] at the same time and not gettin' no help from the community." The perceived constraints put on his early efforts to do good left a strong impression on

Eric: "And this is why I learned still to this day is [that] when you really want to help, you in the way."

The fates of the adolescent boys in Eric's picture tell a familiar story of young Black men in distressed urban neighborhoods across the country since the dawn of what scholars have dubbed the era of mass incarceration. The picture is a reminder of lives lost and families torn apart by the twin tornadoes of the War on Drugs and street violence. It is also a reminder of the failed efforts of many to intervene in the doomed trajectory of these boys' lives. These efforts, whether taken up by individuals or by organizations, are embedded in the social order of the neighborhood, where intersections of race, gender, and class, along with notions of authenticity and legitimacy, play key roles in deciding who is selected by the city or funders to confront the seemingly intractable problem of street violence and how they go about doing so. A closer look at the social organization of these efforts reveals how the various factions of what I describe as the city's crime-fighting community engage in "turf wars" that mimic, in some ways, the block-by-block battles that organize youth violence in the neighborhood.[6] *The Chosen Ones* describes how these battles reinforce the social organization and objectives of the crime-fighting community and, in turn, shape the life trajectories of men like Eric and the lost boys in his photograph.

This book is also a story about transformation and redemption. Eric's experience with the tenants association reveals how the process of redemption is situated in social settings *and* social interactions. Men who are working to change their lives must effectively manage the institutional and interpersonal ties that bind them to the street. They must successfully complete a term of probation or parole. They must resist the pull of loyalty links that might draw them into retaliatory violence. They must also account for the histories of bad relations that may follow them even after they have committed to changing their lives. In addition to this work—and in order for some of this work to be successful—men like Eric must also convince *others* that their commitment to change is sincere: they must act in ways that demonstrate to others, including community gatekeepers, probation officers, program managers, parents, and intimates, that they are no longer the men they once were.[7] They must "make good."[8] Shadd Maruna uses the phrase "making good" to describe the differences between men who give up on criminal activity and those who persist. In his study of the stories that "desisters and persisters" tell, Maruna found that the narratives of those who give up on criminal activity were characterized by tales of finding "reason and purpose in the bleakest of life circumstances." Men who framed their circumstances in this way appeared to be most committed to developing a new sense of self—one that reflected who they are, not who they once were. Making sense of their lives in this way, Maruna explains, helps them to resist the pull to engage in the types of activities that made them targets of punishment from the criminal justice system in the past.

As I learned over the course of field research for this book, people do not make good on their own: people make good *with* others.[9] People make good by *doing good:* by giving back to the neighborhoods or the people they have harmed in the past, as Eric tried to do with his impromptu bake sale. It is in doing good again and again that a person not only finds a personal sense of redemption but also has that redemption recognized and validated by others. In this way, change is best imagined not as an individual accomplishment but as a *group process.*[10]

Embedded in this process is a set of interpersonal practices, activities, and rituals that help to reinforce—or discourage—the bids at change that people make as they work to break free from the street. Eric is working to redeem himself, as others do, in a setting where he was once known as a dealer and a hustler. He is not just working to craft a new identity in his old neighborhood; he is striving to find *a new place* in the neighborhood's social order. It is within this context that Eric works to change his life and the lives of others in the neighborhood; it is also within this context that other members of the community work to make sense of the efforts of men like Eric.

Redemption is also a gendered process. This is not to say that the *process* of redemption is fundamentally different for men and women, boys and girls.[11] Rather, it is to say that *gender ideologies*—normative understandings of what it means to be a "good" or "real" man or woman, boy or girl—shape the process of redemption in important ways.[12] Men's efforts to make good and, in turn, their ability to find a new place in their old neighborhood are influenced and, at times, constrained by mainstream understandings of race and gender and especially Black gender ideologies.[13] These understandings are often reflected either explicitly or implicitly in discussions about how to solve the most pressing problems facing the neighborhood. Often, community members cite the failure of Black men to be real, respectable, or "decent" men as a way to explain the various social problems that affect neighborhood residents, including violence. If only men would "step up" in ways that resonate with mainstream and contemporary Black gender ideologies—by taking control, being the man of the house, or showing boys how to be "real men"—the Black community would be in better shape. For men who are working to break free from the street, however, this narrative of Black masculinity can engender a confusing set of expectations: men are encouraged to relinquish a claim on dominance that helped to order their lives on the street while *holding onto dominance in other areas of their lives.* For some, the pressure to meet the protector-provider expectation that is commonly associated with manhood encouraged their longtime involvement in illegal hustles. Men who make a break from the street soon learn that, even without the hustle, the pressure remains. These challenges highlight how the process of change requires not only a reevaluation of one's behavior but also a reconsideration of one's sense of self *as a man* in ways that challenge common understandings of Black masculinity and encourage "self-definitions, interpersonal relationships and social practices" that are not only redemptive but *liberating.*[14]

THE POLITICS OF REDEMPTION

In general, community-based efforts to save the neighborhood, like Eric's impromptu bake sale, can be divided into two groups: those that are organic and emerge from the informal networks of people most closely associated with the street, and those that are institutionalized and whose workers are accountable not to informal networks within the neighborhood but to a network of public and private funders. In San Francisco, formal caretakers abound. A 2010 resource guide identified over 300 nonprofit organizations that served the 94115 zip code. Among these, twenty-one were identified as youth-serving organizations.[15] Sprinkled among this group are smaller organizations led by community members turned activists, sometimes former gang members or a family member of a loved one slain by street violence. The initial success of these groups often depends on the charisma and code-switching ability of its leader: those who can pull off a more middle-class presentation of self are often better equipped to manage interpersonal interactions with city stakeholders or private funders. Likewise, those with educational credentials are often better suited to manage the bureaucratic work—sometimes described by those in the business as "the paper game" or "the numbers game"—that is required to manage collaborations with the city. Residents-turned-activists who lack a more polished presentation of self or who are not adept at handling the kind of politics and paperwork that comes along with formal organization and funding may continue to engage in organic efforts to save the neighborhood, but they may find themselves struggling to achieve legitimacy in the eyes of local stakeholders. In turn, they often find it difficult to secure the kind of moral or material support that is funneled toward more formal organizations.

This sort of community segmentation is not new; a similar sort of hierarchy has organized urban neighborhoods for decades. In his classic study of a

White, ethnic neighborhood in Boston, conducted on the cusp of the urban renewal era in the twentieth century, sociologist Herbert Gans documents the segmentation and pattern of relations between what he describes as "external caretakers," like those who staffed social welfare institutions in the neighborhood, and "internal caretakers," like families, peers, or neighbors.[16] Gans also highlights the degree to which caretaking work is both transactional and relational. Over time, the social situation of African Americans in contemporary San Francisco shaped these relationships in distinct ways as caretaking work was folded into the sort of "race work" typically taken on by African American community leaders.[17] In *Black on the Block*, Mary Patillo provides an account of how the intersections of race and class shape the social organization of this work in a gentrifying neighborhood in Chicago. Patillo describes African American leaders who act as "middlemen," blending the line between external and internal caretaker with varying degrees of success. Patillo explains that African American middlemen and middlewomen are positioned between the predominantly White stakeholders in the city—from the heads of city government agencies to the heads of nonprofit organizations—and the city's less powerful but still substantial African American community.[18]

In the Fillmore, middlemen and middlewomen play a role in the delivery of services to the city's Black community. Here, I describe this group as the "credentialed class," since it was their acquisition of formal credentials (evidenced in the form of a business card) that was used most often to determine or justify their place in the neighborhood's caretaking hierarchy.[19] These credentials also seemed to serve as a proxy for class position, especially within the Black community. Those with formal credentials could distance themselves from those with what may be better described as street credentials, like a well-known history of involvement in the underground economy or close association with the groups of youth that are typically in the sightlines of law enforcement in the neighborhood. In historically Black urban neighborhoods like the Fillmore, members of the credentialed class typically position themselves as the neighborhood's *problem-solvers*, not part of the problem. Yet, as other scholars have documented, those with street credentials have taken on increasing importance as intermediaries in the delivery of services in neighborhoods that face chronic violence.[20] These intermediaries are often hired by social service organizations as street outreach workers or crisis intervention specialists. It is expected that these workers, when they are paid to do this work, will respect the social order of violence-prevention efforts in the neighborhood. They are expected to act as intermediaries between middlemen and the street. They are not expected to lead violence-prevention efforts on their own.

Beliefs about the proper place and roles of those with street credentials were often revealed in neighborhood meetings and casual conversations. This commonly held belief is illustrated in the following field note entry, which documents an exchange that took place early on in my field research process, before the neighborhood's credentialed class became aware of my close association with Eric and his organization, "Brothers Changing the Hood,"[21] a small, volunteer-based organization Eric founded to help free himself and other Black men in the neighborhood from the violence of the street and the grip of the criminal justice system. The exchange illustrates the relative sense of status that members of the credentialed class derive from their education and related professional achievements and how such members think about the relationships between their credentials and their qualifications vis-à-vis others in the community:

> I am sitting alone at a table in the coffee shop when Donovan, who holds a position as a community organizer for a large, local youth-serving organization, walks up to my table. Donovan does not live in the neighborhood, but he was recently hired to run a program at one of the most troubled housing complexes in the neighborhood. An earlier program housed there ended abruptly after several participants were arrested in the complex's community center.
>
> Donovan approaches my table. "Your name came up," he announces. I am surprised that anyone in his circle would know me well enough for my name to "come up."
>
> "My name came up?" I ask.
>
> "You got to call me to talk about it," he says. I'm suspicious of his claim, but I listen and respond politely. Donovan is with another woman who introduces herself to me. She's working on a new program for youth in the Western Addition, she tells me. She hands me a flyer.
>
> I have met Donovan at a few meetings in the neighborhood. I don't know him well, but from his stance and demeanor I gather that he's troubled about something. Without invitation, he begins a short speech on who should be "at the table," in his words, when it comes to providing services for youth in the Western Addition.
>
> His eyes turn toward Eric and a small group of men at a nearby table.
>
> "They're not educated," he says, "no disrespect to the guys at that table over there. They are just not qualified . . . ." Donovan let the word "qualified" hang in the air, but his message was clear: the guys at the table aren't "qualified" to do the work of running programs for young people in the neighborhood.

Donovan's comments illustrate how, among the city's Black credentialed class, being educated is a way to distinguish oneself as the legitimate provider of caretaking services in the neighborhood. In this way, it is not necessary for one to rack up credentials, although some do; it is only necessary that they be more educated than "the guys at that table over there." At the time of this conversation, Eric had not completed high school. He did not have a GED. His lack of the type of credentials that signal success in formal education informs how others in the neighborhood see him, even after he has given up on street life. Others refer to Eric's lack of formal education, as in the case above, as a reason to keep him in a subjugated position in the neighborhood's formal organizational hierarchy. They also use Eric's lack of sophistication as a way to reinforce their relative sense of status position. The common belief, whether or not it is spoken as explicitly as Donovan shared here, is that the credentialed class and those associated with them ought to be "the chosen ones"—they should be the ones to lead efforts to save the neighborhood. It is this type of sentiment that leads Eric to believe that, as noted above, "when you really want to help, you in the way." Yet men (and women) who are working on redemption may also feel as if they have been chosen, too, as if their efforts to save the neighborhood are more reflective of a calling than a job. These dueling sentiments exacerbate the challenges that confront men who had once had a place on the corner but now want a place at the table.

These tensions and divisions take on particular significance in today's *crime-fighting community*, which relies on an intimate collaboration among law enforcement (federal, state, and local) and a select group of community members, including leaders of youth-based organizations, faith leaders, and street outreach workers, to manage problems associated with public safety in a particular geographic area, especially the persistent problem of violence. The social organization of the crime-fighting community elevates the status of the credentialed class, who are typically relied on to act as intermediaries and interlocutors between "the community" and city government, especially law enforcement. The crime-fighting community provides a more circumscribed place for men (and, in some cases, women) with street credentials who are willing to take on the labor-intensive work (and largely subordinate position) of street outreach worker. The community's close collaboration with law enforcement is often framed as an effort to protect the lives of young Black men, yet its social organization, especially its encouragement to target certain youth for surveillance and punishment, often has the consequence (intended or otherwise) of ceding primary responsibility for the discipline and control of the most vulnerable group of young people in the neighborhood to law enforcement. As I show here, efforts to preserve the social organization of the crime-fighting community on the part of the credentialed class, city stakeholders, and external funders can lead to the alienation and exclusion of community members like Eric, a loss that can ultimately undermine its stated objectives.

THE CONSTRAINTS OF BLACK MASCULINITY: GENDER, VIOLENCE, AND THE CHALLENGES OF CHANGE

As program politics and bureaucratic battles play out in inner-city neighborhoods, youth of color in states across the country, including in California, remain vulnerable to serious violence. In 2005, after three killings in less than two weeks, the Western Addition was labeled in one of the local newspapers as the deadliest area in the city.[22] In 2008, the area was identified as one of five hot-spot zones for serious violence in the city.[23] The murders of young men are marked in ways that are now familiar urban scenes: impromptu memorials near the site of a homicide, RIPs carved into cement sidewalks, and the faces of murdered men and boys printed on the T-shirts of neighborhood youth who mourn them. The concentration of these murders in such a small slice of the city's forty-nine square miles is hard to comprehend. Early on in my fieldwork, I interviewed a former drug dealer who had traded his illegitimate hustle for a legitimate one. He described a T-shirt that he once sold to locals that included the names of 106 people who had been killed on the streets in the Western Addition. Of the 106 names listed on the T-shirt, he knew ninety-six.

Since the start of what scholars have dubbed the Great Crime Decline, which began in the mid-1990s, the dramatic rates of violence that characterized the preceding ten years have dropped significantly. Homicides were at the lowest levels since the early 1960s (4.7 per 100,000) by 2007.[24] Still, youth aged ten to twenty-four in California continued to have homicide rates higher than the national average, with a peak in 2006 of 12.8 per 100,000.[25] Between 2006 and 2010, youth homicide rates in the state were more than five times the national average among males aged fifteen to nineteen (23.1 per 100,000) and males aged twenty to twenty-four (29.0 per 100,000). In California, Black youth remained especially vulnerable to the threat of lethal violence. In 2011, 27.4 percent of all homicide victims known to the police were Black. Of all homicide victims, 80.8 percent of the victims were male. 51.7 percent of Black victims were between the ages of eighteen and twenty-nine.[26]

The persistence of violence in pockets of urban areas since the Great Crime Decline defies easy explanation.[27] According to local residents, the violence has remained persistent but the way the violence plays out across

SAN FRANCISCO

Western Addition deadliest city area

3rd slaying in 8 days prompts response from police, mayor

By Rachel Gordon
CHRONICLE STAFF WRITER

Figure 1. The Western Addition was described as the "deadliest city area" in 2005, when I first began field research in the neighborhood. Source: *San Francisco Chronicle*, Aug. 5, 2005.

Western Addition now deadliest area in city

► HOMICIDES
From Page B1

press conference at the district police station there to announce the statistical decline in homicides as a whole in San Francisco and gang-related fatalities in particular during the first six months of this year compared with the same period last year.

Another killing occurred two days later on July 29. Last Friday, the city installed two anti-crime surveillance cameras outside the Plaza East public housing project where residents report that drug dealing and related gun violence are rampant.

"There's going to be much more of a focus now on the hot spots of the Western Addition," Newsom said.

That is good news to Supervisor Ross Mirkarimi, who represents the Western Addition, the Fillmore and surrounding neighborhoods, where, he said, violence is an epidemic.

"We need to saturate resources immediately in order to stem the rise in violence," said Mirkarimi, who has been holding regular meetings with community groups and the mayor to help craft a blueprint to combat the violence.

Like Mirkarimi, Newsom said "the arm-and-guard strategy is not the solution. It's a temporary Band-Aid."

To that end, city officials will kick off a new program today, called Community Connect, that remakes the city's community policing efforts in which officers get to know the people who live and

S.F. homicides

SINCE 2000
Though the pace of homicides has slowed compared to last year, there is still one slaying nearly every four days on average in San Francisco.

59 64 68 70 85 45*
2000 2001 2002 2003 2004 2005
*Homicides to date
Source: San Francisco Police Department

WESTERN ADDITION BLOODSHED
Rash of killings in the neighborhood is getting the attention of city authorities.

Aug. 3: Fred Ayatch   July 27, Jermaine Williams
July 28, Kenneth Ford

The Chronicle

work in the areas they patrol. They will be expected to get out of their cars and walk the beat.

Fong said the beat program would be sustained and would not falter as similar efforts have in years past.

One officer will oversee the program citywide, and two high-ranking officers from each of the Police Department's 10 precincts will be responsible for implementing a community-policing plan tailored to the specific needs

> "We have got to do more — the police and the community. The killings, the violence have got to stop."
>
> MARY ROGERS, *a Western Addition resident and community activist*

of the surrounding neighborhoods.

In addition, a community organizer, working under city contract, will be assigned to each station. Together, they will work with residents and merchants on ways to reduce violence and coordinate with other city agencies.

The police efforts will be tied into a broader initiative, which has its own name — City Safe — and will focus on youth services, job creation, community develop-

ment, criminal justice and safer streets.

"We have to look at the underlying issues — jobs, vocational training, housing — if we're going to be successful," said Mirkarimi. "Our response cannot rest with the police only."

Rogers, the neighborhood activists, said the new program was on the right track.

"Police aren't a quick fix, and the neighborhood can't be fixed quickly," she said. "This has got to be a community effort. If people don't get involved, it won't work. The killings aren't just going on here, but all over the city. The payoff will be when the killings stop, and we can close the jails."

E-mail Rachel Gordon at rgordon@sfchronicle.com.

and within geographic boundaries represents a break from the recent past. Before the crack epidemic hit the neighborhood in the 1980s, one was more likely to hear about beefs between crews from the Fillmore and crews from other parts of the city, such as Bayview-Hunters Point or Sunnydale. Battles between boys who live blocks away from one another now make the Fillmore, one of just a few historically Black neighborhoods in the city, feel as if it is has turned in on itself. Adults often look upon these lines that divide the neighborhood into mini-fiefdoms with disbelief. For adolescents, the invisible lines that mark the boundaries of their space are as real as any physical geographic boundary. The risk associated with crossing these lines can feel akin to a soldier crossing into enemy territory.

As Robert Vargas explains in *Wounded City*, the eruption and persistence of neighborhood violence (or lack thereof) has as much to do with "gang turf" as "political turf." In this way, the vulnerability of young people to violence is shaped not merely by the behaviors of young people but also by a network of competitive relationships or turf wars among politicians, non-profit organizations, the police, and gang members. Although San Francisco politics differs in a number of ways from Chicago, where Vargas's ethnography is based, violence is politicized in both places. In both settings, violence emerges, at least in part, from a set of social and political relationships between residents in a defined geographic space and the City and not merely from residents' "apathy or lack of will."[28] Put simply, violence emerges where the institutional and the interpersonal meet (or fail to do so).

At the interpersonal level, Elijah Anderson's sociological explanation for the dramatic violence that characterized distressed inner-city neighborhoods at the close of the twentieth century remains a useful framework for understanding much of the violence that continues to mar these neighborhoods today. In such settings, Anderson explains, public interactions, especially violence, are organized around the "code of the street," a form of street justice that takes hold where the presence of civil law is weak and thrives in settings where formal institutions, such as the schools or the police, have abdicated responsibility for protecting inner-city residents: "The code emerges where the influence of the police ends and personal responsibility for one's safety is felt to begin, resulting in a kind of 'people's law,' based on 'street justice.'"[29] Of course, abdication does not necessarily equate with absence, which explains why even residents who live in neighborhoods under routine police surveillance can come to feel as if there is little institutional concern for their well-being. Those who do not abide by the code (and there are many) also carry an awareness of how the code orders daily life, especially the violence that erupts on neighborhood street corners.[30]

Anderson explains that a fundamental element of the code is the development of "a credible reputation for vengeance that works to deter aggression and disrespect, which are sources of great anxiety on the inner-city street."[31] Young men may cultivate this reputation for vengeance in a range of settings or staging areas, from the street corner to social media.[32] The anxiety that young men feel about maintaining a tough front is not unfounded. Young men know better than most that the stakes here are high: young men see other young men, including relatives and peers for whom they care deeply, get killed often enough to reinforce ideas about the need to meet insult or injury with a demonstration of strength and dominance. The quest for vengeance is intertwined with expectations of masculinity, as young men are reluctant to adopt behaviors that may be perceived by others as weak. Emotionally, such incidents send some young men reeling, encouraging them to respond in ways that are consistent with the code, including pursuing vengeance in the wake of the murder of a close friend or relative, even if it means risking their own life.[33]

This pressure to demonstrate dominance, especially in the wake of injury or insult, is not restricted to men who come of age in distressed inner-city neighborhoods. As Patricia Hill Collins explains in *Black Sexual Politics*, the coupling of strength and dominance is central to hegemonic understandings of masculinity; *how* men demonstrate dominance is shaped by their social position. Men in elite positions, like those who lead military or police forces, "have the authority to set policies concerning the legitimate use of force while erasing their own culpability for wars and other violent outcomes."[34] In contrast, men who lack access to such resources "use their bodies, physicality, and a form of masculine aggressiveness" to demonstrate dominance in their everyday lives.[35] The mutually constructive nature of masculinity, respect, strength, and dominance, along with the narrowing of access to educational and employment opportunities and the ongoing and too often unsolved (at least formally) murders of young Black men, continues to encourage poor, inner-city boys and men to resort to physical violence, or to risk their lives, in order to aggrieve slights big and small and, in the end, to be recognized and respected by others *as men*.

It is at this juncture that Black men who are working to change their lives confront the constraints of masculinity: breaking away from street-based hustles and loosening their commitment to the code often requires men to rethink their attachment to certain ideas and beliefs about what it means *to be a man*. As men work to convince those closest to them and others that they have indeed made a change, they often confront a set of challenges shaped by the circumstances of the setting and the gendered understandings that often frame discussions of how to solve the most pressing problems facing the neighborhood. A key contradiction that men confront as they work to change their lives is how to give up on a belief system that organized relations on the street while still being called upon by intimates and others to be protectors and providers, to fulfill expectations of "real" and "respectable" men.[36] For some, the pressure to meet the protector-provider expectation is what encouraged their longtime involvement in illegal hustles in the first place. If the aggression that characterizes the code is a way for marginalized Black men to accomplish masculinity, and if a key way in which men demonstrate masculinity is through the control of violence, then how do marginalized Black men who have given up on street-based hustles and violence retain their claims on manhood? How do men *relinquish* a claim on dominance that helped to order their lives on the street while *holding onto dominance in other areas of their lives?* This tension is especially acute when Black men are called upon to redeem themselves not only as Black men but as Black fathers.

Efforts to address "the crisis of young Black men" often lack an appreciation of how gender, especially Black gender ideologies, shape and complicate men's efforts to change their lives. Yet a gendered analysis of the crisis is necessary, as Collins argues, diagnostically and as a prescription for imagining new gender ideologies that further the project of antiracism and provide a foundation for building a beloved community that is "affirming of all Black people" and accepting of a progressive social justice agenda.[37] Without such an analysis, the ills of the Black community, from the failures of Black educational achievement to shootings on the block, are explained in ways that reflect an uncritical acceptance of (and thus reinforce) hegemonic Black gender ideologies. The crisis is conceptualized as originating in the bodies and minds of Black men and boys, as a consequence of the misplaced values of young Black men and the failings of Black fathers. If men would step up and be real men, as I heard in more than one neighborhood meeting, then the young Black men in the neighborhood would do better too.[38] President Obama echoed this common refrain, which often circulates uncontested in policy circles, in his announcement of the administration's My Brother's Keeper initiative, a public/private collaboration aimed at the crisis of young Black men: "We can reform our criminal justice system to ensure that it's not infected with bias, but nothing keeps a young man out of trouble like a father who takes an active role in his son's life."[39]

The simplicity of the personal responsibility narrative helps to explain its persistence over time, despite its failure to account for how large-scale structural and historical forces influence the attitudes, values, beliefs, and practices that have shaped Black communities over time. The narrative also overlaps with a respectability framework that has shaped much of Black cultural life over the past century. This framework maintains that the betterment of the Black community relies on elevating the morals and behaviors of what is perceived as the community's lower strata. Formal and informal caretakers often draw on a respectability framework when discussing the neighborhood's ongoing struggle with chronic violence, especially in their efforts to get Black men, especially biological fathers, to "step up" into a real and respectable manhood. This respectability framework reflects a popular Black gender ideology that, as Collins explains in *Black Sexual Politics*, relies heavily on a belief in the complementary nature of gender. Such a belief system reinforces assumptions about natural differences between men and women and, in turn, the proper roles that (cisgender) men and women should play in the private and public sphere.

In my field research, comments and ideas shared by and about men in casual conversations as well as during public meetings and community events reflected these deeply rooted beliefs about gender complementarity. At times, women reinforced these messages, echoing the common phrase that "a woman can't teach a man how to be a man." Such comments reinforce a commonly shared diagnosis of what ails the Black community, one that Collins sums up as "too weak" Black men and "too strong" Black women. In such accounts, it is the failure of Black men to be men that even those most interested in saving the neighborhood rely on to explain the problems facing the neighborhood. If only men would "step up" in ways that resonate with contemporary Black gender politics—by taking control, being the man of the house, or showing boys how to be "real men"—the Black community would be in better shape. In order for Black men to "step up," the line of thinking continues, then Black women must relinquish some of the power they have accumulated as gatekeepers: "Women who do not let (Black) men be (Black) men become blamed for Black male behavior."[40] As I highlight in this book, it is not uncommon for men *and* women to exert pressure on Black men to reclaim, even if it means claiming for the first time, their so-called natural place in their families and the neighborhood's social order. That Black women call for this as well reveals how deeply some residents adhere to notions of gender complementarities.

In the following chapters, we see how Eric's efforts to change his own life and the trajectories of other men in his neighborhood intersect not only with the changing landscape of the inner-city but also with Black gender ideologies. The stories of the men in this book also reveal how gender expectations, especially Black gender ideologies, shape—but do not determine—everyday interactions. People in crisis adapt. Men confront and, as I describe in this book, make efforts to reconcile the contradictory messages they receive regarding Black masculinity. At times, men use the apparatus of Black gender ideologies as a way to structure their efforts to find a new place in their families and in their neighborhood. At other moments, men may respond to the confusing set of expectations they confront by redefining in word and deed what it means to be a man worthy of a measure of respect that is not solely rooted in physical dominance.

SETTING AND METHODS

This book draws on field research I conducted in San Francisco's Fillmore neighborhood from 2005 to 2010, including thirty months of continuous residence from July 2007 to December 2009. The selection of the Western Addition area specifically, and San Francisco generally, as the setting in which to ground this study was based on preliminary fieldwork conducted during extended visits to the neighborhood from 2004 to 2006.[41] Through this field research—which included walks and guided tours through the neighborhood, participation in neighborhood events, informal and formal interviews with business owners, community members, and community activists, the collection of print materials and digital images, and the review of limited archival materials—it became clear that the social history of this area follows a trajectory similar to many distressed inner-city neighborhoods across the country. Yet, though much of the literature in urban sociology focuses on post-industrial cities in the Midwest (in recent years, Chicago's Southside has served as the site for a number of significant studies on the Black ghetto) or northeastern cities like Philadelphia, there are relatively few studies that focus on the Black experience in the West, especially in San Francisco.[42] As I discovered during my research for this book, however, the history of Black people in San Francisco makes it an ideal site to study the Black urban experience, especially the experience of African Americans in the later stages of the Great Migration, and the process and consequences of ghettoization.[43]

Before World War II, the Fillmore neighborhood was home to much of the city's Black community, including a number of Black professionals, yet it was not considered "Black space" or "ghetto" in the way it is today.[44] The relatively small Black community shared space in the Fillmore with Irish, Jewish, and Japanese residents. The neighborhood's composition changed dramatically after the start of the war. African Americans, especially those from states like Arkansas, Louisiana, and Texas, were recruited to join the war effort.[45]

African American workers that arrived en masse in the 1940s found crowded but affordable housing in the Fillmore, where they rented rooms or beds in the homes of Japanese American residents who were sent to internment camps by the U.S. government following the start of the war. As sociologist Charles Johnson notes in his 1944 report, *The Negro War Worker in San Francisco*, the arrival of Black migrants in the city changed the demographics of the Fillmore "almost overnight" as "more than five thousand persons of Japanese extraction were lifted from the city's midst, and the area of the city which they occupied taken over by the new Negro residents."[46]

Once in the city, Black migrant workers took up jobs in the war industry and related services, including bars, restaurants, and jazz clubs. As was the case in Black neighborhoods in cities across the country at this time, the Fillmore became a cultural hub.[47] The city's new set of locals would come to describe the area as "the Harlem of the West."[48] Yet, though Black labor was necessary to the wartime effort, it was clear that the city's new Black population presented a social problem for government officials and city elites, as it did in other parts of the country. As Albert Broussard writes in *Black San Francisco*, "For the first time in the city's history, white San Franciscans would have to adjust to a large Black community."[49] In some corners of the city, the response of San Franciscans to this new pattern of migration was characterized by tolerance and ambivalence. In other areas, the response to changing demographics mirrored discriminatory practices used by local officials in other cities. In the area of housing, for example, racial lines were drawn as homeowners adopted restrictive covenants to prevent the sale of homes to African Americans.[50] It was evident to Charles Johnson that the use of racially exclusionary housing practices, if left unchecked, would result in the creation of a "Negro ghetto" in the Fillmore:

> That a concerted effort is being made by neighborhood groups,
> merchant associations and improvement clubs to restrict the area of
> living for Negro families to the present boundaries of the Fillmore
> district, however, seems fairly evident. Further crystallization of these
> efforts has the inevitable consequence of creating a Negro ghetto
> similar to Chinatown.[51]

Johnson's prediction was correct: in the decades after the war, the Fillmore and Hunters Point would become the symbolic and physical representations of the Black ghetto in San Francisco. By and large, the Black community in San Francisco would be moored to these geographic areas for decades. As I document in greater detail in chapter 3, the boundaries of Black space and White space in the city would be maintained, in part, by the actions of law enforcement.[52]

As in other urban industrial centers, the fate of Black workers would turn after the end of the war. In San Francisco, African Americans were largely let go from wartime jobs and excluded from other employment opportunities in the city. More than one city official had hoped that African Americans would leave the city at the end of the war, but many remained, which became a "civic problem" for the city.[53] Like other cities confronted with a large African American population in the post-war period, San Francisco's city officials hoped to solve its problem through "cheap public housing and welfare." This would prove to be an inadequate solution. By the late 1940s, the Fillmore would come to be considered by middle-class Whites and Blacks as a "cesspool of crime and vice."[54] In the decades following the war, as the African American population in the city continued to grow, urban planners and government officials officially categorized the places where poor Black people lived as slums.[55] This official definition was consequential for neighborhood residents.[56] Once slums were officially defined as the problem, institutional solutions, like plans for slum clearance, were developed to remove the slums from the city.[57] The practice of slum removal mirrored the practices used in other industrial centers across the country. Older housing units were destroyed and replaced by public housing projects or other apartment developments, but, as was the case in neighborhoods across the country, "the new developments did not come close to housing the same number of people."[58]

During the first phase of urban renewal, the neighborhood was split in two by a cornerstone of the first wave of redevelopment: Geary Boulevard. The construction of this new road, designed to ease the commute of downtown workers to the city's quickly developing suburbs, cut through the heart of the Black Fillmore. Many lots within the neighborhood would lie vacant for years as a result. In the wake of urban renewal, the African American population would decline substantially both in San Francisco generally and in the Fillmore in particular.

As economic conditions worsened across the country, the Fillmore neighborhood would face other challenges. The lingering history of these challenges continues to shape the spatial identity of the Fillmore, especially what is known as the Western Addition or the Lower Fillmore. Dislocation from the mainstream economy, the deep entrenchment of poverty, and the widening reach of law enforcement in the neighborhood would exacerbate its isolation from the rest of the city.[59] It became clear early on in my fieldwork that, in the minds of many who were familiar with the city, including the residents of the nearby and gentrifying Lower Pacific Heights and Alamo Square neighborhoods as well as the smaller Japantown neighborhood, the Lower Fillmore was largely defined as a "bad" neighborhood marked by crime and violence, a framing that was often reinforced by newspaper reports of shootings and coverage of the city's response to gang activity in the area.[60]

The Fillmore

During the time I conducted field research for this book, many in San Francisco thought of parts of the Lower Fillmore (also described as the Western Addition) as a ghetto (or as "ghetto").[61] African Americans live in higher concentrations there than in other parts of the city. At the start of the new century, African Americans made up 7.8 percent of the city's population (about 60,000 of a total of 776,733 residents). A decade later, Blacks represented just over 6 percent of the city's population. This population is not randomly dispersed across the city. In the area where I lived (described in the census as Tract 159), the percentage of African Americans was a bit over twice the percentage of African Americans in the city (15 percent compared to 6 percent). In the two adjacent census tracts where I conducted the bulk of my fieldwork (158 and 161), a similar trend was observed, with the percentages of African American residents at nearly 29 percent and 37 percent, respectively, both higher than the city's overall African American population. In these adjacent tracks, 38.4 percent and 27 percent of children lived in poverty.[62] The percentage of Black residents, along with the poverty rate, declines sharply as you walk up Fillmore street (or "up the hill," as locals describe it) toward Pacific Heights and the Marina District. By the time you reach California Street, which once marked the northernmost boundary of what was once the Black Fillmore, less than 2 percent of the population is African American.[63]

As is the case in other cities across the country, the area surrounding some of the most troubled parts of the Lower Fillmore is considered, by some, to be "on the rise."[64] Stoked in part by the more recent technology boom in nearby Silicon Valley, which has increased rents and evictions over the past several years, markers of the neighborhood's renewal (or demise, depending on whom you ask) are visible even to newcomers: a Starbucks, a recently renovated Safeway grocery store, a Belgian beer bar, and an edgy urban clothing store targeted at hipsters. Perhaps the most symbolic change is the Fillmore Heritage Center, a condominium and jazz club complex that opened in 2007. The center includes a jazz history museum, a jazz club, and eighty condominium units, twelve of which were slated to sell at under-market rates.

The Fillmore Heritage Center sits across the street from one of the most visible symbols of the second wave of urban redevelopment: the Fillmore Center apartments, where I lived for two-and-a-half years. On the other

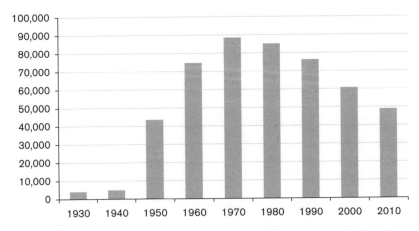

Figure 2. San Francisco's Black population (1930–2010). Source: Based on data from American Community Survey (2010), Day and Abraham (1993).

side of the Fillmore Center stands the housing complex where Eric and Corey spent the bulk of their boyhood years. The Fillmore Center's efforts to attract a new market of residents along with other new projects in the area are slowly pushing the boundaries of the Lower Pacific Heights area into the Lower Fillmore. As a result, the boundaries around what are commonly considered to be the most troubled parts of the Lower Fillmore, especially the government-subsidized housing complexes on Eddy Street, which run perpendicular to Fillmore Street, are becoming more pronounced. As a result of this pending encroachment, daily interactions between newcomers and long-time residents can sometimes be tense, especially in public forums. But long-time residents also cite the presence of newcomers, especially White newcomers, as a sign that the neighborhood is changing, for good or for bad, depending on whom you talk to. People with business stakes in the neighborhood appear more welcoming to this sort of change, even if it means a change in the demographic composition of the area, but some longtime residents view the changes in the neighborhood as the last nail in the coffin of the historically Black Fillmore neighborhood.

Eric's experiences—his successes and his setbacks—along with the community's failure to prevent the deaths of young Black men like Corey, highlight the challenges and contradictions embedded in the efforts of individuals, institutions, and organizations who want to do good in neighborhoods like the Fillmore. The social organization of the crime-fighting community as well as the Black community's relationship to the rest of the

Figure 3. Since World War II, San Francisco's Black residents have been concentrated in the Western Addition (indicated at the top of the map) and the Bayview-Hunters Point area (located in the southeastern portion of the city). Gray shading indicates the percentage of Black residents in each census tract: light gray denotes fewer (less than 15 percent); darker gray more (with darkest areas indicating 40 percent or more). Source: Map created using Social Explorer (www.socialexplorer.com), based on census data; see American Community Survey (2010).

Figure 4 (left). Construction of the Fillmore Heritage Center begins as a worker observes through a chain-link fence. Photo by author in 2005.

Figure 5 (right). The Fillmore Heritage Center opened in 2007. Some of the city's African American residents believe that the Heritage Center was built to attract more desirable populations to the Lower Fillmore. Photo by author.

city is influenced by social forces that have reshaped the social and geographic landscape of the inner city, reordering some relationships within the community and the city while also exacerbating existing fault lines in the city's African American neighborhoods. Key forces shaping the Fillmore over the past thirty years can be grouped into five major areas: the destruction and replacement of federal housing; the increase of public/private ventures that facilitate gentrification; a focus on public safety; an embrace of targeted policing practices; and the inescapable and ever-widening reach of the criminal justice system.[65]

Over the past two decades, federally subsidized high-rise housing projects, once notorious hubs of crime, violence, and other social ills associated with the concentration of poverty, have been demolished. Federal housing programs such as Hope VI have helped to replace these iconic fixtures of the Black ghetto with newly styled, mixed-income housing complexes. These changes often encourage housing authority officials to crack down on units that are associated with crime or violence. In some cases, housing policies, such as the federal "One Strike, You're Out" policy, are used to evict residents, including those not directly involved in criminal activity. These changes often make long-term residents feel as if they have no place in the new neighborhood.

In neighborhoods like the Fillmore, public/private ventures have spurred urban redevelopment and gentrification. Lots that stood vacant for years are now home to mixed-use retail/housing complexes. These complexes bring a stream of new urban migrants into the neighborhood, including many who are not used to living so close to the ghetto. Law enforcement is often called upon to make the sidewalks and city corners safer for the new residents, which puts a spotlight on young Black men in the area. These increased calls for public safety dovetail with a third feature of the new inner city: increased calls to involve the community in public safety projects.

Public safety is now a central piece of governing platforms for politicians at every level and of every stripe. In cities such as San Francisco, which launched a massive effort to target crime and violence in the city in 2007, there is also more pressure than ever to include the so-called community in public safety initiatives. This new political landscape has given rise to a cottage industry of violence prevention specialists, including program directors, counselors, consultants, and outreach workers, whose job it is to save the neighborhood. Securing or maintaining funding for these programs and positions often exposes fault lines in the community, intensifying debates about who is best qualified to solve the problems of crime and violence in poor Black communities.

Throughout the United States, police departments have made what is typically seen as a progressive shift from reactive policing to proactive policing. Instead of responding to calls as they come in, departments that adopt proactive policing practices often rely on data to target their surveillance and enforcement. These targeted policing practices often increase law enforcement surveillance in the most troubled neighborhoods in the city and expose residents in these neighborhoods to unprecedented levels of surveillance, whether or not they are involved in criminal activity. These practices, along with the spread of civil-criminal hybrids like civil gang injunctions (which I describe in more detail in chapter 3), stay-away orders, and the like, raise serious concerns about the erosion of civil rights in the name of public safety.

Finally, neighborhoods like the Fillmore have been on the frontlines of the War on Drugs since the late 1980s. Drug charges and related violent offenses funnel young Black men from the Fillmore into the juvenile and criminal justice systems. Some adolescent boys may spend the bulk of their teenaged years under system control. Once released, these young men return to the neighborhood, often on probation or parole. Some may return to incarceration within weeks or months of their release. Increasingly, cities like San Francisco are under pressure to stem the tide of re-entry, but programs designed to reach this group of young men find it hard to compete with the overwhelming pull of the system and the street.

The intersection of these institutional, cultural, and interpersonal features set the stage for Eric's efforts to change his life and the life trajectories of other Black men in the Fillmore. Eric took on the task of working with young men and fathers from the most troubled housing projects in the neighborhood. He did so at a time when his neighborhood was quickly transforming. The Hope VI housing project where he has led a weekly boys group meeting stands just a block away from a new mixed-use retail center selling condominium units for well over half a million dollars. The new development opened in 2007 and quickly intensified calls for public safety. New policing initiatives, including fixed-post policing and the introduction of a civil gang injunction, left long-time residents and young Black men feeling like targets for removal by incarceration, eviction, or both. In the wake of these changes, community-based organizations petitioned the city for more support to help free young people from the re-entry riptide and to combat violence. Their efforts to secure or maintain city funding for their programs exposed and exacerbated the fault lines of the community, further widening the gap between young men and the resources they need to change their lives.

Brothers Changing the Hood

Shortly after moving to the neighborhood, I met Eric and the men of "Brothers Changing the Hood" (BCH), a small volunteer-based organization started by Eric that is focused on helping Black men with street or criminal histories, especially Black fathers, change their lives: to free them from the violence of the street, the temptation of addiction, or the grip of the criminal justice system. Eric's story is similar to that of many of the men and adolescent boys he seeks to help. As an adolescent, he sold drugs in the neighborhood and joined one of the so-called gangs now included in the gang injunction. Now in his thirties, he is on a mission to make good. Eric sees his efforts in the community as a way to give back and to make up for some of the damage he brought to the neighborhood and its families as a youngster. Like Eric, other men in BCH and the women who support the group's efforts share this motivation.[66] In 2008, their efforts to make good appeared to pay off: BCH received a small grant from the city to help young men on the injunction change their lives. Getting the grant intensified

Eric's efforts to save young men in the neighborhood, but it also catapulted him into a web of community and city politics.

After my first interview with Eric, I explained that I would be in the neighborhood for some time. As an act of reciprocity, I offered to provide assistance to him and his organization in ways that made sense given my skill set. I'm a professor, I explained, so I'm basically good at two things: reading and writing. Eric asked if I would take a look at a grant proposal the organization was working on. I agreed, and a couple of months later Eric called to tell me "we got the grant." My contribution to the group's efforts solidified my position with Eric and the organization, and this allowed me to follow Eric's work closely over the next couple of years. Shadowing Eric's efforts brought me into a world of meetings that organized the neighborhood's crime-fighting community, including meetings at the local coffee shop, the community center, and City Hall, along with other relevant meetings on violence prevention in other parts of the city.

My work with BCH also gained me entrée into the lives of some of the young men in the neighborhood. During this time, I continued to draw on my status and expertise as a researcher and professor to make myself useful to the organization: I prepared a presentation on the gang injunctions that BCH brought to each housing complex listed on the injunction, led a GED study group for young men in one of the neighborhood's housing complexes, sat in on meetings led by the men of BCH, volunteered at BCH events, attended court hearings to support some of the young men, and participated in the rituals that followed the violent deaths of neighborhood residents. I continued to serve as a resource for the organization even after moving out of the neighborhood.

As I followed the work of BCH, I took copious field notes, filling up nearly eight entire composition notebooks, about 1,400 hand-written pages in all. I supplemented these notes with a collection of print materials (flyers, brochures, newspaper clips, etc.) and digital images, including an archive of video recordings shared with me by a local resident. The findings I present here emerged from the iterative process of data collection, memoing, and analytic coding while in the field and in the months and years after I left the field.[67]

ORGANIZATION OF THIS BOOK

This book is not about the paragons of change that are now common characters in the redemptive narratives circulated by antiviolence organizations. Those stories of redemption often provide a neat, linear summary of a man's move from the streets to respectability. A version of this narrative has been popularized by former hustler turned successful rapper, media mogul, and business executive Jay-Z, but other, less sensational versions also circulate in cities across the country as former gang members take on jobs with nonprofit organizations or obtain some other respectable, professional position. Symbolically, these stories are important. Such stories are modern-day Horatio Alger tales used to prove that, with a good dose of grit and determination, it is possible to lift oneself out of poverty and all of its ills. For individuals who are following a similar path, such stories provide a measure of hope. In the end, however, most of us do not live such sensational lives. Our victories are often more modest but no less significant. This is also true for men who are working to change their lives in today's inner-city neighborhoods.

The Chosen Ones is written from the perspective of Black men who see the ghosts of the destruction they brought to their neighborhoods as young boys and who now want to make good. Their stories of change do not take the form of a neat, linear, dramatic narrative arc. Instead, efforts to change their lives and the lives of others are marked by a series of setbacks and successes. For these men, their stories of transformation are neither simple nor celebrated. Sometimes, they are viewed with suspicion. Still, they try. Some do it because they are exhausted by the life they have lived. Some do it because they are now fathers and they want to be around to be parents. For some, faith also plays an important role in their efforts to make good.

In chapter 1, I introduce my key respondent in this study, Eric. This in-depth, ethnographic account of Eric's life story helps to illustrate common experiences shared by men who begin to reconsider their commitment to the underground economy in their early twenties. The chapter illuminates the earliest moments in which Eric begins to imagine pulling himself out of street life—points in his life that I describe as awakening moments. The moments include a commitment to faith, becoming a father at age twenty-three, and a crucial decision about whether to use a gun against a rival group of young men. Each of these moments helped to transform his burgeoning sense of awakening into a commitment to change. Eric's story demonstrates how being "half-and-half," as he describes it, is a key transitional stage in a person's movement away from the street, especially for young adults. As was the case for Eric, a person can spend months or years in this stage before completely giving up on a life in the streets. By the end of the chapter, we come to see Eric's transformation as the accumulation of a gradual series of awakening moments that took place over a period of years. Over time, his sense of awakening becomes a commitment and then a conviction. Eric's awakening is not marked by a total break from the street.[68] Instead, Eric maintains his ties to his old friends and his old neighborhood even as he works to change his life. The chapter ends with a discussion of how Eric's organized efforts to make good led to his entanglement in the community and city politics that have emerged between and within the organizations that serve troubled residents in and around the Fillmore, especially young people.

Chapter 2 examines closely how battles over representation—specifically, battles over who should be chosen to save the neighborhood—have evolved in the city over time. In San Francisco, efforts to respond to violence in the city's Black neighborhoods shifted from "peacekeeping" to crime fighting over the course of the late twentieth and early twenty-first centuries.[69] The social organization of the crime-fighting community elevates the status of the credentialed class, who are typically relied on to act as intermediaries and interlocutors between "the community" and city government, especially law enforcement. Yet the crime-fighting community provides a circumscribed place for men (and, in some cases, women) with street credentials who are willing to take on the labor-intensive work (and largely subordinate position) of street outreach worker. The community's close collaboration with law enforcement is often framed as an effort to protect the lives of young Black men, yet its social organization, especially its encouragement to target certain youth for surveillance and punishment, often has the consequence (intended or otherwise) of ceding primary responsibility for the discipline and control of the most vulnerable group of young people in the neighborhood to law enforcement. As I describe at the end of the chapter, efforts to preserve the social organization of the crime-fighting community can lead to the alienation and exclusion of community members like Eric, a loss that can ultimately undermine its stated objectives.

The crime-fighting community is organized around the bodies of young Black men, yet, as I describe in chapter 3, responsibility for the control of young Black men most vulnerable to violence as either victim or perpetrator is often ceded to the most powerful and punitive member of the crime-fighting community: the criminal justice system. This isolation and vulnerability is evidenced in the daily and routine interactions among a range of law enforcement actors in the neighborhood, from beat cops to task force officers, and young Black men. I focus in particular on the experiences of young Black men in the neighborhood who were born in the 1980s or later, in the decades following Eric and his peers. Although Eric's adolescence intersected with key shifts in criminal justice policy and practices that would *lead to* the rise of mass incarceration and the deep entrenchment of the criminal justice system in neighborhoods like the Western Addition, young people born in the 1980s would *come of age under* a law enforcement regime that would increase the frequency of encounters between the police and local residents without the guarantee of safety or protection from the threat of violence from either group. Under such conditions, the violence committed by young Black men, and the right of the community to be free from such violence, is used to legitimize the efforts and organization of the crime-fighting community. The targeted surveillance and enforcement efforts supported by the crime-fighting community also exposes a large swath of youth to contact with the police. In places where these targeted efforts persist over time, the juvenile and criminal justice system can become the most significant institutional presence in their lives, which can make it even harder to reach young Black men in crisis. In addition to describing the social situation of young Black men in the neighborhood, I also use field notes and video data to illuminate how these practices shape the gender socialization of young men *and* exacerbate the vulnerability of other neighborhood adolescents to gendered forms of violence. In doing so, this chapter reveals how the experience of being a frequent target of police surveillance and intrusion is consequential not just for young Black men *but also for young Black women and girls.*

The institutional shifts and interpersonal challenges outlined in chapters 2 and 3 can complicate efforts to reach young Black men most in need of resources and support. In chapter 4, I highlight the strategies Eric and the men of Brothers Changing the Hood have used in their efforts to help young men in their neighborhood. For Eric and his small organization, the work of saving the neighborhood is intertwined with their own efforts at redemption. This work takes place primarily on the interpersonal level: the group facilitates transformation by building relationships. This is evidenced by how the older men working with Eric's organization organize their efforts to help troubled adolescents in their neighborhood. Specifically, men meet the gendered expectations of being protectors and providers by serving as *buffers* from the various threats that young men in the neighborhood encounter, from violence to the intervention of law enforcement, and as *bridges* between other organizations and the young men these organizations often have difficulty reaching. For some, this work is embedded in their informal work as street mentors or social fathers. The chapter illuminates the ways that men extend understandings of Black masculinity by investing in emotional and relational aspects of caregiving. Their efforts reveal that strength need not always be coupled with dominance—a revelation that holds the seeds of a radically redefined understanding of Black gender ideologies. The chapter also provides evidence of the limits of these efforts, especially the degree to which surveillance and state-sanctioned violence can impede men's efforts to redeem themselves as Black fathers.

The book ends with an extended account of Jay's story. Jay was one of several young men that Eric and his group tried to support shortly after the introduction of the gang injunction in the neighborhood. I first met Jay when he was in his early twenties. He was just beginning to construct the kind of narrative and life that would lead him away from the street. Five years after our first meeting, I found myself speaking at Jay's funeral. This account illustrates how Eric's work, and the work of BCH, intersected with Jay's efforts to change his life. The chapter also reveals the limitations of buffer-and-bridge work when it comes to changing the life trajectory of young men like Jay. The ethnographic tales presented in chapters 4 and 5 highlight the limitations of the crime-fighting community and provide a compelling illustration of how and why individualistic efforts at transformation or narrowly focused calls for the redemption of Black men in general and Black fathers in particular—narratives often embraced by a variety of community residents—will always fall short of delivering young people from the various forms of violence that shape their adolescence.

Ultimately, this book illustrates the role that social institutions, community members, and community politics play not only in encouraging change but also in constructing redemption in neighborhoods that share a history with the Fillmore. The book also illustrates how common understandings of gender, especially Black gender ideologies, shape the process of transformation and redemption. Typically, conversations about re-entry or redemption focus on policy-level changes that can mediate the mark of a criminal record, but anyone who has worked to break free from a street or criminal history knows that everyday interactions matter too. I end the book with a consideration of the most compelling lessons that I took away from this study of how institutional and interpersonal practices can encourage change, or help to maintain it, in the lives of men with street or criminal histories. These lessons are likely to be of interest to practitioners, policymakers, and scholars interested in helping to address what is commonly described as "the crisis" facing young Black men.

At the interpersonal level, these lessons are profound in their simplicity. First, change takes time. Second, change is often framed as an individual's personal journey, but successful change is better imagined as an interactional process. Finally, relationships are transformative. Put simply, an individual's pathway to change may begin with an internal awakening, but successful efforts at change are often sustained with and for others. At the structural level, these lessons challenge the objectives and organization of the crime-fighting community and strengthen calls for a more effective, inclusive, and liberating form of organization that would build buffers and bridges for youth most vulnerable to violence and contact with the criminal justice system.

An appreciation of these lessons can improve current efforts to support people and programs that are committed to helping people change their lives. The conclusion moves beyond the Fillmore to programs that embrace these principles. These lessons are necessary but not sufficient components to addressing the persistence of violence in poor, Black neighborhoods. As I describe in the final pages of this book, reaching that objective requires a commitment from social institutions to create the conditions for change and, more importantly, freedom for those most vulnerable to violence.

1   Eric's Awakening

You either gonna kill someone, get killed, or go to the pen. What
are you goin' do?

—Eric

Eric was born in 1974. Like many other Black residents in San Francisco,
Eric's grandparents migrated to California and the San Francisco Bay Area
from the Deep South.[1] Eric's father, in his mid-twenties at Eric's birth, was
born in California's Central Valley. His mother, about a decade younger
than Eric's father, was born in Louisiana. She moved with her family from
Louisiana to California when she was about twelve years old. Eric's maternal grandmother purchased a home in the Lakeview district of San
Francisco, a former African American enclave near the city's southwestern
borders. Eric remembers little about his maternal grandmother, except for
that she was shot and killed in a bar. Eric grew up in the home that she left
behind. He remembers splitting time between his home and his aunt's
apartment in the Fillmore neighborhood as a child. His aunt's apartment
was in a housing project owned by one of the Black churches in the Western
Addition. Eric remembers the home as the gravitational center of family
gatherings. It was a place where all in the family were welcome. In the early
1980s, Eric's family left his late grandmother's Lakeview home and moved
with his parents and two sisters into a home just a couple of blocks away
from his aunt's apartment—and just footsteps away from the housing complex where he would first enter the neighborhood's drug trade: "That's
where I guess the trouble started."

The "trouble" Eric refers to here would last for over a decade, deepening
as his involvement in the neighborhood's illicit drug market and his commitment to the street family (a phrase he uses as an alternative to gang) he
took up with as an adolescent boy deepened over time. As he neared early
adulthood, Eric realized that if he continued his troubled trajectory, his life
would be limited by the three options he refers to above: kill someone, be
killed, or go to the penitentiary.

In this chapter, I provide a life history account of Eric's turbulent adolescence and early adulthood to illustrate how Eric crafted a *fourth* option for himself—one that would allow him to shed the criminal career and associated lifestyle he had invested so deeply in for over a decade, while continuing to live in the neighborhood he had called home for most of his life. I begin with an account of how experiences in various social settings, like school, the home, and the neighborhood, shaped Eric's drift into delinquency. This account demonstrates how Eric's early life history is shaped by the unique set of social, historical, and economic shifts that came to characterize life in poor, urban, African American neighborhoods from the mid-1980s to the end of the twentieth century. This period marked crack's earliest appearance in the neighborhood to the rise of the War on Drugs, which took aim at the type of open-air drug markets that took root in the Western Addition during Eric's adolescence.[2] Episodes of violence would fracture the neighborhood into warring pockets of youth, and the shockwaves from these violent episodes would reverberate in the neighborhood for years to come. It is within this context that Eric's moral dilemma emerges. It is also within this context that Eric develops a way to break free from the street and to make himself a new man in his old neighborhood.

Eric's account of how key events, like witnessing his uncle's exploitation at the hands of neighborhood drug dealers or becoming a father at age twenty-three, shaped his efforts to break from the street. In particular, his story illustrates the role that *awakening moments*—brief episodes of reflection triggered by external events that encourage a person to think, even in the most fleeting ways, about changing the direction of their lives—can play in the process of change. Eric's account of his turn away from the street as he approached his mid-twenties challenges understandings of change as the result of an epiphany. His process of change was protracted and extended from late adolescence into early adulthood. Through Eric's story, we learn how being "half-and-half," as Eric describes it, can operate as a key phase in a young adult's movement away from the street. Young men who are half-and-half may straddle the line between the street and decency for months or years before completely giving up on the lifestyle associated with the street. By the end of the chapter, we come to see Eric's transformation—his final break from the street—as the result of a gradual awakening over time that was deeply influenced and eventually supported by his relationships with others. In this way, Eric's story helps to reveal how change is a *group* process embedded in distinct situational and relational contexts. Put simply, Eric's story reveals how young men change first for themselves and then *with* and *for* others.

ERIC'S DRIFT INTO DEALING

As I explain in greater detail in chapter 3, the image of the young Black man as "thug," an image that exploited long-held stereotypes of Black men as dangerous or criminal, came to dominate representations of Black masculinity over the course of Eric's adolescence. As Eric grew closer to the "trouble" he alludes to above, beliefs about the inherent criminality of Black men were hardened by now infamous (and wholly unfounded) warnings of the rise of a criminal class of "superpredators." Among the many flaws of such warnings, from the implicit racial bias that lent traction to such a theory to its deeply problematic empirical assumptions, is that such theories simply mischaracterized the problem of crime and violence in inner-city neighborhoods and how young people like Eric were most likely to become involved in the new drug economy of the city and its associated violence. Eric's pathway to dealing drugs and, later, crime was not determined by internal characteristics; rather he, like many others, seemed to drift into delinquency over the course of his early adolescence. In this way, Eric's trajectory is much more consistent with early discussions of delinquency than with the now-defunct "superpredator" theory of the late twentieth century.

As David Matza puts it in a classic study on delinquency, a range of underlying influences or events "so numerous as to defy codification" often guide an adolescent's involvement in delinquency.[3] Though difficult to isolate, as I attempt to do in some part in the following pages, such influences and events operate in ways that "make initiation more probable." Today, such experimentation with delinquency is widely regarded as age-appropriate behavior for most adolescents. However, the circumstances in which youth come of age vary by place and socioeconomic status. These differences shape the forms of deviance one is exposed to at an early age. As is evidenced in the following sketch of Eric's life history, his involvement in the underground economy as a pre-teen was determined, in part, by the circumstances in which he came of age. He was not, as Matza writes, "wholly constrained" by these circumstances. Yet, that he was also not "wholly free" became ever more clear as law enforcement bore down heavily on his neighborhood and peers as Eric entered early adulthood.[4]

For Eric, as it is with many young people who first enter the underground economy, getting into the illicit business of drug selling was as easy as child's play. An older person in the neighborhood might ask a youth to hold something in exchange for some money or to act as a lookout for the police, and, just like that, an adolescent becomes a small part of a much larger market in illegal drugs.[5] It appeared to be this easy for Eric, who once explained his entrance into the drug game this way: you find a person with a little money and a little drugs then you go and get a deal. Fifty dollars buys you a 50 shot of crack-cocaine. From there, you start the process: sell drugs, make money, replenish your supply, and on and on, until it ends. Although getting in appears to be nothing more than the outcome of a simple transaction, it is rather the culmination of a longer process—a final submission to the gradual pull toward participation that began years earlier, building strength as circumstances in other domains of a young person's life, like school or the family, worsen over time.

Trouble at School and Home

Eric says that while his other siblings, two sisters and a brother, "excelled in school, I never really cared for school." His older brother graduated from a local state university. One of his sisters earned a degree from an elite university in the state. Another sister went to college in Southern California and "never came back," he says. As a boy, it was hard for Eric to measure up against his high-achieving siblings. He was held back in second grade. He was "made" "Special Ed," Eric says. He believed this label, and the tracking that comes with it, hindered him in his life and made him question himself, "because I seen my sisters excel and I always wondered why I was in Special Ed." In middle school, Eric felt like he was always in the long shadow of siblings, especially his sisters: "And it was just like my sisters are so educated and I'm sittin' here in Special Ed classes and they in gifted classes. When they [teachers] hearin' my last name immediately it's like, 'Okay, I know your sisters, they gifted and everything,' and I'm just sittin' here in the Special Ed classes and it's like, what am I doing here?"

As an adult, Eric has a much more critical understanding of what Special Education is used for in public school settings: "It's just a place where they shift you to" if you "act up a lot . . . it's just like 'okay, we'll put you in Special Ed.'" The only positive reflection on his early schooling is a class he was referred to after he "got into problems as a juvenile." One of his father's friends taught the class on African American History at the local community center. He remembers learning about the Egyptians and the Moors. "That was interesting to me," Eric says. When he "finally" started going to City College years later, he remembered this experience and enrolled in classes in African American Studies. His interest in these classes helped him to recast himself as a student:

> I'm like okay, well I guess this is the problem. This [African American history] is what is interesting to me, but you're not taught until you go to college and things like that, then you can take the studies. In your

younger years, in elementary, high school you hear about Martin
Luther King and Rosa Parks, but you don't get the detailed history of
who you are. That scared me away from it, or school, or what it was. I
just didn't like the whole school thing.

Eric's sense of disconnection from school was exacerbated by the troubles
he encountered at home, where Eric's father and mother fought often.
When he was around, Eric's father was an imposing force in his life. Eric's
parent's eventually split up, and Eric felt the absence of his father as aban-
donment. He recalls his father, who had already moved out of the family's
home and, by Eric's account, was losing his grip on Eric's life, coming up to
school after he got into trouble:

> He came up to my school, I guess they had called him and he had sat in
> the office and he was just asking me what was going on with my life
> and you know, of course when he came up there he kinda scared me.
> Then he got upset and left and that was the end of it. It was like you're
> not going to be at home when I get home, so I guess this conversation is
> over with.

Even as he engaged in troublesome acts, Eric made attempts at involvement
in more positive social settings, but he found that each institutional actor—
teachers, principals, and even coaches—simply reinforced the negative feelings he already had for himself. He remembers these slights more than
twenty years later: "I tried to join the basketball team and the coach didn't
like me, he said I wouldn't amount to nothin' wouldn't be nothin'." He also
remembers how school officials steered other students away from associat-
ing with him: "The principal, it was a younger class comin' up after me and
the principal was tryin' to steer them away from hangin' out with me. He
said that I'm a loser and all this type of stuff."

Eventually, Eric was kicked out of his middle school "because of the
fights, the horse playing, and things like that that I was involved in. Not
doing my homework, not really going to class, acting up in class." He was
transferred to another school "out in the Avenues" with a history of conflicts between "Asians and the African Americans." "From that," Eric says,
"I got into a lot of trouble because of the racial thing [animosity among
racial groups in the school]": "It was more so as a social hang out up there
than anything. We had to fight with the Asians. It was more so the African
Americans had to stick together because the Asians will clique up. There
were many fights on campus behind that."

Despite his poor performance, Eric eventually graduated to high school.
"That's where I lost all interest," he says. "High school is like okay, well

you're really on your own," Eric explains. "The teachers aren't really on you as much and I found out how to cut class and once I found that out I was like, okay it's on." Notices sent home were not responded to: "The notices and things use to come to the house but my mother was basically trying to get her life together by being abused from the time of her and my father's marriage. So, she just kinda stepped out and I had two older sisters you know so it was the whole thing we were all transforming to and I was like the last of the bunch and it was time for me to grow up and everything was at its point where everybody was trying to get their stuff together." Eric felt as if he was on his own as he entered his high school years. He grew tired of a school system that made him feel badly about himself. These feelings were made worse by financial pressures at home, where Eric struggled to find a way to buy the most basic necessities: "Finances at home wasn't going too well, I didn't have clothes to wear. This impacts this point of your life right there when you're a teenager, you gotta have clothes, you know."[6]

"The Weed Man"

It was during this turbulent adolescent period in his life that Eric became drawn to the activity that buzzed around the housing complex across the street from his new home in the Fillmore. OGs (a colloquial term for "Original Gangsters," or more experienced members of a crew, set, or gang) were hanging out playing dominoes; younger guys were hanging out too. Eric found a level of sociability that drew him closer to a group with a "lifestyle" filled with "cars and things like that." Eric found a "fun environment" among his peers. He also found a way to make money. Eric's association with a new group of youth and OGs, along with his newfound career in the drug economy, helped him to build an identity that carried a positive status among his peers and that made him feel good about himself—a feeling that often eluded him at home and school: "It was like a high itself, just to be known." Eric's entrance into the drug game also helped him to garner a new reputation on his high school campus. Although he rarely attended class, he continued to visit the high school where there was a steady market for marijuana. By his account, he "became the weed man on campus." Eric learned the importance of diversification at an early age. At high school, he sold weed. In the neighborhood, crack.

Over time, hanging out selling dope became Eric's "lifestyle," as he describes it. It also became something of a job for him: "Seven in the morning, I try to get out here before anybody else, make my money, hang out all day and hang out all night, drink. It was the hang out place, and it became the place for me just to have fun." Eric's drift from school to the street was accelerated, by his account, by his father's final departure from his home: "My father is not around to control me, so I'm hangin' around a whole bunch of people that are under no control." Eric's father left the home for good just when Eric was entering his teenaged years. Eric saw his departure as a sort of liberation: "It was open season for me."[7]

Crack Comes to the Fillmore

Eric was one of many young men on the block who, in his words, "got into sellin' crack cocaine" in the mid-1980s. The "easy money" that came along with this new trade was a draw as cash began to flow quickly into the hands of young men who, like Eric, had little financial support at home. The social structure of the new drug economy also strengthened bonds of affiliation among groups of young people, like Eric's newfound street family, who cliqued up so they could offer some protection to one another in the landscape of the new urban drug economy. Eric explained the formation of these groups this way: it's "not really a gang thing, but a set, up here, we call them 'sets' out here, sets." Set is a term that is still used to refer to smaller geographic units—sometimes as small as a block—that fall within a larger geographic area. People who grow up in or around a housing complex, including those not directly involved in the drug trade, may describe themselves as part of that set. Within each set, young people are typically divided into age-ordered cliques. The names of sets change over time, as adolescents move up the age hierarchy that organizes the set and make their own claims on the space.[8]

When Eric was hanging out in the Carter homes (a government-subsidized housing project), the group of young people he associated with was known as the "Young Warriors." A central member of the street family that Eric ran with as an adolescent boy once explained to me how the group emerged to organize young people who had been forgotten by the city and needed protection from players in the new drug economy:

> We created the Young Warriors because it was an extension of our family. You selling drugs and you get robbed on Monday, you got to make a decision: either you going to stop selling drugs or you going to protect yourself. So, the little brother next to you, he selling drugs, the little sister over there she wanna be the lookout. You three or four sit down and say, "Hey, we need to protect each other." We from this area and everybody is claiming they area and now we are forming a group to protect our interests. That's smart. That's intelligent. It's unintelligent *not* to start a gang.

The group's founder no longer engages in the criminal activity that eventually led to his incarceration. His thin short mustache, which must have been just peach fuzz when he founded his street family, is now spotted with gray whiskers. He has traded his career as a hustler for a part-time job at a nearby convenience store and a series of entrepreneurial ventures. He is deeply involved in grassroots activism in the city—fighting for the well-being of the city's Black community at community meetings. Still, like Eric, he resists shedding his association with his "family." He holds tight to the sense of belonging and shared identity that comes along with joining a street family at an early age. He has never removed the simple "YW" tattoo on his arm that marks this association. He won't remove the tattoo, he says, "because that means something." He remains, in his words, "Young Warrior for life."[9]

In addition to serving as an impetus for strengthening bonds among young people at a time in their lives when they are especially susceptible to peer pressure, the new drug economy also reordered the neighborhood's spatial boundaries. Young people in nearby housing complexes joined forces much like the youth of the Carter homes and Eric did. Their conflicts often escalated into feuds that exploded on neighborhood street corners. Eric explains:

> It got [to] a point where it was beyond, it was a drug but you had the money involved, you had the affiliation of the group you was hanging out with. So if we are fighting down here in [another housing complex in the Lower Fillmore], it's not like you gotta stay up here, you got to go down there and fight and go do this thing.

He continues, "It wasn't even the drugs, but the whole mentality of protecting something that's not even ours." The new economy also encouraged fights among older and younger generations. Drug dealers who traded in heroin, for example, had devised a way of doing business in the neighborhood. They typically instructed others involved in the trade not to make the block "hot" by engaging in conflicts that might escalate and attract the attention of the police. Fights between sets in the same neighborhood, which became more common after the introduction of crack, as Eric notes above, violated this rule. According to Eric, OGs also became upset about the loss of business as the drug economy shifted from heroin to crack. Sometimes, Eric explains, you "had to fight with some of the older guys because the money issue, you was taking away some of their clientele, so they didn't like the youngsters out there and things like that."

In addition to the newly erupting battles between sets, involvement in the drug trade also brought a level of risk and danger into Eric's life. Eric was "robbed a couple times" by "stick up kids" who developed a sort of cottage industry out of robbing drug dealers during the crack era: "[I] had a guy put a Tech 9 to my head, take my money, take the dope that I had."[10] Another morning, Eric says, he was on his way down to the Employment Development Department when he was robbed: "I had on my leather coat on, my gold chain" when "these guys jump out of a Jeep and come out with a pistol." The guys took Eric's coat and chain. He jumped into his own car bent on retaliation, "rollin' around tryin' to find them." "That whole lifestyle had its ups and downs," Eric says. Included among "the downs" was the devastation that the new drug trade was having on his and his peers' social networks.

Although much of the moral panic associated with crack addiction has been discredited, many in the neighborhood remember, as Eric does, how crack's arrival damaged already strained social networks, "devastated families," and, in the words of one neighborhood resident, "killed everything." "I could actually see the destroying of families from this new drug," Eric told me. Eric's uncle was among the casualties of this new economy, whose addiction, Eric says, was "destroying the whole family." Other dealers in the neighborhood would exploit his uncle's addiction, selling him crack rock "on credit," charging $50 for what would have been a $10 cash sale. His uncle would buy from sets throughout the neighborhood, racking up debt along the way. Eventually, Eric reached his tipping point, "I'm like, okay, this stuff has to stop." He got into a "situation" with dealers from another set over his uncle's debts. His uncle's addiction and its fallout led Eric to consider how *his* behavior—selling drugs to some of the more vulnerable members of the neighborhood—was "destroying other homes too."

The Changing Urban Landscape

Eric entered the underground economy in 1988, when he was just fourteen years old. In the United States, the mass incarceration era began around 1965 and picked up steam in the 1980s and into the 1990s.[11] Men who lived in neighborhoods like Eric's would become the most vulnerable to the shift toward incarceration as the primary response to drug selling and possession. This new legislation came on the heels of decades of disinvestment in poor, urban neighborhoods and simultaneous investment in the creation of the White suburbs. In the years following World War II, the Fillmore, like Black neighborhoods in cities across the country, became the target of slum clearance efforts. These urban renewal efforts quickened the pace of demographic change in urban neighborhoods as White residents left the city for the suburbs, many taking advantage of FHA mortgages that did not prohibit racial restrictions. After these restrictions were rendered unconstitutional by civil rights legislation in the 1960s, middle-class

African American families also left these neighborhoods. Harvard sociologist William Julius Wilson has provided the most cited account of what happened to those remaining in neighborhoods like the Fillmore from the 1970s onward. Low- and semi-skilled workers were left disconnected from the nation's shift from a manufacturing to a service-based economy. Black workers, especially Black men, were most alienated from the nation's changing economy and much of life in the city beyond the boundaries of the neighborhood.[12]

The mass incarceration era would hit young Black men coming of age in the 1980s—young men like Eric—hard. Tough-on-crime legislation would shift misdemeanor offenses to felonies. Crimes that once led to jail sentences in California would now lead to state or, in some cases, federal prison time. The new legislation introduced the now widely known 100:1 disparity in which the possession of one gram of crack triggers the same punishment as one hundred grams of cocaine, even though the substances are the same. The legislation also introduced "mandatory minimum" sentences that made the possession of five grams of crack a felony punishable by a minimum of five years in prison.[13] Anti-crime bills also funded the development of multi-jurisdictional task forces. The legislation intersected with an overall shift in law enforcement that included the funding and development of para-military SWAT units and special units within police departments, like the San Francisco Gang Task Force. These changes brought the War on Drugs to the streets where Eric grew up, as task forces made up of local, county, state, and federal law enforcement personnel would periodically raid public housing complexes where the making of crack and drug selling were concentrated.[14]

One such raid brought an end to what Eric described as "five good years" of selling in the neighborhood, which spanned from Eric's late teens to his early twenties. From 1993 to 1998, there was "money coming through," Eric explains, and relatively few arrests among his group. But then law enforcement began to crack down more heavily. In 1998, when Eric was twenty-four years old and still in the game, they "had that raid up here, on Carter. I mean they ran in people houses, I mean the Feds came, police came and knocked on people's doors, they kicked in doors." The raid really shook people up, Eric says, and effectively ended the five-year run. The underground economy marched on, the ties to the geographic spaces that took on great meaning during this time carried into the next century, but the crackdown disrupted social networks as some were arrested and others evicted.

Although Eric was not a target of the raid, the dramatic show of force on the part of law enforcement influenced him too. It was clear that the law enforcement regime in the city was changing, as policing practices shifted from abdication to penetration.[15] Eric avoided long-term incarceration, but he realized that he was also in the sightlines of law enforcement. In the late 1990s, Eric participated in what he called Operation Ceasefire, a new program targeting young men involved in the drug trade and violence in the city.[16] The young men identified as the most troublesome in the neighborhood were called in to meet with members of the community, from clergy to people who work in nonprofits. They were told that they must stop what they were doing. If they didn't, then the force of the criminal justice system would come down on them.

Eric was again brought face-to-face with the intense surveillance of the neighborhood's drug economy and his role in it after an arrest. During questioning by an officer, Eric remembers his shock at the degree of detail that officers had in their possession. "They knew my whole operation," he said, "somebody had told them my whole operation." Using confidential informants to get information from neighborhood drug operations was another practice that became more common in the War on Drugs.[17] Typically, informants, even informants with long criminal records of their own, were allowed to remain free as long as they agreed to provide ongoing insider information on the local drug economy and possible related crimes. Over time, others would refer to informants as "snitches." Snitching went against earlier codes of behavior adopted by older OGs. Yet the pressure felt by younger men to provide information was far greater than when heroin dealers were plying their trade on the same streets. In contrast to previous periods, prosecutors now had the power to threaten individuals with decades-long sentences in exchange for information. This information often came at a high price, as residents circulated stories about the murders of people suspected of cooperating with the police.

In the interrogation room, Eric quickly realized that the officers were trying to pressure him to snitch, too: "They said, well, we are giving you a chance to give us something."

Eric refused. He defiantly told the officers that they could just take him down to the county jail.

"So they did," Eric said, "they took me down to [the county jail] and gave me possession and possession of sales. The whole time I was down there I was like I'm on court probation, what am I going to do?" Eric was caught with only a small amount of marijuana and suspected that he would not face long-term incarceration for the charge. "I sat there and they got three days to charge you, so I sat there for three days, they never charged me so they had to release me." Although he evaded long-term incarceration, Eric knew his brief stint of incarceration would cost him. By the time he got back to the neighborhood, his entire stash was gone.

"You Have to Be Ready to Shoot"

In the beginning, Eric's involvement in the underground economy was motivated by financial need as well as an adolescent's search for "fun," as Eric once described it. As Eric got older, he felt more affected by the moral dilemmas that characterized the career of a drug dealer in the city. Eric once explained it to me this way:

> "As you get older [and more] involved, you start seeing more [that] you can't just be out here and just be a part of the drug selling. This [selling drugs] comes with a territorial attitude . . . so you have to be ready for whatever challenges that come through . . . it's not a gang, but you guys are together, so whatever happens to one happens to all of us."
>
> "So you have to be ready to engage in violence?" I ask.
>
> "Right, right," he confirms.

Eric felt the increasing pressure to be ready to use violence at a moment when gun violence was increasing in San Francisco. There were ninety homicides recorded in 1988, the year that Eric entered the drug game. Of those homicides, less than 40 percent were the result of gun injuries. That would change dramatically as Eric entered his late teens. Of the 102 homicides in 1990, 60 percent were the result of gun injuries. Over 80 percent of the 129 homicides recorded in 1993, one year before Eric's twentieth birthday, involved guns. From the early 1990s on, gun homicides would overtake non-gun homicides in the city—and this pattern would remain consistent through the start of the new century. The impact of this shift would be felt especially hard by youth in the city, as the homicide rate for those twenty-four and under doubled from under 20 percent in 1988 to just over 40 percent by 1993.[18] As was the case with the arrival of crack in the neighborhood, friends and family members would be among the casualties of the changing patterns of violence in the neighborhood.

"Now you're seventeen, eighteen [years old]," Eric says, "and you have to be ready to shoot and be involved in gun play if you want to stay out on the street."

This is not what Eric bargained for when he first took up with his crew as a pre-teen, but as he got older, he became convinced, as so many other young men do, that "that's what you had to do and I knew at some point it was either murder or be murdered." This created a moral dilemma for Eric: "I'm really battling with 'do I commit one [a murder]?'" His dilemma was also shaped by an understanding of what it means to shirk away from demonstrations of dominance on the street, especially for a young Black man in his position. If you don't take part (in a shooting), Eric explains, then you're labeled as "a punk"—a label that is likely to make you more vulnerable to exploitation and injury in the future.

The choices before Eric—kill, be killed, or go to the pen—were not theoretical. One moment in particular stands out in Eric's mind. There was a beef going on in the neighborhood, Eric explains. Somebody was shot and killed, and the word on the street was that the shooter was somebody from Eric's crew: "So they was coming for the retaliation." Eric was in his house when his "partna" came to get him. They knew that Eric had a gun in the house, he says, that's why they came to his house. Eric placed the gun in the belt of his pants. The group waited for the others to arrive on the scene. Eric came out of the house. "They was lookin' for one of our partnas," he explained, "and they was asking questions and things." Eric suspected that the group had guns too. He felt that his small group was outnumbered.

A member from the opposing group placed his hand at his waist, took one of Eric's partners, and announced that they were going to look for this guy inside the house. "I was like, you can't take him in there," Eric said, "so he came after me." "One of them hit me," Eric recalls, "and I tripped and fell, so I got jumped." The whole time he was getting jumped, Eric knew that he had a gun on him. Instead of grabbing for his gun and firing at the group, he took the beating: "I still had this gun on me and I was still lookin' like okay, if I start shootin' around here right now, I know that not only am I gonna lose my life, some of my partnas are going to lose they lives." Instead of risking his life, or the life of his friends, Eric waited until the fight eventually broke up. His decision met with different reactions once word hit the street. "Some of the brothas that came up there [said] 'we didn't know you had the pistol, we didn't come up there for that.'" As Eric had predicted, others questioned his reluctance to shoot: "Some people was like man you should have killed them in there." In light of these critiques, Eric felt that he made the right decision. If he had pulled his weapon, he felt that "that was going to take out all of us. It was more of them with more pistols than just mine." Eric knew what was at stake when he decided not to pull his weapon, from his reputation on the street to the lives of his peers. Pulling the trigger may have led to a deeper commitment to the street—the consequences of which, whether it be from street justice or the formal justice system, would be difficult to escape. Eric was not ready to kill someone, but choosing not to do so still left two other undesirable choices on the table: be killed or go the penitentiary.

It is impossible to know how close Eric came to option two—being killed—in the incident described above, but he is well aware that there were other close calls. At times, he seemed to court death. For example, Eric recalls a time when he dared a man who had already pulled a gun on him to pull the trigger:

> He pulled out the pistol and I asked him to shoot me and he shot and I still don't know to this day if there were blanks in the gun or what happened but the gun went off and it was just I don't know what happened to this day. But I thought that I was just that hard to where he wasn't gonna pull the trigger. I thought I was scaring him but, he pulled the trigger and I don't know what happened.

In addition to surviving these sorts of risky encounters, Eric also survived the drive-bys that characterized much of the violence in the 1980s. One shooting took place at a time when the violence in the city was neighborhood-on-neighborhood, not block-on-block: "It was a Fillmore against Hunters Point against Sunnydale."[19] Eric and a "partna" were hanging out in another set's turf. A friend of his, a "show off" as he describes him, began to "do donuts" (spin the car in circles, with tires screeching, leaving skid marks on the asphalt). Eric knew that such an act would be seen as a provocation, "Man, what is wrong with you?" he asked his friend. "You doing donuts on these people's set?" Some time later, the same friend bought a new car and once again "rolled through" the set. They stopped at a coffee shop at the bottom of a hill. Eric walked into the store to buy a sweet potato pie. When he came out of the store, "a guy had a pistol and he was pulling it out." Eric continues, "and before I could even get in the car to tell my partna that he fittin'na shoot, he [the guy] just started shootin'. And the bullet went through the windshield and it just missed where he was sitting at the driver's seat." Eric did not really know who the intended target was: him or his "showoff" friend. Either way, these near misses, along with his observation of the changing law enforcement regime in the neighborhood, encouraged Eric to imagine a *fourth option* for himself, one that would provide an option beyond killing someone, getting killed, or long-term incarceration. As Eric described it, "It's like okay, you gonna have to change your life."

ERIC'S AWAKENING

The teenaged brain is not well suited for the consideration of long-term consequences. That this is true is one of several findings that have fundamentally changed our understanding and, in some settings, our approach to delinquency and crime among youth. We know now that adolescent brains continue to develop into early adulthood. During this period of development, adolescents are more susceptible to peer pressure and impulsivity. As their brains develop, young people get better at imagining the long-term consequences of their behaviors, but their social maturity does not converge with their chronological maturity until their late twenties. This appreciation of the changing adolescent brain across the life course has encouraged key stakeholders in juvenile and criminal justice systems across the country to reconsider culpability when it comes to youth violations and, in turn, appropriate justice-system responses for young people aged twenty-four and younger.[20] As I explain in greater detail in chapter 3, this sort of advanced understanding was not the dominant framing of youth, especially Black youth, during Eric's childhood or adolescence. Consequently, Eric and his peers witnessed and experienced a seemingly universal shift to ever more harsh forms of law enforcement intrusion and punishment as they entered their late teens and early twenties. These shifts shaped the context within which Eric struggled to make sense of what was unfolding before him, which led him to reconsider his behaviors and actions.

Eric began to take notice of the changing patterns of policing and punishment in the neighborhood as he neared his late teens and early twenties. Some of his peers were being processed through the juvenile justice system, he noticed, but others, including those he considered to be at his level, were "going to the pen." These changes encouraged Eric to think seriously about getting out of the streets before it was too late: "So it was like you gotta do somethin'. You don't have any felonies, you haven't been caught with any drugs, you been blessed, you better figure out somethin'."

Over the years that Eric and I discussed his trajectory from adolescence to adulthood, I was struck by how often he punctuated the recollection of particular events with a phrase similar to *"what are you goin' to do?"* Each time he used the phrase it was as if he could feel once again the binds that constrained his choices as an adolescent. It was not uncommon for him to accompany such a reflection with a shake of the head and a long, distant stare, as if he were rethinking each option again, struck by the poor choices that seemed destined to determine his path. I came to think of the reflective moments that Eric included in each recollection as *awakening moments:* brief moments triggered by external events that encourage a person to think, even in the most fleeting of ways, about changing the direction of their lives. These awakening moments do not necessarily operate as "turning points" or "trigger events" in the ways typically imagined by scholars. In perhaps the most prominent study of desistance, for example, Robert Sampson and John Laub introduced a theory of desistance rooted in informal social control—the type of control that is placed on us by ourselves, peers, and intimates. Based on a life-course analysis of a cohort of White, male, "previously criminal youths" from Boston, the authors argue that external events, such as job stability and marital attachment (often referred to as the "good marriage effect") act as "trigger events" that redirected the men in their study toward desistance.[21]

As is apparent in Eric's case, the dramatic events he experienced during his adolescence did not lead him to turn away from the dangers associated with his lifestyle. For the most part, Eric would continue his career for years after some of the most dramatic incidents he describes above. Instead of turning points like a good marriage or conscription into the Armed Forces, the awakening moments I describe here are better imagined as *the moments that precede a turning point;* the accumulation of such moments over time *set the conditions for a turning point to take hold.* These moments are also of a smaller unit than the cognitive shifts described by Peggy Giordano and colleagues in their analysis of the life history narratives of 210 women and men who were incarcerated in Ohio in 1982. In that study, the authors identified what they described as "hooks for change," such as church involvement or a good quality marriage, as key factors in cases of successful desistance. The authors also found that "cognitive shifts" significantly influenced the desistance process and that explanations for desistance varied by gender: "Many of the women who were more successful as desisters crafted highly traditional replacement selves (e.g., child of God, the good wife, involved mother) that they associated with their successful exits from criminal activities." In contrast, "Men more often assigned prominence to prison or treatment, or focused on family more generally (the wife and kids)."[22]

The moments Eric returned to again and again, at times with no prompting from me, seemed to occur long before he had constructed a new "replacement self" or reached any obvious turning point in his life. In some ways, Eric's accounts of these moments were more similar to what has been described as "the crystallization of discontent," a phrase used to describe the linking of single, seemingly unrelated events that become *part of a pattern* that might not easily be fixed, be ignored, or disappear [without] a serious reevaluation or reassessment of one's current situation."[23] The accumulation of seemingly "minor discontents" is said to motivate one to reconsider their path in an effort to avoid becoming a "feared self" in the future: the person who, in Eric's case, kills, gets killed, or goes to the pen. My ability to observe Eric's reference to these moments (rather than his retellings in retrospective interviews) revealed how this crystallization unfolded in a nonlinear way over time and overlapped with key stages in his adolescent development. A close look at these moments also revealed important distinctions, highlighting the moments that matter most when it comes to motivating change.

"Half-and-Half"

The accumulation of awakening moments over time, especially as young people are developing in key ways cognitively over the course of their adolescence, tips a person toward change. Such moments may encourage a young person to seek out experiences or opportunities in other settings that might provide the type of fourth option that Eric was searching for as he entered early adulthood. This sort of seeking behavior may operate *in parallel with* an ongoing commitment to the street. Even as Eric retained some commitment to his lifestyle, for example, he also sought out opportunities to secure the credentials that are typically valued in a legitimate work setting. He tried to go back to school a few times to get his high school diploma, he once told me, but lacked so many credits that he eventually gave up. It took him a few more years to try to get his GED. He passed three of the tests but flunked the math section twice and eventually gave up on that effort, too. That was over a decade ago. He recently found out that they change the test every ten years. When he learned that, he thought, "Man, I missed my opportunity."

Why would a young man like Eric—a young man who, to outsiders, appears to be deeply committed to the street—seek out a credential like a high school equivalency degree? I asked him this question during one of our earliest conversations.

"It's just something that, I don't know, it's just something that I guess I wanted," he said. "You know, somethin' in me said, 'Go get your GED.' It wasn't for no job or anything like that, I had a job."

The job that Eric is referring to was what he had in addition to his job as a drug dealer: part-time work that he secured when he was in his late teens as part of the mayor's program for at-risk youth. He explained that the mayor's office was "giving a lot of the brothas little jobs, you know like at the recreational centers, you know, things like that, then they started this Mayor's Youth-At-Risk thing where you get a job anywhere in the City or County at City Hall or wherever you wanted to work at." Eric explained that he chose to work at the Department of Public Works. He worked there for about six years, but he lost the job when he lost his driver's license after a series of suspensions and an arrest: "So I never went back there." Instead, he says, he "continued to do my thang out here."

To an outsider, Eric may have looked like a typical "gang banger," a person with a deep, unyielding commitment to the street. Yet, during this phase of their lives, adolescent boys and young men may straddle the line between the street and legitimate work opportunities. They might, as Eric did, hold a job with a local agency while continuing to put in time dealing drugs. To others, these kinds of efforts at change may seem disingenuous, yet they represent a key phase for those who are thinking about changing their lives but are unsure about how to do so. Eric now refers to this period of his life, and of the lives of young people he encounters in the neighborhood, as "half-and-half." Using the top of a notebook lying on the coffee shop table where we are sitting, Eric demonstrates what he means by "half-and-half." Sometimes you are over here, he says, placing the notebook on the left side of the table. You know you want to be over here, he continues, dragging the notebook over to the right side of the table, but you are not able to get there yet. Eric puts the notebook in the center of the table. After a brief pause, he moves the notebook back and forth, from left to right, as if crossing over an imaginary line, and concludes, "So you're half-and-half."[24]

Eric's description of "half-and-half" echoes research on desistance that describes it as a slow, gradual process that unfolds over time, a process in which people may "try out" other identities on the road to change. Eric's description of his experience also resonates with writings on religious conversions that describe "the surprising degree to which—and the frequency with which—a transformation of religious identity, behavior, and world view can occur quite tentatively and slowly."[25] In such cases of conversion, a person takes on a "try-it-out" orientation toward the possibility of change; "the actual transformation of identity, behavior, and world view commonly called conversion" can unfold over a "relatively prolonged period—often months or even years."[26] This is the sort of change that is described here. It is a form of situational, behavioral, *and* cognitive adjustment that unfolds over the course of late adolescence and early adulthood and ends, eventually, with a commitment to change. Until then, young men like Eric continue to hustle as a sort of "side bet," something they can fall back on if their efforts to secure legitimate employment fail.[27]

Fatherhood and Change

Awakening moments that accompany key events, like becoming a father, may help to bring young men like Eric more firmly across the dividing line of half-and-half.[28] They may begin to spend more time in a setting other than the street while spending less and less time on the side of half-and-half that is likely to lead to violence, victimization, or incarceration. This was true for Eric, who became a father at age twenty-three. Becoming a father made Eric think ever more deeply about changing his life: "I got my daughter and she is the thing of my life now, so I'm like okay, I don't know what to do." Eric remained half-and-half, seeking out other opportunities beyond the street. During this time, he was offered the opportunity to work as a Black Male Involvement Specialist for a nonprofit agency. A lady who knew his mother, who at one time owned a preschool in the city, gave him a chance. This work allowed him to see fatherhood through a new lens. He met a man there, a professor at a state university who studied fatherhood in the Black community, who would inspire him to think more seriously about the role of fatherhood in his life and his new role as a father, even as he remained somewhat committed to his street lifestyle: "You know, I went through a training with him and he kinda gave me an overview of this fatherhood thing. So, I'm sittin' there listening to him and I'm still selling drugs and still being the weed man, I had people coming to meet me at my job [to buy drugs]. I was the 'Male Involvement Specialist' plus 'Outreach.' You know, my outreach was of course, you know I hang out, still talking to brothas, still selling drugs, still doing these things."

Despite his continued involvement in the underground economy, Eric had been thinking deeply about what it meant to be a good father: "I'm really trying to be a father and impact my daughter's life, so at a certain point that's where it really begins to really hit me, *what am I going to do?*" Eric had been going to court regularly in an effort to secure custody of his daughter. He had also participated in the routine activities associated with caretaking. This new routine shifted his work schedule on the block: "I would hang out at night and take care of her during the day." This pattern continued even after he ended his relationship with his child's mother. The threat of missing those caretaking moments with his daughter seemed to affect Eric more deeply than brief stints of incarceration had in the past: "[It] really starts hitting me after taking care of her and being with her and not being able to pick her up on schedule. [That] really made me think, *man, you got to start doing something.*"

The reality of this threat was driven home during another run-in with the police. Eric recalls driving around with a friend. Eric was driving the car, even though he had a suspended license. The two stopped to greet a friend on the street. A police car came up behind his car. Rather than subject himself to a search that would almost definitely lead to an arrest, Eric took off, leading the officers on a chase through the city's streets. Eventually, he was caught and booked at the city's criminal justice center. The district attorney was pushing for a "real lock-up," Eric says. Unlike thousands of others who funnel through the court system each year, Eric was able make use of a private lawyer. He was placed on three years' court probation.

The real awakening moment for Eric was not his arrest: it was the consequences his arrest had for his daughter. He could not pick up his daughter from school, which troubled him greatly: "All I'm thinking is that I got to pick up my daughter from school." While fatherhood prompted Eric to begin to change some of his routines, he did not immediately sever his ties to the street. Some part of him decided that he wanted to live, and that he wanted a life off the streets, but he still didn't know, as he would tell me, *how* to move beyond half-and-half: "I was like man, you know, something got to give . . . , you either gonna kill someone, get killed, or go to the pen. What are you goin' do?" This silent battle continued, part of the pull that brought Eric back-and-forth across the dividing line of half-and-half.

Bids at Change

The conversion experience is, at times, slow and tentative. For young men like Eric, the effort to seek out experiences and legitimate employment opportunities during the half-and-half stage is a way to gather information or to try out the makings of a new identity. These efforts represent bids at change—how people respond to these bids is consequential for what young men learn from seeking efforts. Perhaps the most transformation-seeking effort for Eric was his agreement to attend a new church with a cousin and a friend (the friend was convinced that the church would be a good place to find potential dates). In contrast to the large Black churches that had acted as a hub for the political and social life of the Black community in San Francisco for decades, this church was a storefront church across the Bay in Oakland.

Eric was now in his mid-twenties; he had been half-and-half for his entire early adulthood. After attending the church for some time, Eric reached out to his pastor for guidance: "I started talking to the pastor." Eric remembers one day when the church called and asked Eric to come down to provide some help. This surprised Eric: "They called me and asked me for my help, and I was just like, what?" Eric went to the church and helped out. Then he got another call. The pastor told him that he was going on his honeymoon and needed Eric to set up the church. Again, Eric was surprised: "I'm like, you want me to do what?" Again, Eric went to the church. He realized that the pastor had a plan for him. He continued to recruit Eric for help, and Eric continued to show up.

After some time, Eric decided to call upon a few other people he knew who had lived the same lifestyle he had lived for years. Eric gathered a small group of men around a table, he says, to figure out, as a group, "a way for some brothas to get some help." Up until that point, nobody at the church really knew the lifestyle that he lived, Eric said, so he shared his story with the group. They then began to meet regularly at the church. Eventually, they named themselves: Brothers Changing the Hood.

Eric was twenty-six years old. He would continue to sell drugs for another two years.

He found it difficult to relinquish the pull of the street, especially the income it provided. The time spent in legitimate settings—work and the church, for example—provided Eric with some space to rethink the trajectory of his life, yet these experiences did not provide all the information Eric needed to break free from the lifestyle he grew up in: "I didn't know how to stop," he said, "even though I had got a job, I didn't know how to stop." In the end, how to stop would be easier than Eric thought; the work of constructing a new identity—and of finding a new place in his old neighborhood—would take much more time.

The Final Act

In Eric's memory, several events clustered together over a short period to mark the end of his days in the underground economy. Efforts to target gang violence had intensified as Eric entered early adulthood. A friend was labeled as a gang member. Eric knew that such a label could have consequences for him, too—the label of gang-associated would make it ever more difficult to avoid long-term incarceration if he were arrested again. Two of Eric's partners were arrested. One was sent to the penitentiary. The other's arrest led to the loss of a significant amount of product. Looking back, Eric sees that he ran into the same sort of trouble that many other dealers run into eventually. The drug economy is a hamster wheel. It takes only a little money—fifty dollars in Eric's case—to get started. From there, the hamster wheel begins to spin. You make money on product; you spend profits on product. If you lose the product to arrest or a robbery, you lose the money too. You get in the hole. "Sooner or later," Eric says, "you ain't got nothin'." The phone call he got about his business partner's arrest, the impounding of his car, and the loss of the product, reinforced this point: "You taking a risk in this whole drug scene. There's nothing that you can really hold onto."

After this setback, Eric would make one last attempt to get back in the game, but it was short lived. The balance of half-and-half was shifting toward his involvement in the church and his commitment to being an active father in his daughter's life. Eric was also wise to how the space he grew up in was changing once again. Another generation was coming up. The behavior of some of the youngsters in the neighborhood was unpredictable. Eric believed that "one of these youngsters would love to say they took you out." That worried him. Instead of fighting to maintain his perch atop the set's pecking order, Eric decided to cede public space to the next generation. After over a decade that spanned early adolescence to early adulthood, Eric decided to end his career as a hustler. He was now twenty-eight years old with a rap sheet, a daughter, and no high school degree.

IDENTIFYING THE MOMENTS THAT MATTER

Eric describes giving it all up on one night, but the process of getting out of the game began years before he made the decision to let it all go. For him, making this change in his life was not the outcome of an epiphany. Eric's account of how he left the lifestyle of the street reveals how changes happen—or begin—over the course of urban adolescence. To summarize: As a boy, Eric drifted into a street family that was fun and exciting. He also learned that he could meet some of the financial necessities that his mother, who was struggling with her husband's departure from the home, could not provide. His new lifestyle brought him positive affirmation from others—he became known in the neighborhood. Becoming known gave him a measure of self-respect and confidence. He felt little of this in his turbulent home or in school. He also felt abandoned by his father; once he left, there was little social control left in Eric's life. It was "open season" for him, as he says. He became committed to developing a career as a drug dealer. He lived this lifestyle for over a decade. Yet, even as he did, he took notice of the circumstances that were changing around him. People were going to the pen. Peers and OGs were now doing serious time for crimes that would have garnered them more lenient sentences in the past. People who grew up together in the same sets and cliques were now turning on each other. The new drug economy was also having a devastating effect on families and friends. His involvement in the drug game also brought him into riskier situations. He was getting robbed, almost killed.

Years after we first met, I sat down with Eric to review what I considered to be key events in his life—the moments that, from his perspective, were central to helping him break free from the street. These events were akin to what John Lofland and Norman Skonovd describe as the "motif experience": the salient thematic elements and key experiences identified by the person "doing" or "undergoing" a conversion and the objective situations in which the conversion unfolds.[29] In my notes, Eric's retelling of these events were often followed by phrases like the following:

"You better figure out somethin'."
"It's like, okay, you gonna have to change your life."
"What are you going to do, man?"

After poring over Eric's timeline again and again, it appeared to me that this internal line of questioning certainly reflected signs of an awakening—an awareness that he needed to pursue a fourth option—but it was not entirely clear which moments mattered most. To answer this question, I decided to review these moments systematically with Eric. Before our meeting, I created a table with columns that included the year in which these moments occurred, Eric's age at the time the moment occurred, a description of the moment, and a column labeled "AM?" to indicate whether a moment was, in fact, considered to be an awakening moment by Eric. In preparation for our meeting, I wrote down a brief shorthand description of each moment that appeared to play a significant role in Eric's life story on the front of an index card. On the back of the card, I included a brief description or a significant quote from Eric's description of the event. I left the year and age columns blank and filled this information in as we went along. This was an opportunity to confirm observations or facts previously recorded in my notes.

Eric and I met in a small room in the main branch of the city's public library on a weekday afternoon to review the cards. I introduced the exercise to Eric.

"It seems like you have these different kind of awakening moments," I began, "[moments] when you're saying to yourself: I gotta figure out a way to do something else." As an example, I described a moment that I wrote about earlier in this chapter, when Eric had to decide if he would use a gun on a group of men who had come to his house bent on retaliation. I suggested that, from the way he tells it, becoming a father was another such moment for him. As I explain what I mean, Eric utters "uh hm" in agreement. I continue, explaining what I would like to do with the stack of cards in front of us: "Let me go through them with you, and you can tell me whether that's true or not."

I began the exercise with fourteen index cards that I had categorized as key moments in Eric's life. As we moved through the list, I also sketched out a timeline so that Eric and I could get a better understanding of the timing of these events in his life. I had organized the cards chronologically before our meeting, but I wanted Eric to provide corrections as necessary. After I selected a card and placed it face up on the table, I would briefly describe the moment in an effort to jog Eric's memory. Eric would look at the card and consider it. We would talk it over and categorize it as an awakening moment or not and then place it in the order in which it occurred chronologically in his life. In asking Eric about the intensity of the moment, I provided strong, medium, or weak as possible selections. I also asked Eric to describe the transformative potential—the degree to which the moment *actually moved him to change his behavior*—of each moment as high,

The Moments That Matter

Intensity	Transformative Potential		
	High	Medium	Low
Strong	Fight, doesn't shoot		
	Becomes a father		
	Witnesses uncle's addiction		
	High-speed chase; can't pick up daughter		
Moderate			Doing donuts
			Carter raid
			Arrest . . . 3 days [in jail]
Weak			Ceasefire*

NOTE: The final table includes only the moments that Eric identified as awakening moments.
* Eric described this event as "Ceasefire," though it was most likely an initiative inspired by Operation Ceasefire that took place in the city in 1997. I provide a more detailed discussion of Operation Ceasefire in chapter 2.

medium, or low. I used these categories to distinguish among those moments that may have encouraged a period of reflection but did not necessarily provide a strong motivation for Eric to change his life and those moments that were perceived by Eric to be deeply transformative. As we made our way through the cards, some key moments came up that I had not included in my batch. I created cards for those moments on the spot, and we placed them along the timeline with the other cards.

In the days following our meeting, I created a new table that documented the intensity level and transformative potential of the moments that Eric had categorized as "awakening moments" (see table). Systematically categorizing these moments with Eric revealed an interesting pattern. First, for Eric, few moments fell in the middle. Instead, moments were most often categorized as strong or weak in intensity and high or low in transformative potential. Also, the most dramatic moments—like Eric having a gun pointed at his face by another young man—were not necessarily awakening moments. Awakening moments *may* be dramatic in nature, but they can also be more mundane, like the time an arrest interfered with his ability to pick up his daughter from daycare.

Reviewing the timeline with Eric also revealed that, for him, the most powerfully transformative awakening moments clustered within a key developmental period in his life and in the lives of adolescents generally. Eric begins making minor bids at change around age eighteen, when he takes a job with a city program for at-risk youth, but his most meaningful awakening moments occur near his mid-twenties, as he enters early adulthood. This exercise also revealed that the moments that mattered most for Eric—the moments that he categorized as high in intensity and transformative potential—were those events that were embedded in the context of personal relationships. Eric's desire to prevent the deaths of members of his street family, becoming a father, witnessing his uncle's addiction, and the risk of not being able to accomplish the fatherhood practices that come along with that role were the four key moments that encouraged Eric to change his life. The exercise revealed a simple yet profound observation regarding the importance of social relationships in the process of desistance, one that has been documented but is still often overlooked in scholarly discussions: people often change *with* and *for* others. Put simply, change is not merely an individual accomplishment; it is a group process.

Understanding Change as a Group Process

Eric's movement beyond the dividing line of "half-and-half" was not only encouraged but also *aided* by his relationships with others. Before joining his street family, Eric was something of an outsider at school. His new street family provided a social setting in which Eric could construct a new identity—a place where he could become, as he has recalled with pride, "known." Over the course of his adolescence and early adulthood, Eric had invested deeply in his reputation as a hustler: each buy, each arrest, reaffirmed this reputation. To secure his place on the other side of half-and-half, Eric would have to find a new setting in which to craft a new identity. Fatherhood and, as I describe below, his assimilation into a new faith community provided a new set of relational contexts within which Eric could prove himself as something other than a dealer. Together, the practices associated with faith and fatherhood operated in concert to push Eric across the dividing line of half-and-half.

"I Had to Step up to the Plate"

Fatherhood provided Eric with a new relational context in which he could revise his sense of self. Becoming a father also reoriented Eric's daily routine in a way that drew him away from the street, much like the seemingly banal tasks he was called upon to perform by his pastor. Eric's commitment to childrearing intensified once his baby's mother returned to work and Eric became the baby's primary caregiver during the day. He describes his new daily routine this way:

> You know, so, it was more, you know, the responsibility was on me because she was a baby so, you know, *I kind of took care of the responsibilities during the day* and when she [the baby's mother] came home at night, you know, I went on about my way. It was more or less that I was becoming more responsible for my daughter. It was like okay, I'm hanging out all day, but *I have to go pick her up by a certain time* and then *I got to feed her by a certain time. I had a whole schedule, you know*. And then finally [his daughter] moved in with me and my mother, so I had to transition from *now I can't just jump out the house and do what I want to do no more*. [emphasis added]

I once asked Eric what made him, at age twenty-three, choose to embrace the various responsibilities associated with parenthood. Although he usually had little difficulty providing a quick answer to my questions, this one, like my question about what motivated him to get his GED, appeared to stump him. When I asked the question a second time, he responded, "I don't know," as if it was a question he had never considered before. "It was just a challenge where I didn't have a choice. You know, I mean it was either that I let someone else take all the responsibility of raising her or, um, I just figured I got one [a child] or something but . . . I felt like, you know, I had to do it; you know, it was my responsibility. I had to step up to the plate."

For those who are at the half-and-half stage, as Eric was for years, becoming a father can help to reorient daily practices in ways that loosen ties to life on the street. For Eric, stepping up to the plate meant that he had to be physically and emotionally present for his child and that he had to provide financially for her. He met the latter responsibility, in part, through his dealings in the underground economy. Since Eric relied on his income from hustling to provide for his daughter, becoming a father did not lead directly to salvation from the streets, but it did alter his daily routines and the set of people to whom he was accountable.

The Relational Role of Faith

The network Eric assimilated into at church and the new organization he created helped to serve a need not dissimilar to what Eric's street family had provided him at an early age. For Eric, fatherhood provided a new relational context within which he could revise his sense of self—he could see himself in a new light. The storefront church community provided Eric with a new set of relationships within which he could establish himself as a new kind of person. Eric did not necessarily go to church *to* change. Yet, when his friend went to the pen, his participation in this new faith community took on greater significance for Eric. He thought he had missed an important opportunity years earlier, when he failed to complete the series of GED tests, but he was not going to miss this one, he thought to himself. Instead of scoffing at the seemingly menial requests made by his pastor, like setting up chairs while his pastor was away, he would perform each one without complaint.

Eric did not share his career as a dealer with people at church, not right away. At church, he once explained, people knew him for something else—something other than "the weed man." He strengthened this new identity with the completion of each task. Eventually, Eric gave up on pretending to be someone without a street history. He asked his pastor for guidance. With his pastor's encouragement, Eric called a group of men together with the objective of helping him to change his life—something he found difficult to do on his own—and to change the lives of other men. Eric believed that this new group would help to reinforce his efforts to construct an identity as a changed man. As Eric moved further beyond half-and-half, he would garner a new credential—as pastor—that would trump the street credentials that he had acquired over more than a decade in the underground economy.[30]

AFTER THE AWAKENING: SHOWING CHANGE

Once Eric made his break from the street, he "took off running" with his commitment to his new identity. Even though he would always be associated with the street family he took up with as a youngster, he was committed to being known for something else now: "I have to be known as change now. Even now I can be identified as a Young Warrior member, so I have to show myself as change."[31] Despite Eric's commitment to change, it did not mean that the street was done with him, at least not right away. Eric's identity as a drug dealer had been constructed over time by a series of situated interactions that played out on the street again and again each day. His efforts at change would also have to be reinforced by a new set of interactions in the neighborhood. In all, he says, it took about three to four years *after he made his cognitive turn away from the street* to secure this new identity in the neighborhood.

Looking back, Eric acknowledges that it took some time to give up on the behaviors, like partying and drinking heavily, that went along with his 24–7 life as a dealer. During this time, Eric would learn that simply giving up on the practices associated with drug dealing was not enough for him to be known as a new man by others—that, too, would be a process. Early on, Eric had to resist the pull back toward his old lifestyle and career. In the days following his commitment to give up on the game, his phone rang constantly, he says, with requests from old clientele. He also had to manage face-to-face confrontations with people in the neighborhood who knew him only as the man he used to be: "Everywhere I go, it don't matter where I'm at, everybody knew I sold marijuana. So, it's like I can't go anywhere. If I see somebody, they want some marijuana. [I tell them] I don't sell that anymore. I don't do that anymore. It's just everywhere I went. 'Do you have any marijuana?'"[32]

For Eric to change his reputation, he had to change his routine behaviors. He tempered his association with people and places that might pull him into past behaviors. In the neighborhood, he cut off his involvement with certain people, including those that he "grew up with all my life." Not that these people didn't support his efforts to change—they did, by Eric's account. "That's what you're doing now, no problem," they would say. At the same time, as an act of sociability, friends or family members might offer an opportunity to engage in the sort of activities associated with his old lifestyle, like smoking marijuana or drinking, which were activities that Eric was now trying to avoid.

Eric is distant from the drug scene now. Since his exit, he says, the game has evolved to yet another level in the neighborhood. The violence there appears to have little to do with drugs; it is about beefs between adolescent boys in different sets in the neighborhood. Eric's expertise is no longer in the game but in the challenges that come along with exiting the game, especially the barriers facing Black fathers with criminal histories. Eric now wants to draw on this expertise to make good in the neighborhood. In the same way that it took time for Eric to build up his reputation on the street, it would take some time and work for others to accept Eric's efforts to change his reputation. It would take even longer for him to find a new place in the neighborhood's crime-fighting community.

2 The Crime-Fighting Community

> Institutions deliver goods and services; they are the legitimate
> satisfiers of legitimate human wants.
>
> **—Sociologist Everett C. Hughes**

My familiarity with the neighborhood and my relationship to Brothers Changing the Hood deepened over my first few months in the Fillmore. I came to recognize people by sight and found myself returning their greetings as I ran daily errands. During this time, I also began to do the things that Eric and his small group of friends did together. The group held many meetings. Initially, they were at "the office," the nickname Eric and his peers used for a local coffee shop on Fillmore Street. One afternoon, while walking by the café, I glanced inside and noticed Eric seated at a table with several other men. I stopped in to greet Eric and the group. Eric greeted me warmly and then introduced me to the men at the table.

"This is Nikki," he announced to the group. "She's a professor."

The men in the group smiled and nodded approvingly, a greeting similar to others I would receive after being introduced by Eric to his peers. This attitude of acceptance contrasted with the skepticism I would receive from some members of the credentialed class, especially early on when it seemed that my status was tainted by my association with Eric and his peers.[1]

"She's been helping us," Eric continued, but then paused, as if he was searching for the right words to describe my relationship to him and his organization over the previous several months.

"She's been helping us save the neighborhood."

As I described in chapter 1, "saving the neighborhood," as Eric calls it, is part of his redemptive journey. "I know the destruction that I put out in this community," he told me in an early interview. As a grown man, he lives with the belief that he may be "responsible right now for somebody that might have lost their life. I can be responsible for that. So, I'm giving back now."

For men like Eric, the work of saving the neighborhood is part of a larger effort to move decidedly beyond what he described in chapter 1 as "half-and-half." His mission to save the neighborhood is an outgrowth of his commitment to showing and maintaining change in his own life—to continue to "make good" by doing good.[2] "Showing change," as Eric called it, or making good, as Maruna describes it, is not merely a narrative framework; in sociological terms, it is a situated and ongoing interactional accomplishment. In this way, showing change is not merely an act; it is an *activity* performed *with* others. In order for Eric to show and maintain change, others in the neighborhood must, at some level, validate the new self that he is constructing.

Eric's challenges with the community gatekeepers reveal that others outside of Eric's organization, including at times those who are officially charged with the work of saving the neighborhood, do not always embrace or support his efforts to make good. As described in the introduction, Donovan, a community organizer for a local youth-serving organization, dismissed Eric and his group as "not educated" and, in turn, not "qualified" to lead violence-prevention efforts in the community. This is but one example of how men's efforts to make good are sometimes overlooked, discounted, or viewed as suspect. These evaluations have consequences not only for Eric's "making good" efforts but also for his place in the neighborhood's social hierarchy.[3]

In this chapter, I examine how battles over who should be chosen and what they are chosen to do have evolved over time. In San Francisco, for instance, efforts to respond to violence in the city's Black neighborhoods shifted from "peacekeeping" to crime fighting over the course of the late twentieth and early twenty-first centuries.[4] This shift had consequences not only for men like Eric but also for the young people, particularly Black youth, at the heart of what I describe as the city's *crime-fighting community*. Perhaps more than any other time in the city's history, members of the credentialed class are now called on to represent "the community." In turn, these members of the community are deeply implicated in efforts to manage problems associated with public safety, especially the persistent problem of violence. The social organization of the crime-fighting community elevates the status of the credentialed class, yet it provides a circumscribed place for men (and, in some cases, women) with street credentials who are willing to take on the laborious work of street outreach worker. The community's close collaboration with law enforcement is often framed as an effort to protect the lives of young Black men. Although the actions of many in the credentialed class are intended to *help*, not hurt, Black youth, the social organization of the crime-fighting community, especially its reliance on targeting certain youth for surveillance and punishment, often has the consequence (intended or otherwise) of ceding primary responsibility for the discipline and control of the most vulnerable group of young people in the neighborhood to law enforcement.

The rigid social structure of the crime-fighting community presents challenges for men like Eric, whose efforts to make good are more of a calling than a job. In general, community-based efforts to "save the neighborhood" can be divided into at least two groups. There are efforts that are organic and emerge from the informal networks of those most closely associated with the street. Members of this group tend to be more interested in working directly with people to solve the range of problems they may confront, including the problem of increased surveillance and enforcement that are often ushered into a community with the support of the credentialed class. This group may also be somewhat resistant to having these efforts institutionalized; the paperwork associated with institutional efforts to save the neighborhood can seem overwhelming, constraining, and, ultimately, quite distant from what they believe is really needed to save the neighborhood.

The crime-fighting community is, to be sure, an *institutionalized* effort to save the neighborhood from crime and violence. The work of the crime-fighting community relies heavily on paid workers who are accountable to external public and private funding agencies. For many in this group, the work is, quite literally, a job. At times, the organic, emergent work taken on by groups like Eric's may be seen as a threat to the system of accountability that lies at the heart of the crime-fighting community, especially members of the credentialed class who, like Donovan, see themselves as the "legitimate satisfier" of the neighborhood's and the city's "legitimate human want": a crime-free community. Efforts to preserve the social organization of the crime-fighting community on the part of the credentialed class, city stakeholders, and external funders can lead to the alienation and exclusion of community members like Eric, a loss that, as I show near the end of this chapter, can ultimately undermine its stated objectives.

RACE AND THE POLITICS OF REPRESENTATION

Every society has its caretakers, "institutions and individuals who provide services to people."[5] Although caretaking may seem purely altruistic, it is, at its root, a reciprocal relationship: "The caretaker gives [their] services in exchange for a material or nonmaterial return. The doctor receives a fee; the social worker, deference."[6] For nonprofessional caretakers, the fee may be a psychic or social one, like a feeling of doing good in the community or having a place among one's peers. Caretaking work also has a structure—

a particular social organization that orders the interactions between those giving care, those receiving care, and external stakeholders like city officials or funders.

As I worked to better understand the structure of what I originally thought of as caretaking work in San Francisco, I returned to classic and contemporary urban ethnographies that document the social organization of similar efforts at different points in time, especially studies from Herbert Gans, St. Clair Drake and Horace Cayton, Elijah Anderson, and Mary Patillo. Often, the interpersonal conflicts that play out at community meetings in the neighborhood, or during meetings at City Hall, are attributed to characteristics of particular individuals, especially activists. Yet these classic and contemporary works, which I review briefly in the next few pages, help to provide a conceptual framework for understanding the evolving objectives of caretaking work in the city over time and the ways that a community's caretaking efforts are shaped by external forces, internal divisions, and the politics of race and representation.

Among the lessons learned from these works is that, though lots of people do caretaking work, all caretaking work is not the same. Gans divided caretakers into two groups: internal caretakers and external caretakers. *Internal caretakers* embed their efforts in informal networks made up of family members, peers, and neighbors who may be called upon to provide assistance to someone in need of medical care or to act as an "informal counselor" to those in need.[7] In contrast, *external caretakers* are typically outsiders who work in social welfare institutions and agencies in a neighborhood and are charged with the task of changing the behavior of their clients in some way. Like many people who work in these agencies today, the group of external caretakers that Gans observed in his study of a White, ethnic neighborhood in Boston at the onset of urban renewal seemed "genuinely interested in providing service to their clients." Yet, as Gans also observed, some staff members lacked a level of "insight and empathy" for the youth in their care. Some external caretakers were afraid of their charges. The social distance between this group and their "clients," as Gans describes them, led to a reliance on intermediaries: staff members who could negotiate relationships with segments of the community that other staff members felt ill-prepared to reach. In Gans's study, intermediaries were valued by organizations and staff members for their ability to garner respect from youth while maintaining a commitment to the moral order of the organization.

African Americans have a long history of caretaking that has been intertwined with survival. The Great Migration of Black people from the U.S. South to urban, industrial centers over the greater part of the twentieth century marked a splintering of caretaking work, from intimate and community-based to institutionalized. Organizations were created to facilitate the incorporation of newly arriving migrants from the South, including youth who were excluded from racially segregated institutions and opportunities in their new hometowns.[8] Caretaking became an attempt at racial uplift for some middle-class Black people. In Drake and Cayton's *Black Metropolis*, a classic urban ethnography of Bronzeville, home to Chicago's Black community in the 1930s, this particular form of caretaking was taken on by "Race Leaders" to whom "the masses" left the management of "the burden of The Race." The lives of Race Leaders "were oriented around 'service.'" For some, this service was restricted to participation in "charitable organizations or associations for racial advancement" during their "leisure time," whereas for others, "solving the race problem [was] a full-time job." As Drake and Cayton write, "a score or so individuals in Bronzeville are elected and appointed politicians who 'represent The Race.' There are also a few civic leaders who earn their living administering social agencies such as the Urban League, the YMCA, the YWCA, settlement houses, and similar organizations."[9]

The social organization of caretaking work is also shaped by the racial politics of any given moment.[10] The quickening of ghettoization in the post-war period, along with the urban uprisings of the late 1960s and the emergence of the Black Power movement of the 1960s and early 1970s, influenced the evolution of caretaking work in Black communities across the country. For some, race work (concerted efforts to lift up the race) would become, increasingly, paid work. Social agencies from the neighborhood needed intermediaries who were trusted and also aligned with the values of the institution. The social, institutional, and financial investment in quelling disorder would give rise to a new organization of caretaking work that would exploit and exacerbate inter- and intra-racial tensions.

Anderson tells the story of a divided Black political structure whose ability to represent the Black community's interests was constrained by unbalanced power relations among Black representatives and White elites in a Midwestern city. He found "black representation [to be] discordant, unstable, and unreliable" and "divided among factions, each with its own ideas and approaches for the resolution of community problems."[11] Anderson called these factions "the insiders," "the outsiders," and "the militant young."

Insiders included Black politicians and professionals who were often selected by powerful Whites to represent the Black community. The outsiders included African Americans who came to Midwestville looking for a better life. Insiders often found themselves in a bind when called upon to advance the interests of the Black community, since their authenticity and legitimacy within the Black community was commonly questioned by others, perhaps especially the militant young.

In contrast to the more middle-class aspirations of the insiders and the outsiders, the "militant young included formerly delinquent youth turned activists and, in some cases, spokespersons, who were intent on helping the black community in the wake of the civil unrest of the late 1960s."[12] For this group, engagement with the city's power structure occasionally offered some social mobility—for example, as a former-gang-member-turned-activist was folded into the paid work of a caretaking career. Yet this type of mobility often came with a paradox: as a person moved from activist to spokesperson, he (most often he) became increasingly "sustained and constrained by his 'respectable' position."[13] That is, he became more accountable to institutions than to the people he was called upon to represent.

The emergence of Black shadow politics was not spontaneous or random. As Anderson explains, the Black political structure was deeply influenced by external pressures, interventions, and investments, especially financial support that flowed from a range of government-sponsored programs, such as the Model Cities program and urban renewal efforts. Powerful, White elites exploited the tensions among factions within the community "through the meting out of rewards, psychic and material, to 'acceptable' black representatives." This exploitation came with a consequence revealed in Anderson's conclusion on the structure of Black politics in the city: "black representation thus amounts to little more than black followership—followership of powerful external elements."[14]

The lingering history and politics of urban renewal and rising gentrification in neighborhoods that were once considered no-go zones has complicated and transformed caretaking. The work of saving neighborhood youth from incarceration, injury, or death was supported increasingly by public funding; as more well-off people move to neighborhoods such as the Fillmore, pressure mounts to take care of violent crime. Patillo's *Black on the Block*, a study that brings us back to Chicago six decades after the original publication of *Black Metropolis*, reveals how contemporary social forces around housing, safety, and education puts pressure on the Black middle class and Black leaders who act as intermediaries between the community and city governments. Patillo describes this group as "middlemen" or "middlewomen." Black middlemen and middlewomen are typically members of the Black middle class. Their demeanor in public and their collection of credentials are crafted in a way that demonstrates to others their orientation toward decency and respectability. Their formal credentials also help to shore up their legitimacy as "brokers of a wide variety of resources" to those outsiders who require some participation from the community in order to meet organizational objectives. They too face the dilemmas of representing the race as they work to reconcile the contradictions that come along with their insider position. The orientation of their interests tends to influence how they are seen by others in the city: "When directed upward, [middlemen] can be either supplicants or claimants, and when looking downward, they may be suppliers or enforcers."[15] The selected spokespersons and social workers are sometimes viewed by community members as mere tokens, Uncle Toms or overseers who generally lack a deep engagement with the segments of the Black community they are supposed to serve.[16]

The exploitation of Black leadership has long been evident in San Francisco. In September 1966, for instance, a police officer shot and killed a young man from Hunters Point. The outcome, an uprising in the wake of the young man's death, was made worse by a fundamental misunderstanding on the part of the police and the mayor of the role of Black middle-class leadership in the city, explains Arthur Hippler, who was conducting an ethnography of Hunters Point at the time. Hippler's assessment echoes Anderson's description of Black shadow politics in Midwestville:

> The major error in judgment, of course, was thinking that their presence could do any good at all, which itself was based on a series of misperceptions—i.e., that they were in any sense leaders of Hunter's Point or even respected there, that they even understood what the disturbance was about at its core, and, finally, that they had any real power to change the social situation that underlay the disorders.[17]

In the years following the shooting, a group of service agency personnel charged with addressing the problems of the city's Black ghettos would take the place of selected leaders. Their efforts, however, were often ineffective, "buried beneath the glacier like movement of bureaucratic adaptation, lack of understanding, fear and powerlessness to change even so simple a thing as the hiring habits of San Francisco employers."[18] The question of who could deliver a peaceful Black community, which was especially acute in the 1950s and 1960s, would linger as violence and urban uprisings made peacekeeping a key objective of caretaking efforts in the city.

THE POLITICS OF PEACEKEEPING IN SAN FRANCISCO

In *The Streets of San Francisco*, historian Christopher Agee documents the rise of two organizations formed in the 1950s and 1960s: Youth for Service (YFS) and Young Men of Action (YMA). Tensions over who was best suited to represent the Black community, along with the ebb and flow of external funding, shaped the objectives and social organization of peacekeeping efforts in the city, according to Agee. Early peacekeeping efforts emerged in response to three main problems: interpersonal violence among Black youth; police violence against Black youth; and quelling the uprisings that followed such incidents. In order to respond to these problems, peacekeeping work was organized around three key objectives: reducing community violence, including police violence; securing job grants; and achieving civic legitimacy for gang-involved youth.[19]

Peacekeeping was a pathway to employment. One early effort, Neighborhood Youth Corps, led to over 200 jobs for low-income youth. Peacekeeping efforts also sought to make legitimate leaders out of the leaders of gangs in the neighborhood.[20] In this way, peacekeeping efforts were imagined as a pathway to mobility and civic legitimacy.

Peacekeeping efforts also relied heavily on street outreach workers, a network of intermediaries that could influence gang-associated youth. These intermediaries were most often men who represented a specific form of Black masculinity: one that demonstrated strength and a generally tough demeanor that youth on the street would respect.[21] They did earn respect from youth. They were not, however, given a similar level of respect by the city's elites, who instead favored middle-class representatives and ministers in the wake of crises in the neighborhood, even though their efforts to serve the neighborhood paled in contrast to the work of internal caretakers.[22]

Tension between those the city designated as leaders and the leaders chosen by the communities came to a head in the aftermath of the Hunters Point uprising of 1966. During the uprising, outreach workers acted as mediators between police and rioters, placing themselves in harm's way. It was a moment when, Agee writes, "the young men of Hunters Point stepped forward as potential partners in the city's pursuit of a common good." These efforts were praised in the media. In his public address to the city after the uprising, however, the mayor ignored the peacekeeping efforts of street outreach workers and instead stood with "liberal black spokespersons to his side and riot-geared police to his back."[23]

In the late 1960s, the peacekeeping network in the city's Black neighborhoods would finally receive some recognition from City Hall, though not in the way originally imagined. The peacekeeping network developed over the 1950s and 1960s would be exploited by soon-to-be mayor Joseph Alioto. He relied heavily on Black youth to spread the word of his promise for more programs, Agee writes, programs supported by the federally funded Model Cities program following Alioto's election. Black voters also helped Alioto's victory in the election. In return, Alioto shifted to a law-and-order politics that would secure support from the more suburban parts of the city during his re-election campaign. In the early 1970s, the street outreach workers at the center of peacekeeping efforts over the previous decade would be overwhelmed by the arrival of the heroin industry in the city. San Francisco politics would go on to mirror the law-and-order politics spreading across the nation in the 1970s.[24]

FROM PEACEKEEPING TO CRIME FIGHTING

For most people, today's U.S. cities are the safest they have been in five decades. Rates of violent crime in the United States peaked in the mid-1990s, and violent crime has continued to drop precipitously since then. Yet violence continues to be concentrated and chronic in certain pockets of the city, most often those areas in which poor people of color have lived for generations, such as in San Francisco's Lower Fillmore and parts of Hunters Point.[25] The question of what the nation, the city, and the community should do about violence in these communities has been hotly debated for decades. Eventually, support has coalesced for a response I refer to as the crime-fighting community, where broader swaths of community members and representatives are recruited into the work of surveillance and punishment. Meanwhile, the power of law enforcement has punished a targeted set of members in the community. Middlewomen, intermediaries, and other neighborhood residents have been drawn into the crime-fighting community, which came into its own in the 1990s and early 2000s, once again shifting caretaking work by leaving peacekeeping behind.

Street outreach workers of the 1960s and 1970s called on young people to explain the consequences of police abuse to officers. By the 1980s, intermediates who billed themselves as representatives of the community stood with law enforcement, calling on the police to "do something" about the persistent problem of violence in the neighborhood.[26] Early academic advocates of this approach stood confidently on the side of community residents who wanted more, not less, intrusive forms of surveillance from law enforcement, like youth curfews and gang loitering ordinances, even as both were struck down as unconstitutional. Scholars and other stakeholders argued that residents in neighborhoods with high rates of violent crime were entitled to a crime-free community, a right that ought to trump certain constitutional protections, like freedom from unreasonable or unwarranted searches.[27]

Calls for more stringent policing and punishment argued that the wants of a crime-free community were a matter of police accountability—a right that Black people had been denied historically. The increase in Black political representation, proponents argued, should strengthen calls to hold the police accountable for ensuring public safety. "Reduction of crime is one of the primary purposes to which minority communities are putting their new-found political power," write Tracey Meares and Dan Kahan, early propo-nents of this call. Advocates of the crime-fighting community typically underestimated or ignored the potential for police abuse or the consequences that the expansion of surveillance would have for all neighborhood resi-dents, not just those labeled as thugs or gang members by community repre-sentatives.[28] Likely, these representatives believed that the heavy hand of law enforcement would come down not on the heads of good, decent people like them but rather on the heads of those who, from their perspective, needed or deserved it: street-oriented, gang-associated, ghetto youth, includ-ing seemingly out-of-control youth in their family or on their block.[29]

The rhetorical strategy of pitting some community members against others to advocate for more aggressive enforcement in their communities proved to be powerful and durable. Programs like Operation Ceasefire, enshrined by an influential *New Yorker* profile of David Kennedy and by Kennedy's subsequent account of the program, contribute to this durability.[30]

Those who are familiar with the landscape of violence prevention know that "the Boston Miracle" is a term popularized by the media to describe the dramatic drop in homicides in Boston over the 1990s—from an average of one hundred homicides per year in the mid-1990s to thirty-two in 1999. Operation Ceasefire has earned top billing in the story of this dramatic reduction. Kennedy, an architect of Operation Ceasefire, documents the rise and organizing principles of the program in his first-person account, *Don't Shoot*. His account embraces "the wants-of-the-community" rhetoric while also expanding the discussion of "community." Kennedy asserts that three distinct but overlapping communities play a role in violence preven-tion. The first community, he writes, is law enforcement. The second is the community that exists "in even the poorest, hardest-hit black neighbor-hoods," whose members want "to be safe, to prosper, for its sons and daugh-ters to prosper." The third community is the "community of the streets." It is within the last community, Kennedy argues, that "a small, superheated world of gangs and drug crews and drug markets . . . with its own rules, its own understandings . . . kill for their brothers, die for their brothers."[31] Based on this understanding, Kennedy and his collaborators developed an innovative approach with a simple end in mind: to get the shooters and their crews to stop shooting—or else.

The "or else" would leverage the power of the first community, law enforcement, which relies heavily on the participation of the second community, especially faith leaders, to target and control members of the third community, the small group of people known to be committing acts of interpersonal violence in the neighborhood. The approach was innovative in targeting a small group of individuals for surveillance and aggressive enforcement. The approach could even be described as progressive in some aspects, for instance in framing those involved in violence as rational thinkers, instead of "super-predators" or a new breed of violent youth. Yet it was still organized to align two communities against the third. Youth who did not abide by the program's warnings faced the force of federal law enforcement agencies, who had already begun an effort to ratchet up penalties for a host of drug and violent offenses and became key partners in Operation Ceasefire. Street violence was no longer a local issue; it was now the concern of the federal government.[32]

Word of this new approach to crime fighting in the neighborhood was delivered during forums where groups of identified troublemakers were called in by probation or parole officers for a meeting with the newly formed crime-fighting community.[33] The early effort in Boston provided dramatic examples of "or else" for the young men to consider, including a case in which a notorious gang member who had avoided long-term incarceration was arrested and sentenced to nineteen years and seven months in federal prison with no possibility of parole for the possession of *one* bullet. A representative of the city's Streetworkers program also played a role in these forums, echoing the message that the community wanted an end to violence. Then and only then would the young men called in be provided with assistance and services.

In the wake of the "Boston Miracle," cities across the country tried to replicate parts of the city's crime-fighting strategy.[34] Early evaluations of Operation Ceasefire pointed to dramatic crime reductions in cities that replicated the Ceasefire model.[35] That violence persists at chronic rates in some cities, including in areas that once adopted a Ceasefire model, suggests its limited ability to end gun violence across generations of young people. Nevertheless, the Ceasefire model—specifically, the idea of targeting a small group of people in a defined geographic space—continues to shape approaches to violence prevention today.

THE FILLMORE'S CRIME-FIGHTING COMMUNITY

It is now widely recognized that the tough-on-crime turn of the 1980s and 1990s sparked the rise of mass imprisonment in the United States.[36] What is less commonly understood, however, is how justice system and community-level responses to the problems of drugs and violence in inner-city neighborhoods altered the social organization of a particular type of caretaking—violence prevention—in neighborhoods like the Fillmore. Changes in the landscape of community caretaking professions, including the seemingly rapid emergence of new positions, like Violence Intervention Specialist, were influenced, in part, by changes in funding streams that filled the vacuum left by the erosion of the social safety net. The 1994 Violent Crime Act, for example, not only increased penalties for violent offenses but also directed millions of dollars to community-level programs and laid the foundation for funding the caretaking economy for years to come. As was the case in early peacekeeping efforts in San Francisco, this funding often exacerbated existing fault lines in the community and has transformed much of the work of "saving the neighborhood," as Eric described it early on, into "paperwork" and the management of bureaucratic demands and obligations.[37]

As a consequence of these pecuniary shifts in funding and philosophical shifts in the privileging of the rights of some community members over others, the credentialed class would become ever more involved in managing community-based responses to the problems of the street, like drug trafficking and violence in urban neighborhoods.[38]

During the course of my field research in the neighborhood, the crime-fighting perspective was institutionalized in San Francisco's Mayor's Office of Criminal Justice, which was created by the city in response to protests to stop the violence, as well as a plethora of youth-serving nonprofit organizations. These largely grant-funded nonprofits may work in collaboration with key stakeholders in law enforcement and corrections to effect a crime-free community. For the credentialed class, collaborations with law enforcement would deepen, exploiting and reinforcing longstanding social and moral distinctions in the Black community. Meanwhile, some members of the community—for example, those labeled as gang members or serious youth offenders—became more vulnerable to contact with law enforcement and entry in the juvenile or criminal justice system.

The crime-fighting community I encountered in the Fillmore was composed of several distinct but mutually reinforcing subgroups of (typically) Black San Franciscans: *spokespersons*, usually members of what I refer to as the credentialed class; *street brokers*, who act as intermediaries between the street and the credentialed class; and *activists*.[39] Below, I provide a brief description of the defining characteristics of each group before moving on to an ethnographic account of the neighborhood's crime-fighting community in action.

Spokespersons

In the neighborhood, divisions along axes of class and education, along with evaluations of cultural, social, and moral behavior are reflected in considerations of who is qualified to do the work of saving the neighborhood. I describe this group of middlemen as the "credentialed class" because, as noted previously, it is their acquisition of formal credentials that seems to determine or justify their place in the neighborhood's crime-fighting community. For members of this group, credentials—especially advanced degrees—seem to serve as a proxy for class position, especially within the Black community. Those formal credentials distance them from those with street credentials, such as a well-known history of involvement in the underground economy or close association with the crews in the sightlines of area law enforcement.[40]

The credentialed class plays a key role in the delivery of services to the city's Black community. They hold positions such as executive directors, program directors, or program managers in community-based organizations (CBOs).[41] The work of the credentialed class is to manage the social problems of lower-income Blacks in the neighborhood. The names attached to these social problems often change, depending on which areas are of interest to funders. Over my time in the neighborhood, the problem shifted from violence prevention to disconnected youth to gang-involved youth and back again. The credentialed class also takes on some responsibility for managing overly passionate, less articulate residents whom they view as less than ideal spokespeople or leaders. Members of the credentialed class position themselves—and are positioned by powerful others—as the *legitimate* problem-solvers in the community.

Acquiring the credentials of a formal education does prepare professional caretakers to accomplish some of the important tasks related to the work of saving the neighborhood. These tasks are typically text- and numbers-based and require the preparation of reports to public or private funders. This kind of paperwork is crucial for continued funding from a variety of local, state, and federal organizations. Although members of the credentialed class may be motivated by a desire to serve their communities, the social organization of this work requires that the credentialed class hold themselves accountable not to men like Eric, or troubled youth, but to funders. They know that if they fail to achieve successful outcomes, then their funding and in turn their jobs are at risk.

Street Brokers or Other Intermediaries

In most cases, the Black credentialed class is a degree (or, at times, decades) removed from the most troubled youth in the neighborhood, and the street in general. They often rely on a network of workers who can connect with youth to meet the objective of their programs. In today's inner city, intermediaries are often hired by social service organizations as street outreach workers.[42] The credentialed class recruits a stable of part-time workers for temporary employment, offering official titles (printed on business cards that they hand out readily) like "Outreach Coordinator," "Community Organizer," or "Violence Prevention Specialist." Here, I describe this class of workers—those with street credentials but not formal credentials—as street brokers: individuals with connections to the street that are more salient than those held by the credentialed class. Today's street brokers often have varying degrees of commitment to the institution that employs them. Some are, as Eric was in his early twenties, half-and-half and so have not fully left their criminal past behind them. Like the peacekeepers of a previous era, street brokers are crucial to the success of caretaking agencies and institutions in urban neighborhoods with histories of violence.

Like the intermediaries in Gans's *Urban Villagers*, these street outreach workers are of particular value to the credentialed class because they are able to garner some measure of respect from youth while performing the work of the institution; they too are able to share in some of the ways of the youth while maintaining their authority. It is expected that these workers, when they are paid to do this work, will respect the social order of caretaking work and, in particular, their subservient role in the hierarchy. They are not expected to lead caretaking efforts on their own.[43]

These positions are not nearly as secure as the positions of the professional credentialed class, despite their crucial role. They are typically non-salaried, temporary appointments reliant on the ebb and flow of grant funding. Although tensions may exist among the credentialed class and street brokers, it should be noted that the two groups share a common concern: addressing the persistent problem of violence and its related consequences.

The Activists

Activists are the third important group in the social order of the caretaking community in San Francisco more broadly, and the neighborhood's crime-fighting community in particular. The term is often used in a derogatory or dismissive way to distinguish serious, rational, and respectable members of

the community from those they perceive as frivolous, disorderly, and igno-
rant. During my time in the Fillmore, this group was most often composed
of men, including some men associated with Eric and his organization, who
supposedly lacked the civility required to effectively negotiate with members of the credentialed class or other city stakeholders.[44] At times, activists
have been seen as a threat to the bureaucratic efforts of the crime-fighting
community, whose leaders value a respectable and rational representation
of Blackness in relations with city stakeholders.

The headline for an *SF Weekly* cover story about the acrimonious history of redevelopment in the neighborhood captured this disdain. It posed
the provocative question: "What's really wrong with the Lower Fillmore?"
The answer was phrased with an equally provocative question: "Could it
be the activists who claim they are trying to rebuild it?"[45] In the article,
which traces the history of urban redevelopment in the neighborhood over
a period of nearly forty years, contemporary "activists"—the term is often
set in quotes in the article, suggesting the dubious nature of the term—are
described as disruptive, disrespectful, and disinterested in the real concerns
of city and neighborhood representatives who are working to distribute
redevelopment funding prior to the Redevelopment Agency's official
departure from the neighborhood on January 1, 2009. Whereas committee
members attempt to focus on shoring up local businesses and developing a
marketable identity for the Fillmore, "the activists" use public forums to
redirect the conversation to seemingly unrelated or "irrelevant" concerns,
like the neighborhood's "youth problem" and other "social ills" like drugs,
violence, and unemployment, which, the activists argue, are intertwined
with the neighborhood's history of urban redevelopment (also referred to
as "Negro removal"). The activists are portrayed as crass opportunists who
"contributed to and prolonged the infightings, sometimes for financial
gain." The article was referencing the practice of distributing Redevelopment
Agency consulting contracts to particularly disruptive activists. The article
concludes with a response to the questions posed in its headline, one that
lays much of the blame for what is wrong with the Lower Fillmore at the
feet of neighborhood activists: "But to prosper—even to survive—new
blood and a lot less of the nasty 'activism' that has long characterized the
neighborhood might be just what the Lower Fillmore needs."

The appeals and actions of the activists, scorned as they are, serve an
important role in reinforcing the social order of the neighborhood's crime-
fighting community. Many of the members of the credentialed class who
were involved in redevelopment efforts, for example, are the same people
who are now involved in violence-prevention efforts. They are the

spokespersons called upon again and again. Their currency and appeal is rooted, in part, in their difference from activists and, simultaneously, in their ability to work with the activists, when needed. In this way, a symbiotic relationship exists not only among the spokespersons, outreach workers, and the activists but also between this group and other city and business stakeholders who prefer to engage with a class of Black people they deem to be more acquiescent and rational than the activists.

The bureaucratic battles and infighting that defines the crime-fighting community in San Francisco has consequences for the most vulnerable youth in the city and others working to change their lives. At times, the bureaucratic pressures of the crime-fighting community supersede sustained efforts to incorporate troubled youth more fully into civic life. It is far more common for youth to be pushed out of civic life—through death, detention, incarceration, or a web of bureaucratic paperwork, like gang injunctions or stay-away orders—than lifted up into the realm of civic legitimacy, a phenomenon I observed firsthand during my time in the neighborhood.

THE CRIME-FIGHTING COMMUNITY IN ACTION

Today's crime-fighting community is shored up by targeted and collaborative efforts among the criminal justice system and the community. At times, these efforts leverage the punitive power of law enforcement to coerce moral and behavioral change from young Black men while offering little chance of social mobility for youth in exchange. Other collaborative efforts are designed to minimize the political and interpersonal friction that comes along with violence-prevention efforts in the city. In both types of arrangements, youth run the risk of being treated as mere pawns in a paper game. The social organization of the crime-fighting community also runs the risk of ceding primary responsibility for the control, surveillance, and punishment of a segment of Black youth to law enforcement at a moment that is historically unique for its commitment to incarceration and harsh punishment.

The collaborative relationship between law enforcement and Black spokespersons was revealed in meetings I attended while conducting fieldwork in the neighborhood, including meetings held by Safe More, a nonprofit organization supported by funding from the public defender's office that held a regular convening of youth-serving organizations in the neighborhood. Safe More organized bi-weekly, lunch-time meetings that were open to the public but were attended mainly by staff members of local nonprofits along with a handful of residents of the community, including Eric.

The nonprofit also sponsored a range of activities in the neighborhood, from school supply giveaways at the start of the year to holiday parties and health clinics. Mary Cook, an African American woman and member of the credentialed class, led each meeting. The agenda would often include updates from each subcommittee, which focused on areas of social justice, social development, community health, education, and economic and vocational advancement.

During my time in the neighborhood, I attended these meetings sometimes on my own and other times with Eric, who attended as a representative of Brothers Changing the Hood (BCH). I attended one such meeting in the fall of 2007, several months after a preliminary gang injunction was implemented in the neighborhood. A gang injunction is a civil injunction issued by the city attorney that restricts the lawful and unlawful behavior and association of people named on the injunction within a specific geographic area. Two gang-injunction zones were created in the Western Addition; the zones covered the areas surrounding three government-subsidized housing projects. The introduction of the gang injunction along with the introduction of a Ceasefire-inspired effort led to a good deal of confusion, frustration, and anxiety among some members of the community, including young men who were the primary targets of these surveillance and enforcement efforts. This anxiety and confusion was evident in a Safe More meeting about the injunction. This meeting, which I describe in greater detail below, highlights the role that spokespersons and street brokers play in the crime-fighting community. Here, we see how more organic and potentially disruptive efforts to address the problem of violence in the neighborhood are subsumed and constrained by bureaucratic logics.

In many ways, the meeting was typical. The agenda included updates from the subcommittees along with a review of the community calendar, among other items. The meeting took place a month before the Western Addition gang injunction was made permanent. It was the second meeting called to address the gang injunction, which was the first business item on the agenda. A representative from the Lawyer's Committee on Civil Rights passed out a copy of the preliminary injunction for the group to review. The gang injunction was added to the agenda so the group could discuss and select a process for opting out of the injunction. Once a person is named on the injunction, they remain there *for life*. At the moment, no opt-out process had been written into the injunction.

As often happens during community meetings, especially when the topic comes to crime or justice, the conversation strays, with some community members expressing concern and frustration with issues ranging from police practices to the "madness" that is going on in the streets. That day, in contrast to other meetings I attended, three young Black men were seated at the table. By this time, I had noticed that although community meetings would often turn to the topic of violence and young Black men, there were rarely any young Black men in the room. The three young men at the table on this afternoon were brought to the meeting by George, a man who looked to be in his mid- to late thirties, with a dark brown complexion and a muscular build. George grew up in the neighborhood and had recently taken on a leadership role at a local community center. Of the three young men at the meeting, two of them, aged twenty-five and twenty, were listed on the preliminary injunction. During the meeting, George acted as intermediary for the young men, indicating when they should share their stories with the group.

Others contributed to the conversation on their own volition. One woman spoke about her experience working with probationers as part of a focused violence-deterrence program that began in the Western Addition in the early summer and included what people in the neighborhood referred to as the "call in." Following this discussion, one of the young men, the twenty-five-year-old, raised his hand. "'Scuse me," he said, somewhat tentatively, before sharing his experience with the group of professionals around the table, which I then recorded in my fieldnotes:

> Derrick is twenty-five years old. He has a medium brown complexion and is wearing a white T-shirt underneath an oversized black sweatshirt, slightly baggy denim jeans, and sneakers. His face twists up in anxiety, frustration, and anger as he discloses what his interactions with his probation officer have been like. He begins by telling the group about his troubled interactions with his probation officer, who seems to be using the gang injunction and the call in to harass or intimidate him. [His description of his probation officer is similar to accounts I would hear from other young men in the neighborhood who shared the same P.O. over the course of my time in the neighborhood.] He complains that his probation officer is trying to get into his head. He tells the group that his P.O. makes him take off his shirt and searches him every time he goes to his office. His P.O. tells him that he is being watched all the time and that the police can't wait until Nov. 9th. He says that his probation officer tells him that if he does just one [wrong] thing, he is going to "take [him] down."
>
> "Do ya'll know of anything happening November 9th," he asks. "Is that another call-in?"
>
> It's clear that Derrick is upset. He asks if there is anything that he can do to "shake" this guy. One of the participants who works closely with Eric's organization speaks out on Derrick's behalf to direct the

group's focus to the substance of the young man's concerns. He asks the group if there is any way that Derrick can switch P.O.s because at this point it doesn't even seem to be about business with this guy, he says, it is personal. It's like he has a vendetta against him.

Derrick says that his P.O. told him that "I have to be out of my mama's house in forty-five days," just days before the Christmas holiday.

I ask Derrick if his P.O. gave him a reason for him having to get out of his mother's house. He explains that he has a "stay-away order" from another case.

Derrick seems trapped by legal troubles. It is clear that he feels the tightening of constraints from the stepped up surveillance and enforcement efforts. At the same time, he says, he is trying to do "something positive" and he appears quite fearful of his trajectory being complicated by his P.O. Members of the group express an interest in getting young people like Derrick, who are trying to do something positive, to talk to other young people facing similar challenges. The group talks about the need to document the positive work that young people are doing with evaluations and assessments.

The twenty-year-old also talks during the meeting. In contrast to what seems like the general acceptance of the inevitability of the gang injunction, the young man questions the legitimacy of the gang injunction's implementation altogether. He asks the group questions that challenge the legitimacy of the process, such as asking the group if we really think that the judge really looked through those four thousand pages of documents (referring to the pages of expert declarations provided by law enforcement as evidence of gang association) and then decided who he was going to put on the list? He says that his record is no longer than a single piece of paper and he's on the list. George, the man who brought the young people to the meeting, says that he was on the list too before he got his name removed.

The representative from the Lawyer's Committee on Civil Rights says that she wished she had learned of this group earlier in the process, when the City Attorney first announced his plans to extend the gang injunction into the Western Addition over the summer. She says that she's been having trouble getting lawyers to volunteer to sign up to take on cases and that law firms that she contacted are hesitant to get involved. No one wants to take the cases pro bono because the case is about "gangs."

This meeting, particularly the conversation about local crime-fighting efforts like the gang injunction and the "call in," illustrates the new contours of the crime-fighting community. That the setting for the convening existed at all was a consequence of the persistence of violence in the neighborhood *and* funding that flowed through the criminal justice system (albeit the public defender's office) that either required or encouraged the involvement of the community.

The people around the table represented different factions of the crime-fighting community. The leader of the convening, a member of the credentialed class, was frequently called upon by the city to act as a middlewoman for the Black community, even though, by her own account, she occupied a position that was somewhat distant from the street. As such, George, acting as a *street broker*, stepped up to serve the role of bringing youth to the table. The young men represented the street, albeit a particular version of the young men who are often at the center of crime-fighting politics in the neighborhood.[46] If these young men were, as they say, trying to do "something positive," it is likely that the group would use them as exemplars of change for other young people in the neighborhood, thus providing them with a place in the hierarchy of the crime-fighting community.

The young men's accounts and appeals also demonstrated the limits of the crime-fighting community. Their comments suggested that institutional actors in the criminal justice system, like the probation officer the young men referred to, may use their newfound leverage to increase their control and dominance over young men in the system, or as a cover for a set of practices that young men may interpret as degrading and disrespectful. As was evidenced in the failure of the credentialed class to offer to take up the young men's concerns over their treatment by their probation officer at this meeting, their role in the crime-fighting community was to operate *in concert with* and *not in opposition to* the crime-fighting objectives of law enforcement—a departure from the peacekeeping community of the past.

This commitment was revealed in a description of the implementation of the gang injunction that Mrs. Cook once shared with the group. The comments came at the end of a nearly two-hour meeting, after an attendee brought up the issue of the gang injunction, which had not yet been discussed by the convener or the head of the social justice committee. The convener suggested taking up the issue during the next meeting, but an attendee intervened before the meeting came to an official end: "How do we find out about the updates on the injunction?"

The head of the committee to which the gang injunction had been assigned said that a lawyer had contacted him to discuss the injunction. The convener interrupted to say that she may ask somebody from the public defender's office to visit the group to discuss the injunction. She said that they were working on ways to help people who were demonstrating an effort to get off the list. An attendee asked if people were being evicted because they were on the list. The convener replied that there was other stuff—referring to other law enforcement efforts, like the call in—going on that was not directly related to the gang injunction.

"Definitely the heat is on," she said, "there's movement."

In addition to the public defender, she suggested having an officer at the next meeting talk about how the injunction was being handled. She said that some of the people named on the injunction had been told that they would only be arrested if they returned to their mother's house, but then some of those people had been arrested anyway.

She warned the group that "senses are heightened" among officers in the neighborhood because of the injunction. "People are much more aware now," she said, with police reacting to unremarkable infractions like jaywalking. Her advice: if you're on the injunction, stay clean.

These warnings were packaged as helpful advice to be distributed by others to certain youth in the neighborhood. Yet the warnings also suggested that the convener was aligned with the objectives of those in charge of issuing and enforcing the gang injunction: "We're really trying to leverage the injunction," she told the group. She suggested that "we" (i.e., the first and second community of Kennedy's description) were trying to use the injunction in a certain way, echoing the logic of the gang injunction shared by scholars, the city attorney, and law enforcement.[47]

The convener's handling of the discussion regarding the gang injunction illustrates ties that bind the crime-fighting community together. The convener seemed in the know when it came to the various law enforcement efforts taking place in the community. She revealed this privileged knowledge in her explanation of how "they" were using the injunction. Near the end of the discussion, she also revealed her alignment with the objectives of law enforcement and other city stakeholders who had supported the implementation of the gang injunction in the neighborhood: *we* are trying to leverage the injunction, she said, to use it to increase the surveillance, to turn up the pressure, for those on "the list." The convener did not address the injunction as a civil rights issue, as some community activists have done. Instead, she operated as a middlewoman. She facilitated the objectives of the city and law enforcement by passing along information to a segment of the community in a way that minimized any concerns regarding the legality of the injunction, its racist roots, or the potential negative impact on families or individuals named on the list. The bureaucratic work of the crime-fighting community and its futility was highlighted in its assignment to the social justice committee, without discussion of how it seemed to violate the fundamental civil rights of those named on the injunction.

The handling of the gang injunction at this regular convening also revealed the implicit pact among the credentialed class, the city, and law enforcement: community-based organizations will largely cede control over those most likely to be involved in violence to law enforcement, whereas other youth-serving organizations will focus on "at-risk" youth at the margins of the community. These efforts may draw some young people away from the eye of the storm of violence, but those most vulnerable to violence and incarceration, young people like the young men at the table, are often left to negotiate their interactions with law enforcement, along with any efforts to change the direction of their young lives, largely on their own.

THE CRIME-FIGHTING COMMUNITY
AND THE NUMBERS GAME

The crime-fighting community's preoccupation with bureaucracy presents a dilemma for internal caretakers for whom the work of saving the neighborhood is less of a job and more of a calling. As it was for Eric, this work is often intertwined with efforts to make good. Yet there seems to be little space within the crime-fighting community for members of this group to emerge as legitimate providers of services on their own. Because of these constraints, their efforts to do good and make good are limited by the politics of the crime-fighting community.

To return to the statement from Everett Hughes at the start of this chapter: once institutionalized, legitimacy and credibility are granted or manufactured by an institution. Even though Eric described himself as an executive director of an organization, neither he nor his organization was legitimate in the eyes of the credentialed class. He simply did not have the right sort of credentials. As Donovan commented, Eric is not "educated." From the outside, the organization did not appear organized. The lack of educational credentials or an apparent organizational structure made others reluctant to see Eric and BCH as legitimate purveyors of services in the community. Since Eric started the organization to change his life, he does the work anyway. Still, he aspires to be if not a *member* of the Black credentialed class then at least to be treated with the same level of respect that they receive from others. Eric had hoped that securing a small grant from the city to do outreach work around the gang injunction might help to legitimize his status and the status of BCH. Instead, he found that getting the grant served to intensify the efforts of the credentialed class to get him to "play the game," as it was once described to Eric by a local politician.

The game that Eric refers to—often known as the "numbers game"—is political in nature, but it also flows from the competition among programs for funding that has structured violence-prevention work in the city for decades. The Safe More convening was intended to minimize this competition. Yet the institutionalization of these efforts did little to eliminate a problem that was common to the settlement houses Herbert Gans studied decades ago. The crime-fighting community of today must prove that there is a legitimate need for its services. One way to demonstrate this need is to "stress the numbers" to funders and benefactors, as Gans explains in *Urban Villagers:*

> With respect to adolescents, the settlement houses stressed the numbers
> they attracted, rather than the way they [youth] behaved once they
> came. This not only assured board members that their settlement house
> was earning its keep, but reassured its staff that, despite all of the
> frustration, it was performing a useful function.[48]

The stakes have since increased. The pressure to get the numbers is perhaps greater than the pressure placed on settlement houses described by Gans because of changes in the provision of funding for social services that has taken place over the past sixty years. The work of applying for funding to finance the nonprofit and proving to the funding agency that you are serving the community takes up much of an organization's energy. Getting the numbers is crucial to the organization's survival. Eric summed up the present manifestation of the pressure to get the numbers this way during an early interview: "It's all about the mighty dollar in which I can get funded for starting a youth program and it's also about numbers."

Organizations must prove that they are indeed serving the target population that they said they would serve in their grant, Eric explained to me. In order to continue to receive funding for programs targeting youth, he said, "They have to prove that kids are coming through the door." This pressure to get the numbers fosters organizational anxiety. If organizations do not get the numbers, then they are likely to lose their funding and, in turn, the jobs that are supported by that funding stream. Among their colleagues and community members, they are also likely to lose some sense of their standing and status. Efforts to get the numbers can, at times, undermine the legitimacy of these institutions. In the minds of some people, organizations that continue to receive "city money" year after year come to look less like a legitimate institution delivering services and more like "poverty pimps."[49]

The numbers game is embedded in a larger "paper game," as the director of a city office charged with handling (and handing out) federal money once described it. This is where credentials become currency.[50] In the end, an organization must present well on paper and demonstrate that it can handle the administrative burden of managing grant money. This is especially challenging for smaller organizations. The city offices that are charged with handing out money are accountable to others—auditors, city attorneys, or federal funding agencies. Of the seven hundred community-based organizations in San Francisco, a handful of large anchor institutions stand out as capable of handling this administrative burden. The paper game does not favor small organizations like BCH. For a small, volunteer-based organization without funding to pay grant writers to prepare grants or hire IT staff to supervise intake and assessment, managing the paperwork tied to the smallest of grants can be a burden.

Eric was also reluctant to play the game. He found that constant politicking frustrated his efforts to make good. It also made it difficult for Eric to find a place in the community that allowed him to do the work he wanted to do. Eric wanted to change lives, not play games. In the end, he was accountable to the group he grew up with, not to funders.

The numbers game is, at its heart, about accountability. Eric felt pressured to relinquish his accountability to his peers and extended primary group, and to take up the cause of the Black credentialed class and its backers in city government. He was encouraged to learn the rules of a new hustle and to play by those rules. Playing by the rules meant that Eric should fold his efforts to save the neighborhood into the larger objectives of city-funded organizations in the neighborhood. There was a particular pressure for him to fold his work into the efforts of Safe More. Eric understood the logic of the game, but he thought that playing the game was nothing more than a hustle. After a decade putting in work on the streets, he was done with hustles. He was also reluctant to treat his calling like a job, instead of a mission. His reluctance to play the game sometimes led to trouble, especially when his efforts to save the neighborhood intersected with the work of organizations like Safe More.

In the final section of this chapter, I draw on my participant observation with BCH to illustrate the sort of bureaucratic combat that emerges from the social organization of caretaking work as I have described it here. The story of the flyer, as I call it, reveals the consequences of these battles for men like Eric and others in the neighborhood who are motivated to make good.

THE STORY OF "THE FLYER"

At times, Eric's organization does what looks a lot like outreach work, but the group also has a strong sense of itself as a collection of independent actors. Eric started the group years ago as a way to break free from the street. He was not hired to do this work—he was simply trying to change the trajectory of his own life. Over time—about a decade—he shed his identity as a hustler. People in the neighborhood came to know him for the positive work he was doing in the neighborhood. He became a pastor in a local storefront church. Some people began to call him "Rev." Others looking for help or to change their lives in the same way they saw him doing would seek him out. This is how he met and came to work with a man named Lincoln.

Lincoln attended a meeting that Eric's organization held on the gang injunction in the neighborhood. At the time, one of Lincoln's sons was in custody and was being pressured, according to Lincoln, to claim gang membership. Lincoln attended the meeting Eric was hosting because he wanted to help his son. Eric told him that if he really wanted to help his son, he had to start with changing his own life: then he could be a model for his sons. Lincoln took that message to heart. He began to volunteer regularly with Eric's group. He took up the (very challenging) task of organizing a Monday night boys group that was held in one of the more notorious housing complexes in the neighborhood. The group was typical in many ways—it was something of an introduction to life skills for the boys—but it was also a setting in which Lincoln could carve out this new place for himself in the neighborhood.

As I describe in greater detail in chapter 4, the work that Lincoln performed as a volunteer was important not only to his own effort to change his life but also to the young boys in the group, many of whom were not connected to more mainstream youth-serving organizations in the community. Over time (I observed the group over a period of a year), Lincoln and the boys could connect the youth to these institutions, including institutions that were once wary about having young men from the nearby projects in their programs. Once the young men began to attend programs hosted at these institutions, Lincoln was called upon again and again to act as a mediator of sorts between the young people and the institutions. When the boys caused trouble, he was called upon to show up and de-escalate conflicts or discipline the boys. Lincoln took on this role as a volunteer. Like others in similar positions, Lincoln took on this role as a way to find—or create for himself—a new place in the neighborhood. In doing so, he provided an important service for the community. Several months into Lincoln's efforts with the group, I received a phone call from Eric.

"Hey, Nikki," he says. I sense a note of dejection in the tone of his voice. "I don't know what's going on," he continues. "It never fails to surprise me."

"What happened?" I ask.

Eric tells me that we have been summoned to a meeting at the local community center. He goes on to explain that the director of Safe More is upset and wants to talk to us about our work in the housing complex where we have been holding the boys group. I agree to meet Eric at the community center. Mary Cook is there along with Lisa, a community leader from the housing complex where the boys group is held who also acts as something of an assistant to Mrs. Cook. The executive director of the community center is there, too, as well as Eric's sister, who has worked with community-based organizations that serve the neighborhood in the past and who now works at the community center. Lincoln also shows up for the meeting. He had to make his way through one of the open-air drug corridors in the neighborhood. When he arrives, he says to Eric, "I'm glad I'm not in that life no more. I don't know how I survived it man. People come up to me [looking to buy drugs] and I'm like, 'I don't do that no more.'"

"I like what I'm doing now. I'm going to be doing this whether or not I get paid. I got kids out there," he says as he grabs Eric by the shoulders. "This brother got me into this. I like it. I'm not going back."

After a few minutes, we get to why the impromptu meeting was called. Lisa, the president of the tenants association, is upset because Eric and his group did not come to her when they developed an outline for programming at the housing complex (the programming included the boys group and a GED course that I led with a graduate student). Lisa pulls out a copy of the outline. Eric is told that the outline went to the head of public housing, and when housing came to the outreach coordinator, she was held accountable because she did not know what was going on in the housing complex. Housing asked her why her organization was not listed on the flyer as a partner in the programming. There were consequences for not knowing the answers to these questions, Mrs. Cook said, for her and her organization: she had to let a paid outreach worker go because he did not know what was going on. The outreach coordinator might have to stop paying Lisa, too, for the work she was doing there. Lisa makes a point that highlights the system of accountability when it comes to programs in the neighborhoods: decisions about what happens in the housing complex must go through the Tenants Association, which means going through her.

As I sat in on this meeting, I was struck by how petty it all seemed. With all that was going on in the neighborhood, why is it that all of us are around this table to talk about a flyer? After months of the men coming together as volunteers to work with some of the most troubled young people in the neighborhood, this was their reward: admonished like children over a flyer, scolded for not getting the paperwork right. From Eric's perspective, not including the organization's name on the flyer was just an oversight. But this minor oversight triggered a set of *institutional* consequences for members of the credentialed class and their allies in the neighborhood.[51] It also engendered some frustration on Eric's part regarding his place in the community's caretaking hierarchy and exposed a common tension among individuals and institutions working to "save the neighborhood."

The meeting over the flyer also sent a message that reinforced a story that many people shared with me during my fieldwork in the neighborhood: that paperwork was more important than people. These bureaucratic skirmishes send a message to men like Eric and Lincoln. Each time their efforts to make good bump up against the politics of programs in the neighborhood, it affirms Eric's belief that he has to "fight to do right" or that, as he has said before about similar experiences with gatekeepers in the community, "when you really want to help, you in the way."

As is evidenced by the story of the flyer, the social organization of caretaking work engenders a latent sense of competition among individuals and organizations. The allocation of funding is largely a bureaucratic process. Caretaking agencies and institutions that receive funding to save the neighborhood are expected to handle the paperwork associated with receiving such funding. This puts others who also perform caretaking work at a disadvantage, especially internal caretakers, like Eric, whose mission to save the neighborhood is part of a larger personal mission to make good.

In *A Place on the Corner*, Elijah Anderson writes "social order exists because people stay in their place, and they do so because other people keep them there."[52] The seemingly inconsequential dispute over a flyer reveals how men like Eric, *as well as members of the credentialed class*, are kept in their place both by the institutional constraints of funding streams and by the interpersonal enforcement of boundaries by the credentialed class. The story of the flyer illustrates how the social organization of institutional resources in the neighborhood can make it difficult for men like Eric and Lincoln to find a legitimate place in the neighborhood after they break free from the street. Such disputes over paperwork miss the importance of the work that men like Eric and Lincoln do, and in doing so miss an opportunity to magnify the impact of their work—*work that they will likely do even if there is no funding to do it.*

To be sure, the disputes that erupt among members of the crime-fighting community are shaped by the social history and racial politics I described earlier in this chapter. As such, these disputes are not trivial, despite their pettiness. The social organization of any caretaking community is consequential for the delivery of services to those in need, including the young

Black men in the Western Addition who were most vulnerable to victimization at the hands of their peers and targeted policing practices. The rise of the crime-fighting community was facilitated, in large part, by identifying these young men as the problem, even in one of the most liberal cities in the nation. In the following chapter, I describe the social situation of the young people who are the targets of the crime-fighting community, which has essentially ceded primary responsibility for the control, surveillance, and punishment of the most vulnerable group of young people in the neighborhood to law enforcement.

3   **Targets**

The persistence of gun violence in small pockets of the city legitimizes the institutionalized efforts of the crime-fighting community. One such episode of violence erupted just two weeks before I made the Fillmore my home. "7 injured as feud rages in the Western Addition," blared a headline in the local paper, "2 attacks in 12 hours." Another article reported that the shootings were the "latest sign of a neighborhood under siege by brazen young thugs with guns." The shootings erupted just a short distance from a local community center. According to the news report, the fallout from the shooting spread over an unusually wide radius: "The shootings left nearby cars and homes scarred by bullet holes. Yellow chalk circles on the pavement, which typically indicate where a bullet casing has been found, were scattered over a wide area, as if the victims of the second shooting had been chased."[1]

This was not the first time that the Fillmore had drawn attention for gun violence. Two years earlier, a local paper had dubbed the Western Addition the "deadliest city area." This came after predawn shootings killed two young men, aged nineteen and twenty-six, along with a three-year-old child, in less than two weeks. In the wake of that shooting, then Mayor Gavin Newsom announced that there would be "much more of a focus now on the hot spots of the Western Addition."[2] The killings represented the forty-third, forty-fourth, and forty-fifth homicide victims of 2005. By the end of 2007, San Francisco would record one hundred homicides, four more homicides than recorded in 2005 and the highest number of homicides in the city since the beginning of the new millennium.[3]

In both 2005 and 2007, the vast majority of homicides involved young men and guns.[4] In 2007, over half of the homicide victims were Black, and a third were younger than twenty-five.[5] Still, despite the regularity of gun violence in the city generally and in the Fillmore specifically, the summer

2007 shooting stood out for several reasons: the number of people injured; the quick escalation to retaliation; and the harm done to a bystander. Jason Steinberg, a thirty-two-year-old White male resident, was injured when a stray bullet burst through a metal gate and struck him in his left thigh. Steinberg's injury suggested that the violence in the neighborhood threatened to extend beyond its usual networks of young Black men. The shooting conveyed that the quickly gentrifying neighborhood might not be safe for newcomers, a conclusion that Steinberg came to after his injury. "I'm looking to move out immediately," he told a reporter following the shooting.

The early morning shoot-out triggered what is now a familiar set of responses from the city, law enforcement, and local residents. The explosion of violence on the city's streets intensified calls for the city to "do something" about gun violence in neighborhoods like the Fillmore.[6] In the wake of the shootings, police presence in the neighborhood intensified. The local newspaper reported that the move was met with both relief and skepticism on the part of residents: "Vonne [an elderly neighborhood resident] and her neighbors welcomed the Police Department's beefed-up presence, but wondered why the police don't give more attention to the neighborhood prior to the most recent eruption of violence. 'I saw two policemen walking the beat down here,' [Vonne] said. 'Why not do this all the time?'" Another resident, a young woman who withheld her name from the reporter out of fear, shared her frustration with the city's response to the shooting: "I don't want to be racist, but I'll say this," she said. "All year, kids have been getting shot, but the police don't do anything about it until that White man got shot."[7] Her comment reveals a commonly held belief among African Americans regarding the value placed on Black life by the city and especially the police: violence is only a problem when it spills *outside* of the Black community.[8]

It may not have been obvious to the anonymous resident quoted by the reporter, but law enforcement and other city officials had, in fact, been doing something about the violence in the neighborhood. Among these initiatives, including hiring and reassigning officers as well as the installation of cameras on reportedly high-crime corners,[9] were the efforts of the city attorney who, working in collaboration with local law enforcement, had been using the power of his office to target so-called gangs in the neighborhood. In the weeks following the early morning shooting in 2007, the city attorney issued a preliminary gang injunction (preliminary to the permanent injunction discussed in the previous chapter) that relied heavily on evidence provided by local law enforcement. The preliminary injunction included the names of over one hundred men. Of the forty-two men named on what would eventually become a permanent injunction, over 80 percent were under the age of thirty; half were between the ages of eighteen and twenty-four.[10]

The gang injunction restricted the behavior and association of those named. Although issued in a civil court, the injunction operated as what Katherine Beckett and Steve Herbert have described as a "civil-criminal hybrid": a violation of the civil gang injunction could lead to criminal penalty, including a fine, up to six months in jail, or both.[11] The gang injunction was but one of a host of efforts the city launched in an effort to suppress violence and gang activity. As Mayor Newsom suggested in 2005, the city had begun to focus the attention of law enforcement on "hot spots" of violence. In 2007, the city developed a "hot spot" policing and enforcement strategy. In 2008, as San Francisco was on its way to recording ninety-eight homicides for the second year in a row, the city implemented its hot-spot policing effort in five neighborhoods, including the Western Addition, where "officers from patrol, gang, narcotics and other units team with probation officers, the California Highway Patrol and others to saturate the hot spots."[12]

In this chapter, I explain how young Black men become targets of anti-violence, anti-gang, and anti-crime efforts in the crime-fighting community. I draw on multiple data sources to illustrate the ways that the social situation of young Black men in the neighborhood has changed over time in ways that both overlap and contrast with Eric's experience as a youth and young adult in the same neighborhood. Eric's adolescence overlapped with key shifts in criminal justice policy and practices that would lead to the rise of mass incarceration and the deep entrenchment of the criminal justice system in neighborhoods like the Western Addition. In contrast, young people born in the 1980s would come of age under a law enforcement regime that would increase the frequency of encounters between the police and local residents without the guarantee of safety or protection from the threat of violence from either group. In the discourse of the crime-fighting community, young Black men's experiences as victims of lethal violence are used to legitimize the penetration and expansion of criminal justice surveillance in the neighborhood, which has consequences not only for young men's vulnerability to violence and justice system involvement but also for the gender socialization of Black youth.[13] A consequence of this sustained focus by police on a particular group of people in a particular geographic area over a series of decades is that the young Black men living there face a double bind: they come of age under the persistent presence of criminal justice surveillance, yet they remain vulnerable to injury or death as a result of violence in the city. This surveillance takes two forms: the increased *physical presence* of a range of law enforcement actors in the neighborhood, from "black-and-whites" patrolling the beat to task force officers stopping and searching young men in public, and the *expansion of bureaucratic forms of surveillance,* such as the gang injunction handed down by the city attorney in the wake of the summer shootings and other forms of bureaucracy that keep young people tied to the juvenile or criminal justice system. Efforts to resist these forms of bodily and bureaucratic control are likely to be met with a range of sanctions, including fines, physical coercion, and periods of incarceration.

The justice system's response to violence contributes to a troubling contradiction. Each shooting that makes the pages of the local paper legitimizes the entrenchment of law enforcement in the neighborhood, which, in turn, leads to more frequent and potentially more aggressive encounters between residents and the police. In many neighborhoods, these frequent encounters have contributed to the erosion of faith in the criminal justice system.[14] A lack of trust in the criminal justice system as a protector or adjudicator of wrongs allows, as Elijah Anderson has documented, a form of street justice based on respect, reputation, and retaliation to fill the void.[15] The deeper and broader the penetration of what is perceived to be an unjust system, the more likely it is that residents will take justice into their own hands. The shootings or killings that erupt over seemingly trivial matters only serve to reinforce the belief that young Black men are, as one Bay Area city attorney once described it, "bullet magnets," whose bodies and behaviors require the type of aggressive policing practices called for by city officials, law enforcement, and some neighborhood residents.[16] In this way, aggressive policing practices have, over the past thirty years, become co-constructors of the acts of violence that they are called upon to prevent—a contradiction that is not lost on many neighborhood residents.

Typically, scholars, policy makers, and city officials will evaluate the efficacy of these types of targeted policing practices solely through the lens of public safety while overlooking how aggressive policing practices can potentially make some members of the community less safe. These residents are more likely not only to come under the control of the justice system but also to witness or experience violence. Also overlooked is the social and psychological impact that such practices may have on residents, especially youth. In the second half of this chapter, I bring attention to a set of consequences that emerge from the penetration and expansion of the criminal justice system in what I describe as *high-surveillance neighborhoods:* neighborhoods that are the frequent targets of hot-spot policing and other forms of targeted and aggressive policing practices.[17] In contrast to the experiences of youth in settings without a substantial law enforcement presence, such routine contact with the police shapes adolescence for youth in high-surveillance neighborhoods in ways that extend far beyond their involvement with the justice system.

Put simply, law enforcement has taken on a key role as an agent of socialization for youth of color in high-surveillance neighborhoods.[18] Young people, especially those who are most disconnected from various pro-social institutions (e.g., schools, faith communities, or youth organizations), learn important lessons about authority, status, and dominance through their daily encounters with police. For young men, these lessons shape understandings of what it means to be respected not simply as a person but *as a man* in these settings. During face-to-face encounters with the police, young men are, over the course of their adolescence, socialized into submission—a gendered lesson that runs counter to mainstream expectations of masculinity, which are typically rooted in dominance. For example, the stop-and-search encounter, once described to me as "the regular routine" by a respondent, demands that a young man accept a "submissive or supplicant" role, since any challenge to an officer's authority (intended or perceived) can lead to a loss of liberty or, in extreme cases, loss of life. Examined in this way, the stop-and-search and other routine forms of contact with law enforcement become the frontline of a gendered battle, one in which a civilian, especially an adolescent, is ill-positioned to win since officers possess a monopoly over violence that almost always trumps that of any civilian. Indeed, that is what makes police officers different from the rest of us.

Close attention to young men's frequent encounters with the police in high-surveillance neighborhoods reveals a striking similarity to the range of formal and informal social constraints that operate to keep women and girls (and other gendered outsiders) "in their place." As Patricia Hill Collins explains in *Black Sexual Politics,* the forms of constraint experienced by Black women and girls, especially the omnipresent threat of sexual violence, are often hidden from public view or silenced during public discussions regarding the problems facing the Black community. This silencing allows the violence to continue as if it is a natural or normal dimension of social life. This silencing, Collins explains, confines Black women in an invisible cage of control, which only compounds the pain and vulnerability that comes along with confinement: "[B]eing confined in a cage that seems invisible to everyone else nullifies a woman's suffering and exacerbates her isolation."[19]

For young Black men in high-surveillance neighborhoods, the penetration and expansion of law enforcement in their daily lives *also operates as an invisible cage,* one that constrains their bodies and behaviors, shaping what they do, who they do it with, where they do it, and how, while reinforcing notions of manhood that are deeply rooted in the coupling of strength and dominance. The gendered lessons that young Black men learn from how officers handle their bodies and the bodies of others who look like them are consequential not only for young Black men but also for the women and adolescent girls who share space and time with them, since efforts to repair or redeem a young man's sense of self are all too often played out on the bodies of Black women and girls (or other gendered outsiders).

During my time in the Fillmore, I learned that routine encounters with the police, whether they unfold in public or private or are experienced directly or indirectly (e.g., the witnessing of aggressive encounters), hold the potential to send ripples of aggression throughout the community.[20] Acts of physical aggression may manifest in the actions of young Black men, especially in their relations with peers, family members, intimates, or other authority figures in ways that reinforce stereotypical ideas about Black masculinity and fortify efforts to constrain and contain their bodies. The hand that local policing efforts play in the distribution of this aggression is often made invisible, buried in calls to contain the violence that is presumed to originate in the bodies of Black men, which, to borrow from Collins, only exacerbates the isolation and vulnerability of Black men *and* those close to them.

RACE AND POLICING IN SAN FRANCISCO: FROM ABDICATION TO ENTRENCHMENT

San Francisco is widely known as a liberal and tolerant city. In *Culture and Civility in San Francisco,* a collection of ethnographic essays published in the early 1970s, Howard Becker and Irving Horowitz comment on the city's cosmopolitan reputation: "San Francisco prides itself on its sophistication, on being the most European of American cities, on its picturesque cosmopolitanism. The picturesque quality, indeed the quaintness, rests in part on physical beauty." At the time, the city's sense of cosmopolitanism also rested on its treatment of ethnic minorities—"a panoply of ethnic differences"—and its general tolerance for deviance: "Deviants of many kinds live well in San Francisco—natives and tourists alike make that observation." Becker and Horowitz describe this tolerance for ethnic difference and social deviance as a "culture of civility." This "low-key approach" to deviance extended, for the most part, to law enforcement as well: "Because its politicians and police allow and can live with activities that would freak their opposite numbers elsewhere, San Francisco is a natural experiment in the consequences of tolerating deviance."[21]

Although the city did not yet, according to Becker and Horowitz, embrace the law-and-order approach that would become popular among conservatives in the wake of the urban uprisings of the late 1960s, it was, as the authors note, as capable as any other metropolis of policing the boundaries of acceptable behavior in the city—including the boundaries of race relations in the city.[22] At the time, law enforcement's treatment of African Americans in the city was much more consistent with a culture of containment than a culture of cosmopolitanism. This approach would harden as the nation and the city's embrace of "law and order" and "tough on crime" politics intensified over the latter part of the twentieth century.

As the influx of African Americans in the post-war period continued to increase well into the 1960s and 1970s, the local police force, which was "nearly all-white, all-Catholic and all-male" at the time, adopted a quarantine approach to policing the city's Black community, especially the groups of young people who had formed "bopping gangs" (cliques of adolescents from different "turfs" in Hunters Point) in the residential areas to which they had been restricted.[23] In *Hunter's Point: A Black Ghetto*, an ethnography published in 1974, Arthur Hippler explained it this way:

> Under the quarantine procedure, black youths who were recognized as Hunter's Pointers and found in other areas of the city were rousted and sent back to Hunter's Point. In practice, this meant that groups of young boys or girls who appeared anywhere west of Third Street—the "boundary" of Hunter's Point—were given the alternatives of going "back up on the Hill where you niggers belong" or being arrested on a variety of charges that police save for such situations.[24]

The quarantine approach "made 'turf' (local territory) boundaries even more important," exacerbated the Black community's isolation from the rest of the city, and engendered a distrust of law enforcement that lingers today.[25]

The response of law enforcement to the Hunters Point uprising in 1966 marked a nadir in the relationship between law enforcement and the city's Black residents. Like the Watts rebellion in Los Angeles in 1965 and those that would follow in cities across the country as the decade neared its end, the Hunters Point uprising was sparked by an aggressive encounter with the police. The unrest began after a patrol officer "fatally shot in the back an unarmed teenager suspected of auto theft."[26] In the wake of the uprising, law enforcement adopted a strategy of both quarantine and abdication by "removing themselves from the neighborhood and establishing a perimeter designed to contain but not extinguish the violence."[27] The abdication of responsibility for protecting and serving the city's Black neighborhoods would characterize policing in San Francisco for years following the riots. In the 1980s, this approach would change dramatically, shifting from abdication to entrenchment and bureaucratic expansion in the wake of the arrival of crack in the city.[28]

CRACK AND THE RISE OF "GET TOUGH" POLICING IN SAN FRANCISCO

On Thursday, April 7, 1988, the *San Francisco Chronicle* published a special report on crack cocaine, "SF Crack Dealers Tell Their Story," alongside news about surrogate mother Mary Beth Whitehead's battle to visit "Baby M," the stoning of an Israeli girl, and the shooting of two Palestinian youths half a world away.[29] The special report begins with the story of Tommy G., a sixteen-year-old from Hunters Point serving time in the city's juvenile detention facility. From the beginning of the article, Tommy G. and other Black youth like him are set apart as unlike other youth in the city: "At a time when others his age are worried about going steady, pep rallies and proms, Tommy G. sits in an isolated detention camp and contemplates a return to the life of crime that put him there." The article then highlights how the youth of the "crack generation" are different not only from other youth in the city but also from any group of young people the city has ever seen: "a new breed of impoverished, angry kids—some as young as ten and eleven—who are willing to take up arms and lay down their lives for a piece of the Bay Area's lucrative crack market." Although the youth made up the lower strata of the city's drug market, they reportedly loomed large in the intensity with which they defied authority, especially law enforcement, and their casual embrace of violence: "Juvenile justice experts say they have never seen a group as lawless or violent as the new generation of teenage crack criminals."[30]

By the time the special report was published, the crack epidemic had already begun to pummel cities across the country. A report from the Drug Enforcement Agency warned that the crack epidemic threatened to spread beyond the boundaries of the city and into suburban and rural areas.[31] In San Francisco, criminal and juvenile justice officials warned that the crack epidemic threatened not only to "wipe out a whole generation of these kids," in the words of one Superior Court judge, but also "to produce (in their offspring) a new generation of children who will have to be raised by the state." The framing of youth of the crack generation as a uniquely and immutably different "breed" of adolescents who posed a threat to society and the state foreshadowed the rise and dominance of the "superpredator thesis" of the 1990s, which warned of an emerging class of criminal youth who would respond only to the most punitive of sanctions, if at all. The dire threat to the city, the state, and the nation was summed up in comments from a veteran probation officer in the *Chronicle*'s special report: "We have the potential here of a social atomic bomb going off."[32]

Decades after the epidemic, the mythical rise of a "superpredator" class and the warnings of the doomed trajectories of so-called crack babies have proven to be baseless.[33] Less than a decade after the *Chronicle*'s special report, the country would find itself at the beginning of the Great Crime Decline as rates of violent crime began what would be a precipitous drop that would extend well into the new millennium. A recent longitudinal study followed 200 babies born to low-income, African American women in Philadelphia between 1989 and 1992. One hundred of the babies in the study were exposed to cocaine in utero and half had no exposure; the study found no significant differences between the two groups. The most consequential differences, the study found, were associated not with exposure to cocaine but rather exposure to poverty and violence.[34]

Although the epidemic did not follow the path predicted by researchers and some scholars, the arrival of crack did shake the social and relational foundations of San Francisco's Black community in significant ways. Decades later, the arrival of crack in the city features prominently in the stories residents tell about the origins of the problems facing San Francisco's Black neighborhoods and the problems with Black youth in the city today. One young woman I interviewed early on in my fieldwork put it to me quite bluntly: "Crack killed everything." Eric, too, recalls how the arrival of crack disrupted family and peer networks as youth sold to the friends or older family relatives of their peers and, as in the case of Eric's uncle, family members' struggles with addictions were exploited by young people selling crack in the neighborhood.

The consequences of the justice system's response to Black youth involved in drug markets during the 1980s and 1990s are still felt in neighborhoods like the Fillmore and Hunters Point, especially decisions to place young Black men directly in the sightlines of local law enforcement. In the *Chronicle*'s special report, a brief mention of the racialized dimensions of the Bay Area's drug market appeared alongside news of the "new breed" of poor, Black, criminal youth. "Affluent Whites" were also deeply implicated in the rise of the Bay Area's crack market: "[W]hites often play key roles at the top of the pyramid." One youth disclosed to a reporter that "his suppliers were 'fancy people, and they weren't black.'" Yet affluent Whites would not become the poster child of the nation's drug war. Instead, young Black men in their teens and early twenties would become the targets of the nation's and the city's embrace of geographically targeted, "get tough" policing and punishment.

Apart from the emotional and relational devastation often attributed to crack by those who lived in the neighborhood in the 1980s, the justice system's response to the arrival of crack in the city marked an important turning point in policing, especially in law enforcement's interactions with Black youth in the city. As Doris Marie Provine writes in *Unequal Under Law*, crack became the "centerpiece of the federal war on drugs," a war that would be fought on street corners like those in the Fillmore.[35] The justice system's response to the city's crack epidemic would change the composition of its juvenile and criminal justice systems. In San Francisco, the number of juvenile crack arrests would more than triple in just one year, from 184 in 1986 to 632 in 1987.[36] The surge followed, according to one newspaper article, a "police crackdown" over the summer of 1987. The city would go on to double its narcotics division as it readied itself to fight a new war, one that quite knowingly pit the city against its youth: "a new regimen of strict rules and discipline" would be used "against young crack dealers and users who seem immune to more gentle methods of rehabilitation."[37]

These new efforts would come to rely heavily on institutions and actors outside of the criminal justice system.[38] Just a few months after the special report was published, another headline announced a new effort to increase and intensify the surveillance of alleged drug gangs in the Western Addition, Hunters Point, Visitacion Valley, and Portrero Hill. The effort was reportedly triggered by a "streak of shootings among black youth gangs." The new effort would include the San Francisco Housing Authority in "a major police effort to 'win back' its low-income rental units from drug dealers and other criminals."[39] The "new get-tough program," as it was described in the *San Francisco Chronicle*, would include "intensive surveillance by undercover police and stepped-up arrests of crack cocaine dealers" for nearly half of the agency's twenty-three housing projects, including one in the Western Addition.[40] The age of the crack cocaine dealers—the ten- and eleven-year-old "kids who peddle crack" mentioned in the paper's earlier report—was not mentioned in the announcement of this new effort. The focus on youth in public housing complexes would continue for decades.

At the time, the description of the policing strategy to be used by law enforcement was consistent with the practice of random patrol, a policing strategy that was believed to increase the likelihood of apprehending offenders, since dealers would not be able to predict when or where the police might arrive: "The police teams will not be at the projects all of the time. Instead, they will work at selected locations at different times."[41] This approach would give way to the rise of data-driven, targeted policing practices in the 1990s. This new practice of "hot spot" policing would provide the logic for the persistent presence of the police in poor, Black neighborhoods well into the twenty-first century.

EMBRACING TARGETED POLICING

In San Francisco, the degree of law enforcement's involvement with the city's Black neighborhoods shifted, as it did in cities across the country, from abdication in the 1960s and 1970s, to penetration in the 1980s, to deep entrenchment and bureaucratic expansion during the 1990s and into the new century. This shift relied on new sets of institutional arrangements, including the formation of anti-drug, anti-gang, or anti-violence task forces that leaned heavily on relationships among local, state, and federal law enforcement agencies. Support—both financial and political—was encouraged by the "superpredator panic," by the embrace of Broken Windows policing in the 1980s, and, in part, by scholarly research that supported the introduction of place-based policing efforts, typically described as "hot spot" policing.

In contrast to the random patrols that dominated policing at the time, Broken Windows policing encouraged law enforcement to focus its efforts on low-level offenses committed by "disreputable or obstreperous or unpredictable people," including "rowdy teenagers."[42] This shift to targeted policing would also rely on the underlying logic of place-based policing, which encouraged law enforcement to focus policing resources on those geographic areas where much of the reported crime occurred, or "hot spots." Given the persistence of residential segregation in the city, it comes as no surprise that, in San Francisco, serious violence is concentrated in 2.1 percent of the city's forty-nine square miles, an area that includes neighborhoods that have borne the brunt of racially discriminatory residential and labor practices for decades. It should also come as no surprise that the Lower Fillmore, a neighborhood that was thrust onto the frontlines of the War on Drugs in the 1980s, is, three decades later, one of five officially designated "hot-spot zones" for violence in the city.[43] The designation of the neighborhood as a hot-spot zone provides a color-blind logic that legitimizes the persistence of a range of targeted surveillance and enforcement efforts, many of which continue to target Black youth living there.[44]

Targeted, proactive policing practices like hot-spot policing, which often operate in tandem with gang injunctions and other forms of exclusionary paperwork (like stay-away orders), have produced mixed results: some evaluations report short-term effects on crime reduction, but the research is still out on whether or not targeted policing practices actually prevent crime over the long term.[45] There are also potential adverse effects of proactive policing practices that are often overlooked during the course of implementation or evaluation, including the effect of targeted policing practices on already precarious police-community relations.[46] Recent ethnographic research suggests that aggressive, targeted enforcement may systematically erode trust in the police, especially among minority youth who are the frequent targets of these encounters: "Hot spots policing, because it has been operationally defined as aggressive enforcement in specific areas, runs the risk of weakening police-community relations."[47] This risk is especially acute in poor, minority neighborhoods.[48]

The erosion of trust in the police is consequential for law-abiding behavior. It is now well accepted in criminological circles that trust in the police is paramount for public safety: people who trust the police tend to obey the law.[49] Further, researchers have found that encounters that are perceived as fair and just are likely to strengthen citizens' beliefs in the legitimacy of law enforcement.[50] Yet many studies show that police legitimacy is lower among minority groups and in settings in which proactive policing practices are focused.[51] Frequent searches and the failure to find evidence that would lead to an arrest exacerbates tension between neighborhood residents and the police, making young men believe that they are arbitrary targets of police surveillance.[52]

The embrace of targeted police practices is based on a framing of Black youth (along with Latino youth) that resembles the damaging narratives that were circulated at the rise of the crack epidemic. Newspaper reports describe youth as "brazen young thugs" who fight to the death over seemingly trivial matters, which serves to legitimize the persistent presence of law enforcement in the neighborhood. Today, this logic exists in concert with a more paternalistic (and patronizing) logic that emphasizes the need to protect Black youth not from aggressive or intrusive policing practices but from themselves. Framed as a cost-benefit analysis, which has become ever more popular in contemporary discussions of the unintended consequences of mass incarceration, this new narrative posits that men of color may pay more when it comes to the degree of intrusion of law enforcement in their daily lives, but that they may "also gain more in lower rates of death and injury."[53] Yet the *persistence* of violence in poor neighborhoods, perhaps especially in neighborhoods where the police have held sway for decades, strongly suggests that the justice system is failing youth on both counts—a fact that is not lost on young people in neighborhoods like the Lower Fillmore.

Over the past three decades, policing practices in San Francisco have shifted in ways that stand in stark contrast to the quarantine approach embraced in the mid-twentieth century. These shifts in policing practices are revealed in the police encounters that unfold in public spaces every day. For a young man coming of age in the Fillmore today, especially a man "on paperwork," a short walk to the store or a visit to a family member in a local housing project is likely to put him in the sightlines of law enforcement, opening him up to a range of intrusive encounters that are not experienced by youth in neighborhoods that lack a heavy law enforcement presence. These shifts have important consequences for the socialization of young people in the neighborhood and their exposure to various forms of violence.

THE SOCIAL CONSEQUENCES OF TARGETED SURVEILLANCE

For most Americans, encounters with law enforcement are infrequent and typically limited to brief exchanges related to traffic violations. Moreover, the participants—the officer and the citizen—usually are strangers to each other, and neither is likely to encounter the other in the future. For residents in high-surveillance neighborhoods, however, interactions with the police are far more regular and much more intimate than the typical police-civilian encounter. As a result, the participants in these encounters are known to each other in a way that is uncommon in other, low-surveillance settings.

In the Fillmore, targeted policing practices do more than shape young people's perceptions of the police in negative ways: targeted policing practices also shape their life space—affecting what they do, where, and with whom. This is true not only for those with official criminal histories but also for other young residents, including those who have yet to have any formal contact with the justice system. Developmental psychologists highlight the significant relationship between "life space"—a term used to describe the environment that surrounds an individual—and healthy adolescent development this way: "How young people spend their waking hours defines the fund of developmental experiences in each culture; they circumscribe what a boy or girl learns, and for better or worse, shape the men and women these children become."[54] If this is true, then for young Black men who live in high-surveillance neighborhoods, law enforcement officers are now key agents of socialization with a level of authority that, depending on the strength of one's contacts with other pro-social institutions and the frequency with which they encounter the police, may surpass that of teachers, pastors, or parents.

Targeted police practices thus potentially have serious institutional, social, and psychological consequences for adolescent boys and girls as they transition into adulthood. Yet we know very little about these patterns or their effects. Young men's encounters with law enforcement are rarely subject to observation or evaluation by outsiders with an interest in the well-being of youth. Consequently, adolescent boys must learn to negotiate directly with police officers who may be a decade or more their senior and who have the authority to use lethal violence. To what extent these experiences shape young men's behaviors and beliefs is unclear, since few researchers have systematically examined the impact of popular policing interventions on adolescent development. In the following section, I provide an account of the types of routine encounters that occur between young men and the police, then consider the consequences of these types of encounters for the gender socialization of Black youth more broadly.

ROUTINE ENCOUNTERS WITH THE POLICE

By the time they enter their teens, boys who grow up in neighborhoods like the Fillmore are aware that the gaze of the police is most frequently targeted at them. The following transcription of a video-recorded exchange illustrates how, in this setting, some youth perceive even nonverbal interaction with the police as intrusive and threatening.[55] The clip opens with the camera focused on a police officer leaning against his squad car, which is parked at a street corner that is a popular hangout for neighborhood youth. The voice of a young man calls out to the videographer:

"Get 'em, Ray. They [the police] was harassing me the whole day. You feel me? Get all that Ray, he was harassing me," the young man says.
"This one cat [officer]—right here?" [the videographer] asks.
"Both of 'em," the young man explains.
"Oh it's two in there [the car]?"
"There's another one. They was both harassing me. He right there in the car. Get all of it [on camera]."
"What was they talking about?" the videographer asks.
"They talking 'bout we can't stand by the bus stop. First they came searching right there for nothing. Then we can't stand at the bus stop."
"They say you can't stand at the bus stop?"
"Yeah and they just sat here and watched us for a good, what, five, ten minutes?"
"Right."
"They sat right there."

"Watch to see if a bus come or something."

"Uh, huh. Man, they crazy."

"Yeah."

"Wow."

"Ya'll got to call me sooner."

After a few moments of being filmed, the officer gets back in his car and drives off.

In high-surveillance neighborhoods such as the Fillmore, officers are typically encouraged to spend time in areas where crime or violence is concentrated even if it appears as if nothing is happening.[56] As a result, encounters like the above are routine. It is impossible for the young man to truly know the officer's intention, yet his framing of the officer's presence and gaze as harassment is illustrative of how even the most minimally intrusive encounters—a look, a stare—can signal to young men that they are locked in "a forced social relationship" with law enforcement.[57] In this case, the young man reports feeling watched while engaging in a routine act like hanging out at a bus stop; his encouragement of the videographer to "get" the officer on camera is not merely a form of retaliation, it is also an act of resistance.[58] The young man perceived the officer's gaze as a deliberate intrusion on his life space, and he now wants the cameraman to make the officer experience a similar level of discomfort. Yet the gaze of law enforcement is quite different from the gaze of a citizen. A look or stare from a police officer can coerce a citizen into participating in what sociologist Harold Garfinkel describes as a public degradation ceremony "whereby the public identity of an actor is transformed into something looked on as lower in the local scheme of social types."[59] The young man's interpretation of the officer's gaze as "harassment" suggests that he understands the officer's behavior as a message: He is not free to hang out on the block without becoming a subject of law enforcement surveillance. He is, even if not a suspect, always suspect.

That these sorts of interactions are unwelcome and potentially injurious is revealed in the effort young men put into *avoiding* them. Young people in troubled neighborhoods often develop situated survival strategies that help them successfully navigate their environment.[60] The strategies that adolescents in the Fillmore use are similar, but they are distinguished by their specific relationship to the presence of law enforcement. One common defensive strategy is what I refer to as "the walk around." The goal of this maneuver is to keep out of the sightlines of police officers. As the police approach, young men, especially if they are in a group, disperse and walk in the other direction. In some cases, the young men may be fulfilling an informal deal made with local beat officers: they avoid direct interaction with the police and potentially an arrest for involvement in illegal behavior, and the police officers avoid investing the time and energy required to process a nonfelony arrest.[61] In other cases, officers are simply sending a silent message: leave the block or face an increased level of intrusion. Avoidance strategies do not always work. In the housing complex nearest my home, young men escaped view by slipping into the gated interior area of the complex. This would offer some respite from the police, but it would frequently place them in the sightlines of housing security personnel, who also were intent on displacing them from public space.

Outside of the gates, young men are sometimes caught in what feels to them like "surprise attacks" in which police cars pull up quickly and officers aggressively confront an individual or a small group of young people. Boys as young as twelve and fifteen shared accounts of police officers "jumping out [of their cars] on us," weapons drawn.[62] During a meeting held in the neighborhood, one young man described his experience with a surprise attack. After he shared his story, I asked him how he responded when officers jumped out on him with weapons drawn. The teenager leaned back in his chair, extended his arms outward, and raised his palms in the air: "I don't do nothing," he said with a resigned shrug.

Currently, we know little about the developmental consequences of young men's encounters with the police. From a sociological perspective, however, we know that such interactions are intended to injure a person's self. In the military, the objective is to break down the self and then build up a new self in service to the institution: a soldier. In prisons, the objective is to reaffirm the lower status of the incarcerated in order to reinforce the social hierarchy and, in turn, to maintain the social order of the institution. But what are the consequences of such encounters for young men in a neighborhood like the Fillmore? In these settings, such encounters, especially if they are regular features of daily life, are likely to injure a young person's sense of self. Since these interactions with law enforcement are likely to occur at a key stage in a young person's developmental trajectory, they may do more than influence what a young man does, with whom, and how.[63] These encounters can inform a young man's sense of who he is, who he can become, his commitment to mainstream society, and, ultimately, his beliefs in the fairness and legitimacy of policing. Given the intimate nature and often emotional intensity of these encounters, each search sends a message to a young man regarding his place in a larger raced and gendered social hierarchy.

In a setting that embraces proactive policing practices, body searches are common. "Going in my pockets" is a term local youths use to describe these routine searches. Routine searches can lead to an arrest, but often they do not.[64] In some jurisdictions, law enforcement may record such encounters as a "stop-and-frisk" or a "pat down." Legal scholars typically describe these encounters as "Terry stops," a reference to the 1968 precedent-setting Supreme Court decision in *Terry v. Ohio*. The Fourth Amendment protects the rights of citizens from unreasonable searches and seizures. Reaching into a person's pockets or patting down their clothing constitutes a search. Whenever a police officer stops an individual and restrains his freedom to walk away, that person is effectively "seized." Prior to *Terry v. Ohio*, the Supreme Court held that police officers must have probable cause to initiate such encounters. In *Terry v. Ohio*, the justices ruled that the initiation of such interactions could meet a lesser standard, namely "whether a man of reasonable caution is warranted in believing that the action taken was appropriate."[65] This standard is commonly referred to as "reasonable suspicion." In some settings, the stop-and-search is now used with a regularity that defies reason.[66] For many young Black men in these settings, the stop-and-search has become a regular routine.

The stories young men shared in public meetings and in formal and informal conversations reveal common characteristics in the unfolding of a "going in my pockets" kind of encounter. Officers initiate these searches by approaching an individual or a small group of young men who are hanging out on the block. Once within arm's distance or so, the officer asks the young man for identification.[67] If he has it, the young man shows his identification. The officer may review the identification, call into the station for verification, or check it against lists accessible from his squad car. Alternatively, the officer may simply glance at the ID to check the address shown against the address where the young man has been stopped. Over the past decade, government-subsidized housing complexes have increased the enforcement of trespassing laws in and around their properties. Violations of these laws can be grounds for citation or arrest.[68]

During the search, the officer might refer to the target in informal ways, such as "dog" or "G"; doing so signals the officer's sovereign power to "automatically assume the right to employ an intimate form of address or truncated formal ones."[69] If the young man protests or complains during an encounter, the officer may choose to address some concerns, but not others, or may simply ignore complaints and conduct the search largely in silence. If the ID is valid and the search continues without escalation to arrest, then the officer will release the young man.[70]

In other cases, the officer might not request identification but instead direct a young man to hold his arms up in the air or place his hands against a nearby wall. The officer may then pat down the individual's outer cloth-ing. The young man might acquiesce to the search in an effort to bring the encounter to an end more quickly. An officer who intends to place his hands deep inside a young man's pockets may first ask if the person has anything (e.g., a weapon or anything sharp) in his pockets. Otherwise, he might just squeeze the outside of the pockets first. If the officer finds no illegal sub-stances, he may ask the young person a series of questions, seeking infor-mation about other people or other cases, or he may just let him go.[71]

Through being subjected to multiple stop-and-search encounters, young Black men learn to behave like professional suspects. A stop-and-search encounter demands either explicitly or implicitly that a young man accept a submissive role. Confronting an officer or questioning their actions can have dire consequences ranging from imprisonment to physical harm, including death. By the time they are in their late teens, young men who are frequent targets of the police have learned how to perform during stops. In some cases, the stop-and-search can be accomplished with little more than nonverbal communication. The search I describe below is part of the video archive of interactions between police and Fillmore residents. The clip illustrates how young men have been socialized into participating in these encounters:

> The clip begins with two people in the frame—a White male officer dressed in plain clothes and a young Black man wearing a black hoodie. [In this neighborhood, the black hoodie is a standard part of the urban youth uniform.] The officer's blue striped polo-shirt makes him stand out as an outsider. The officer has the build of an outside linebacker and is about a foot taller than the young man. The two stand chest-to-chest. The young man, who appears to be in his late teens, looks directly at the officer, but the officer's gaze is directed at the young man's left pocket. The officer's right hand grips the young man's outstretched right arm. The teen's other arm is lifted slightly above a 90-degree angle.
>
> "What?" says the young man, as he drops his arm to his side. "What the fuck you talking about?"
>
> The officer keeps his hold on the teen's right arm and begins lifting the hoodie. The young man grabs his sweatshirt and lifts it himself, exposing his belly and part of his lower chest. The two look toward the young man's right pants pocket. The officer moves his left hand to the teen's jeans, which hang slightly below his hip, exposing an inch or two of his boxer shorts. The teen holds his sweatshirt up near his mid-chest line. The officer holds his right hand in the air as he moves his own left hand across the young man's pockets.
>
> "Did I talk about anything?" the officer asks, in response to the question the teen posed a couple of seconds earlier.

The officer glances at the camera and continues the search. The teen is still using both hands to hold his sweatshirt up. The officer places his right hand on the teen's upper right arm, and the teen turns around. The two are now standing back to chest. The officer's back is to the camera. The officer reaches his hand down the right leg of the teen.

"I ain't got nu'n' sharp, nigga. I don't carry weapons, nigga," says the teen as he is turned around.

The two begin to turn to their left. The young man's sweatshirt starts to drop back down toward his waist. His pants have slipped, so that his studded black belt now hangs below his buttocks. The officer places his left hand on the teen's left arm.

"Don't use that word. It's a bad word," the officer says to the teen.

For a moment, the officer turns chest-to-chest toward the teen. As he does, the teen lifts both arms directly above his head. The officer offers a quick, dismissive glance and then turns and walks quickly away from the teen.

"That's just my slang," the young man says, and begins to follow the officer, who is walking toward his partner (who is searching one of the teen's peers).

"It's still a bad word," says the officer over his shoulder.

"Man, right," says the youth.

The portion of the search described above lasts less than fifteen seconds, but the interactions embody the routine encounters between police and youth, and they reveal the accompanying patterns of degradation. As the officer moves silently through each step of the search, the teen moves along with him, following the officer's nonverbal direction at each turn. The officer does not tell the youth to keep his arms raised, but he does; he does not tell the young man to hold up his sweatshirt, but he does so, seemingly anticipating the officer's next move. The officer does not tell the youth to turn around, but he follows the pull of the officer's arm, as if the two are in an intimate dance. The teen also seems aware that the officer is looking for weapons. He anticipates a body search: "I ain't got nu'n' sharp, nigga. I don't carry weapons, nigga." Carefully reviewing this recorded encounter makes clear that the stop-and-search is "a set of structured social routines understood and enacted by the various parties involved."[72] In short, it is a "regular routine."

In addition to the nonverbal messages about how to play his role in the stop-and-search, the teen at each turn also receives messages about his relative inferiority vis-à-vis the police: He is, sometimes physically, constrained in a submissive role. He may offer some verbal challenges, but officers have a great deal of discretion in choosing a response. The officer in the clip does not address the substance of the teen's complaints. Instead, he responds in the most literal sense ("Did I talk about anything?") and adds an admonishment against using a "bad word." Alternatives to dismissing the complaints of targets of stop-and-search encounters include teasing the targets, denying their complaints, or deliberately lengthening encounters with repeated questioning. In these situations, the targeted individuals find themselves enmeshed in a "developing tissue of constraint."[73] They are released from these constraints only at the direction and authority of the officer—who may demonstrate that authority with no more than a quick final glance before walking away from the targeted individual.

SHIFTING TARGETS: POLICE AGGRESSION AND GENDERED VIOLENCE

The stop-and-search is a meaningful encounter for the young people who are directly involved in the encounter. Likewise, witnessing an encounter significantly affects young onlookers.[74] Beyond reaffirming negative attitudes toward the police, a vicarious encounter exposes neighborhood residents to a secondary shame and degradation. Adolescents may be especially vulnerable. Typically, bystanders are aware that there is little they can do to stop an unfolding police encounter. This powerlessness results in what sociologist Erving Goffman has described as an experiential mortification: "[A]n individual witnesses a physical assault upon someone to whom he has ties and suffers the permanent mortification of having (and being known to have) taken no action."[75] Repeated experiences are likely to erode witnesses' trust in the police.

An example of young bystanders' sense of powerlessness emerged during a weekly meeting for adolescent boys that I attended in an effort to observe one former hustler's changing role in the neighborhood. Lincoln, an African American man, acted as a social father to several local youth, helping them and their peers process difficult events in the neighborhood, including the social meaning of arrests. I wrote this fieldnote shortly after one of the meetings that Lincoln led:

> I arrive at one of the meetings and a group of about twelve boys is arranged around the tables, which are shaped like an L. When Lincoln asks if I have anything to say to the boys, I say I do not. Lincoln does. He asks the group what they think about Ed getting beat up. When I ask who Ed is, Lincoln tells me he is the son of the housing complex's maintenance worker, and that it was the police who beat him. He explains that the police got a call that a Black man wearing a white T-shirt had a gun. That description (as Lincoln notes) is broad enough to

fit everyone present. When the police arrived, they arrested Ed, handcuffed him, and then slammed him to the ground. Lincoln says he has never seen that (slamming a cuffed suspect to the ground) happen before. Ed had a cut on his head, above his eyebrow, and he resisted getting thrown into the back of the police car. Once forced inside, he kicked out the back window.

Some of the boys at the meeting witnessed this dramatic scene; they seem saddened and frustrated by the events. I ask the whole group how that kind of an event makes them feel. One boy says that it makes you feel like you want to hurt the police. When I say that I can understand that feeling, Lincoln counters quickly, reminding the boys that they cannot hurt the police. He then returns to my original question, asking about their feelings. One of the younger boys, about twelve years old, answers, saying that what happened to Ed makes him feel like it is racist, like the police do not like Black people, like they deliberately go after the older Black men, so that just young boys like them are going to be left, and then they will need a pass to get on housing complex property.

I ask if the treatment of Ed makes them feel like the police are there for them. They say no, adding that the police do not care if somebody gets shot. When I question how it makes them feel about power, one boy says he feels like he has no power. I probe, repeating his answer, which he confirms. Then I ask the group what they can do if they have no power. Stay out of trouble, do well in school, one boy suggests. Pressing, I ask, what else? The often boisterous group falls silent.

Shortly after this conversation, I said my good-byes to the group so that I could prepare for an early flight from San Francisco to Santa Barbara, where I was scheduled to teach a class the next day. I rose from the table and made my way to the door. As I placed my hand on the door's handle, one of the young men from the group—a teenager that I had interacted with previously and who had always treated me with deference and respect—lofted a loud farewell into the air: "Bye, sexy." I was stunned by the young man's transgression, but I did not respond. Instead, I let the inappropriate comment hang in the air as I completed my exit from the room. I was sure that Lincoln would scold the young man for his lack of respect—a lesson that he sometimes punctuated with a swift jab to a boy's chest. In the moment, however, I understood the young man's actions with a clarity that I had never had before. The source of the young man's sense of powerlessness was palpable. I had just participated in a conversation that exposed his vulnerability to dominance and aggression at the hands of the police. I understood that, in that moment, "Bye, sexy" was merely a desperate grasp at a semblance of power and control after having his sense of power-*less*-ness laid bare before me. Although young, he has already learned that his effort to regain a sense of dominance—to save the face of his budding manhood—required a female body. My status as a professor or, as Lincoln implored repeatedly during the group's tenure, a "lady," could not withstand this pressure.[76]

Understood in this way, "Bye, sexy" is more than an adolescent's effort to prove his manhood among his peers. It is an effort to *escape his own vulnerability*—the same sort of vulnerability that women and girls are exposed to regularly. If he had not made such an effort, then he would have to settle in with a social fact that is contrary to his understanding of what it means to be a man—that he is, in fact, embedded in a set of power relations that make him more like a woman or a girl than he would like to admit. His one-off comment demonstrates that he (and, by proxy, the group, since he is something of a leader among his peers) still has a hold on manhood. The routine interventions of the police may threaten the neighborhood's gendered hierarchy, but in that room, for that moment, the hierarchy still stands.

For me, moments like these did not happen often among the young men I knew in the neighborhood, but it is a dynamic that plays out much more regularly for many Black women and girls in public space. The omnipresence of law enforcement in the neighborhood can exacerbate the vulnerability already experienced by women and girls in these settings. A video clip of what appears to be an arrest in the neighborhood illustrates how one young Black woman's detention makes her more vulnerable to harassment at the hands of her peers and essentially aligns young Black men with the dominance-oriented principles of an institution that often handles their bodies in similar ways.

In the clip, a young Black woman is being led through the courtyard of one of the neighborhood's government-subsidized housing projects. She shuffles in front of a male officer with her hands cuffed behind her back. Her back is slightly arched, which makes her chest jut out in front of her. She is dressed in a fitted red polo shirt and jean shorts that stop at the top of her thigh. The young woman is led past a group of young men hanging on a nearby ledge. This clip stands out as much for what happens as for what does not happen when the girl moves past the group. One young man comments on her clothing—"with some Daisy Dukes on," he says—which results in hoots and hollers from his peers. "Shit, I wish I was locked up with you, man," says another teenaged boy, " . . . you'd be really locked up, for real." This comment, of course, acknowledges his own exposure to incarceration—"*I wish I was locked up with you*" treats incarceration as something of a normal occurrence—but, because of the sexual innuendo embedded in his comment, also reinforces his claim to a superior position on the gendered hierarchy: I would be locked up but you, he suggests, by virtue of his presence in a shared cell, would be *"really locked up, for real."*

As I reviewed the clip, I was also struck by the officers' silence as the young woman is harassed. If the other side of manhood—the other side of dominating women and girls—is to protect women and girls, then it is clear that this young woman, at least in this moment, is not the type of woman deserving of protection from *either* the police or the young men on the block. In the moment, the young men do not object to the handling of the young woman in handcuffs. The young men do not launch taunts and insults at the male officers, as they sometimes do on other occasions. Instead, in this moment, they align themselves with the male officers who are demonstrating their own form of dominance over the young woman by marching her through the complex in handcuffs—a position that is routinely taken by young men in the neighborhood. Like the adolescent boy at the meeting, the young men on the stoop make their claims to manhood vis-à-vis the subjugation of the female body before them.[77] These claims to manhood are tenuous, as one of the male callers implies, since young Black men in the neighborhood *share a vulnerability* to being handled by the police in the same way.

Strip Searches

This shared vulnerability among young Black men is illustrated in a type of encounter with the police that is rarely the focus of public conversation: body searches. Such searches are a powerful illustration of how young Black men in distressed neighborhoods share a vulnerability to aggression, violence, and dominance. In total institutions, such as prisons or jails, routine body searches communicate dispossession.[78] In the neighborhood, these routine body searches send the message that a Black male body is state property.[79] This is perhaps most evident in the cases of strip searches, which routinely occur prior to a period of incarceration. The strip search, however, is not always followed with long-term detention.[80]

During a strip search, the male suspect is coerced to bend over, spread his buttocks, and manipulate his genitalia (or have it done so by an officer) in order to demonstrate that he is not carrying contraband or weapons in or on his body. His failure to comply is likely to be seen as resistance, to be met with coercive force. As a practice, the strip search is objectifying and degrading: it requires that both the officer and the subject of the search treat a man's body as an object. The strip search is emasculating; each aspect troubles normative understandings of manhood and Black masculinity, particularly the coupling of strength and dominance that shape normative understandings of Black men in general and policing as a masculine institution.

The largely hidden nature of this invasive practice mirrors Black women's experience with sexual violence as a form of social control.[81] In this way, as Collins explains in her analysis of race, masculinity, and sexual violence in prisons, "police treatment of Black men demonstrates how the command to 'assume the position' can be about much more than simple policing."[82] In *Asylums*, Goffman offers that such practices are part of a "trimming procedure": an institutional practice intended to shape captives into the "administrative machinery of the establishment . . . to be worked on smoothly by routine operations."[83] The enactment of these practices by institutional actors acting on the behalf of "large, allegedly impartial bureaucracies," coupled with the overwhelming regularity with which these practices occur, hides the violence done with each search and, as Collins notes, gives the sense that the treatment of Black male bodies in this way is "natural and normal."[84]

Taken together, the work of Collins and Goffman suggests that the routine practices associated with the policing of high-surveillance neighborhoods, from the search on the street to more invasive practices like the strip search, can be seen as a larger institutional effort to trim Black men into submissive subjects. In effect, the bodies of poor or working-class men are *made to be like* the bodies of poor or working-class women: bodies that can be penetrated and controlled at will and without recourse.

Much like the search on the street, the strip search is degrading, dehumanizing, and humiliating. This is true whether or not an institutional actor—an officer or a prison guard—intends it to be so; any difference in the injury to one's dignity is merely a matter of degree. In situations that are not followed by a long period of detention, the humiliation experienced by a young man during the course of a search is likely to be magnified upon his release, when he must confront officers, including, perhaps, officers who have seen the most intimate parts of his body, patrolling the neighborhood the next day. Even if not the same officer, the omnipresence of officers in the neighborhood can remind young men of the possibility of violation. The degree to which young men may come to interpret this type of handling by law enforcement as a violation, along with the lingering effects of the perceived violation, was revealed one night during a tenants meeting at one of the public housing complexes in the neighborhood.

The meeting was called to address a recent wave of evictions from the housing complex. The notices informed the tenants that they were being evicted because they had committed, permitted, or failed to prevent criminal activity either in or near their unit. Over the course of the night, the mainly low-income residents in attendance also discussed the gang injunction and the relationship between the community and the police in general.

Near the end of the meeting, Larry, one of Lincoln's sons, shared his account of what he believed to be an overly harsh and intrusive encounter with the police during his recent detention at the local police station. He told the group that he was taken to the local station and, as he described it, "strip-searched." He looked saddened and frustrated as he shared his experience and searched for possible remedies from the group. Several weeks after Larry's public disclosure of this intrusive encounter with the police, he and I attended a boys' group meeting. There, I witnessed how Larry's feelings of frustration and anger lingered nearly a month after the initial incident:

> It is about 7:30 at night. It's dark outside. The meeting has ended. The boys finish the plates of food that are provided at each meeting and, one-by-one or in pairs, begin to trickle out of the meeting area. As they exit, the attention of the group is drawn to two police cars that have pulled into the parking lot adjacent to the meeting room's entrance. The group then begins to move outside en masse.
>
> "What's going on?" I ask into the crowd of bystanders that has quickly gathered to observe the impending scene.
>
> I notice Lincoln has taken a stand near the officers. . . .
>
> Four officers are on the scene. Lincoln says that the officers are claiming that three of the boys attending the meeting broke into a resident's home, but he says the boys were in the room the whole time. . . . A small group of kids, between the ages of eight and eleven, gather around the officers.
>
> "Who's snitching, who's a snitch," they yell at the officer. "You a snitch," the officer responds as he points to one of the kids.
>
> Lincoln orders the kids to run on. As Lincoln engages the officers, the older boys in the group walk away, spreading out like water on pavement as they make their way across the street and away from the officers.
>
> As I observe the scene, I hear Larry's voice rise from the crowd of observers. Larry is a senior in high school. He's been studying for the state-mandated exit exam. I've provided some support for him along the way.
>
> "Not tonight, not tonight," he repeats in a monotone chant. "Ya'll ain't taking me in tonight," bouncing on his toes like a boxer getting ready for a match. "You're not going to strip search me," he says, "that's illegal."
>
> Larry makes his way over to me. He continues to bounce and chant as we observe the scene from the railing that separates the entrance from the parking lot. He raises his voice and begins to yell in the direction of the officers. I turn to him to get his attention and adopt a low, soft tone as I encourage him to calm down. He pauses for a moment to share the source of his frustration with me directly.
>
> "It's frustrating," he says. "They can come up in here, take me to the station, strip search me and I can't do anything back to them." I tell him

that I understand, but that the way to get back at them is by taking and passing his exit exam. "You're trying to go somewhere," I say. I encourage him not to court the police into disrupting his path. He takes my suggestion in before retreating back into the crowd of bystanders.

Larry's behavior that night was among the most memorable observations from my time in the neighborhood. It stood out not simply because Larry was challenging the legitimacy of the police—it is not entirely uncommon for bystanders to launch accusations in the direction of officers from the outskirts of an encounter. Rather, I was struck by the specificity of Larry's accusation: "You're not going to strip search me, that's illegal." His accusation made public an intimate violation experienced by Larry at the hands of the police. Larry's display of frustration and anger also stood out because of the public way in which he broadcast his vulnerability, a departure from the silence that typically surrounds the experience of sexual violence experienced by women and some forms of violent victimization experienced by Black men. In a study of the victims of gun violence, for example, Jooyoung Lee found that a heavy silence hung around injuries that threatened one's manhood in actual or symbolic ways, since "an injury in (or near) a man's genitalia might jeopardize his elite status [as a 'badass'] and transform him into a 'freak' in the eyes of his peers."[85]

Here, Larry risked any threat to his manhood that might accompany his public disclosure and instead shared his experience of being strip-searched with all within earshot. In doing so, he made clear that his effort to confront the police was motivated by this past violation—a violation that is often hidden from the public. Now, on his home turf, Larry provoked the police in an effort not only to repair the injury done to him during the strip search but also to right the power imbalance that had lingered since the incident.

Larry's effort to break this silence came with a risk. In fighting against this otherwise invisible cage of constraint, Larry opened himself up to the potential for harsher forms of bodily control, including the possibility of lethal violence at the hands of the police—a threat from which I hoped to insulate him in my efforts to redirect his frustration. In hindsight, my attempts to protect him also acted as a form of constraint. By encouraging him to retreat, I forestalled any revolutionary potential that may have existed in his efforts to directly confront the police. Historically, such responses have triggered urban uprisings and, eventually, reforms in policing. The more recent #BlackLivesMatter movement may not have erupted had the tragic encounter between Ferguson, Missouri, resident Michael Brown and then-officer Darren Wilson gone differently on that summer day in August 2014. A Department of Justice report published seven months after Brown's killing found frequent and compelling evidence of an overly aggressive and racially discriminatory pattern of policing that targeted men like Brown and others in the community.[86]

Half a country away, residents of the Fillmore share the experience of being targeted and, at times, aggressively surveilled by local law enforcement.[87] This is especially true for young Black men like Larry. His conciliatory retreat may have protected him in the moment, but my encouragement for him to give up his protest did little to weaken the invisible constraints, stitched together with the strands of dominance that surround him and his peers each day.

The ethnographic findings presented in this chapter provide a framework for understanding how the shift to targeted policing practices in the 1980s changed the nature of daily life for Black youth in poor, Black neighborhoods in San Francisco. The relationship of law enforcement to the city's Black community has shifted from the abdication of the "quarantine approach" to entrenchment, characterized by the seemingly constant presence of law enforcement, the normalization of stops and body searches, the infiltration and manipulation of personal relationships, and bureaucratic expansion, which serves to strengthen the bars of the invisible cage surrounding Black youth in the city. These shifts were facilitated and legitimized by the crime-fighting community. Three decades after the arrival of crack in the neighborhood, adolescent boys, especially those in their late teens and early twenties, remain targets for local law enforcement across its various iterations, from "black and whites" (a term used to describe uniformed patrol officers) to undercover or plain-clothes gang task-force members, private and sometimes armed security guards, and housing authority police, who are also armed. Together, these layers of public and private security form a seemingly all-encompassing web of surveillance for youth to negotiate as they engage in legitimate or illegitimate activities in the Fillmore.

This shift has had a range of often-overlooked consequences for the socialization of young men who live in neighborhoods like the Fillmore. These routine interactions with law enforcement, whether experienced directly or observed, not only injure a youth's developing sense of self but also reinforce an adolescent's understanding of the central roles that strength, dominance, and respect play in the construction of manhood. It is through these interactions that many young Black men come to learn their value *as* men and their place in the "pecking order" of their neighborhood's gender hierarchy. These patterns of interaction between institutional authorities and residents, especially adolescents, reflect and reinforce the crudest notions of masculinity and dominance. As such, these routine encounters with the police encourage a young person's socialization into a particular sort of masculinity over the course of adolescence, a form of masculinity that is consistent with hegemonic forms of masculinity but that overemphasizes the expression of manhood through physical dominance. Just as importantly, this physical dominance has clear consequences for women and girls in these neighborhoods: as state violence is absorbed by the bodies and minds of Black men, it gets shifted onto the bodies of Black women, girls, and others who occupy the lower rungs of the gender hierarchy.[88]

Law enforcement officials all but ignore the complicated consequences of targeted policing practices in their efforts to embrace them. Advocates, especially members of the crime-fighting community, frame targeted policing as necessary for public safety and, more recently—in a logic that mimics the arguments against the abolition of slavery—policy makers and scholars claim that these intrusive policing practices are not punitive but rather protective of young Black men and their communities. In addition, the consequences of these encounters are erased when the problems facing youth are framed as originating in a set of moral or cultural deficits—as if they originate in the bodies and minds of young Black men. Here, the personal responsibility narrative subsumes any efforts to address the structural forms of violence that adolescents are exposed to in their neighborhoods. Instead, Black elders may scold young men for not pulling up their pants, young women for not behaving in a "ladylike" manner, or both groups for not acting in otherwise more respectable ways. This framing influences the development of so-called solutions to the problem of violence in the neighborhood, as young men who find themselves as targets of violence at the hands of other young Black men, law enforcement, or both, are recruited into manhood development programs while those who may be most in need of the social support that could be provided by a youth organization are often discouraged or flat out prohibited from participation for fear that doing so would sacrifice efforts to "get the numbers" and secure future funding for an organization.

The institutional and interpersonal challenges outlined in this and the preceding chapter complicate efforts to reach young Black men. This leaves us with the question of *who* and *how?* If not members of the credentialed class, then who in the neighborhood, to borrow from Donovan's accusation in the introduction, is most "qualified" to do the work of saving the neighborhood? Who is best positioned to connect with the young men who live their lives as targets? Once they connect, how can they help to move young people out of the sightlines of law enforcement or others who wish to do them harm? What does this caretaking work look like? What are the challenges of this type of work, and what do victories look like for those involved in these efforts? In the next chapter, I use the work of Brothers Changing the Hood to provide answers to these questions. The answers not only challenge our understanding of what it means to be "qualified" to do this work but also complicate our understanding of the limits of the logics that inform this work, including ideas about manhood and Black masculinity.

4 Buffers and Bridges

"Can we get a family up here?"

Eric is onstage in Bethel Park on a sunny Saturday afternoon in September. A decade ago, Eric was a drug dealer. Now in his thirties, he is a pastor and the director of Brothers Changing the Hood (BCH). He stands onstage dressed in a baggy white T-shirt emblazoned with the organization's logo, long denim shorts that fall below his knees, and blue leather ankle boots. Eric's organization is hosting a celebration of Black families in the neighborhood, designed in part to draw local low-income residents out of their homes. Many are reluctant to spend much time in public space, a lingering consequence of the violence that once earned the neighborhood the dubious distinction of being the deadliest in San Francisco.[1] The BCH grassroots event is organized each year by a small network of volunteers, family members, and friends. Local performers, praise dancers, and Christian rap artists take turns entertaining the crowd throughout the day.

During a break in the performance schedule, Eric grabs the microphone and calls out to the audience. He wants a man to bring his family onstage. He specifies that he is looking for a "husband, wife, and children." After a few moments, a man steps up to the stage, followed by his wife and seven children, one still in a stroller. The children are dressed neatly in jeans and T-shirts. The group is greeted with applause from the audience. The family poses for a picture. "This is the model that we trying to get to," Eric says.

A man calls out from the crowd, and Eric responds, "A real man do take care of his family. Come on up here. Come on. Come represent the family then," he calls to the man. "Come represent the family then."

"This is my family," the man says, after joining a small group of women and children already gathered onstage. "This is my son, his little brother, my daughter, they little cousins, mommy, and my girl, my momma. We all one big family and I'm doing this," he says, with a mixture of confidence and defiance as the crowd applauds for him and his family.

A third group comes to the stage. Eric hands the microphone to a woman who is joined by five small children and several adults. The woman introduces the adults and adolescents in the group. She points to a man who is also standing on the stage but does not introduce him by name. "This is our family," declares the mother, looking toward Eric.

As Eric steps across the stage, the man in the group points to the mother's cousin and says, "That's my wife right there and these are my kids." "Now, this is what I'm looking for," Eric says, turning to the man.

THE GOOD BLACK FATHER

Since the 1970s, disconnection from the mainstream labor market and disproportionately high rates of incarceration among African American men have reshaped the low-income African American family.[2] The pressures associated with exclusion from the labor market and incarceration, along with the embarrassment and shame that often accompany addiction, have led some men to remove themselves from their families altogether; families hit hard by incarceration, street violence, or addiction reconfigure into alternative family formations that work for them.[3] The groups who join Eric onstage each represent a form of family now common among low-income African Americans. What Eric says he is "looking for," however, is a particular form of family that others, from scholars to politicians to members of the general public of all political persuasions, often call for too: a family composed of a "husband, wife, and children."

In the public imagination, the ideal Black family is one that models the traditional nuclear family and reflects certain normative expectations of gender. The fictional, upper-middle-class Huxtable family featured in the popular sitcom "The Cosby Show" once epitomized this image of the Black family. Today, the Obama family, once described by a political strategist as "the Huxtables in the White House," represents the good, decent, and respectable Black family.[4] In this idealized version of the Black family, husband and wife may be partners and friends, but the Black man as father is still expected to "take care of his family." The inability or unwillingness of Black men to meet these expectations—their failure to act like "real men"—is often cited as a source of the "crisis" facing Black communities today. If only Black men would "step up" in ways that resonate with contemporary Black gender politics—by taking control, being the man of the house, or showing boys how to be real men—the Black community would be in better shape. President Obama echoed this logic, which often circulates uncontested in policy circles, in his announcement of the administration's My Brother's Keeper initiative, a public/private collaboration aimed at addressing the crisis of young Black men: "We can reform our criminal justice system to ensure that it's not infected with bias, but nothing keeps a young man out of trouble like a father who takes an active role in his son's life."[5]

To be sure, men *and* women exert pressure on Black men to reclaim, even if it means claiming for the first time, their so-called natural place in their families and the neighborhood's social order. During my field research, comments and ideas shared by and about men in casual conversations as well as during public meetings and community events reflected these deeply rooted beliefs about gender complementarity. It was not uncommon, for example, to hear a woman repeat the common refrain that "a woman can't teach a man how to be a man." In order for Black men to "step up," the line of thinking continues, then Black women must relinquish some of the power they have accumulated as gatekeepers: "Women who do not let (Black) men be (Black) men become blamed for Black male behavior."[6] Such comments reinforce a commonly shared diagnosis of what ails the Black community, one that Patricia Hill Collins sums up as "too weak" Black men and "too strong" Black women. That Black women call for this as well reveals how strongly some residents invest in notions of gender complementarities.

Today, it is far more common for Black men of the mass incarceration generation to become *fathers* at early ages than it is for them to become *husbands*. Efforts to meet the expectations of the good Black father—or to challenge stereotypical images of the absent Black father—can act as both catalyst and constraint for Black men working to change their lives. Such efforts are also rife with contradictions. A key contradiction that men confront as they work to change their lives is how to give up on a belief system that organized relations on the street while still being called upon by intimates and others to be protectors and providers, to fulfill expectations of "real" and "respectable" men. For some, the pressure to meet the protector-provider expectation is why they became involved in illegal hustles in the first place. This pressure does not relent simply because a man has decided to change his life. Eric once explained the dilemma to me in this way: "I know on one hand I can pick up the phone and someone will shoot me some money or shoot me some dope to make some money. So the more pressure I get, it's like well you know what let me just go back over here [to selling drugs]." In this way, the pressure to be the father that others expect may turn a man back to the street.[7]

Eric's mission is, in part, to "take the pressure" off of men who are working to change their lives. Eric believes that other men, including men with a history of criminal activity or incarceration, can gain a sense of confidence if they are able to fulfill their obligations as a father. In order to do so, however, men may have to redefine some of these expectations. He explains: "These men and all these expectations of being a man if we can give them a little bit of help then it takes the pressure off." He would like them to know that they do not have to just "provide the money" or "do the scolding." Bonding is important, too, "hugs and stuff like that." Eric believes that the "little things would help them out more than someone beating them up telling them, 'well you need to get yourself a job.'[8]

For Eric and his organization, the work of becoming a good father and encouraging others to do the same is intertwined with the work of saving the neighborhood. In contrast to the institutionalized efforts of the crime-fighting community, much of this work takes place on the interpersonal level through the building of relationships among men. The work men put into redeeming themselves as Black fathers was revealed to me in the efforts and accounts of older men who volunteer with Eric's organization. At times, men used the apparatus of Black gender ideologies as a way to structure their efforts to find a new place in their families and in their neighborhood. At other moments, men responded to the confusing set of expectations they confronted by redefining in word and deed what it means to be a man worthy of a measure of respect not solely rooted in physical dominance. As other scholars have reported, men who lack the resources—either personal, social, or financial—to accomplish more traditional expectations of fatherhood often reclaim or redefine fatherhood in ways that allow them to maintain some "mastery" of their social worlds and, to be sure, some measure of dignity.[9]

As I illustrate in the following pages, men who, for a variety of reasons, cannot meet the expectations of absolute protector or primary provider, roles that rely on the coupling of strength and dominance and, to a large degree, some degree of financial stability, instead act as *buffers and bridges*. Specifically, men who give up on dominance in other aspects of their lives can still use their physical strength and, at times, their bodies to act as buffers from the various threats that young men encounter in the neighborhood, from violence to the intrusions of law enforcement. Men who lack economic resources to "provide" in a purely economic fashion can still act as bridges for young people, connecting young men with organizational and institutional resources that seem out of their reach, including access to some organizations in their neighborhood that have grown wary of interacting with troubled youth. Whereas other scholars have reported on the ways that men do this for children in their homes, the efforts of BCH reveal how buffer-and-bridge work is embedded in their public yet informal roles as street mentors or social fathers, where they help children throughout the neighborhood. This work has distinct benefits for the young people BCH worked with; for the men who volunteer with Eric's organization, this work also serves as a hook on which the men can hang their efforts to change their own lives.

MAKING WORK, REMAKING MEN

That men must work is one of the most basic expectations associated with manhood.[10] For Eric and men with similar histories, attachment to stable work opportunities is often elusive. Since breaking free from the street, Eric has pieced together paid work selling newspaper ads for a local paper and working security. This work allows him to meet certain financial obligations, but it is not the work he feels called to do; it is not the work that helps him to stay free. The work of BCH is the work that tends to structure his day. That he and others dubbed the local coffee shop "the office" reveals something about how they see what others might consider to be their off time. It is here that Eric and other volunteers sit and discuss short-term and long-term goals. Regular events, like the picnic in the park or a series of breakfasts for Black fathers, help to provide Eric and those who serve with him a purpose. This work also helps to construct a relational context that men can latch onto as they work through transitions in their own lives.

For Eric and others, BCH provides a caring community for Black men not only to redeem themselves for past wrongs but also to redeem themselves as men and as fathers.[11] The group provides a community of accountability, one that is not based on the threat of punitive sanctions, as programs mandated by probation or parole tend to be, but is instead built on a set of positive social bonds embedded in informal networks. That the group continues over time is, to be sure, a consequence of Eric's persistence, but that the community exists year after year is a consequence of what the men (mostly men) do together each day; the group's solidarity and efficacy at any given moment is the result of men's voluntary commitment to the work of the organization and the work of saving the neighborhood. It was through this work that I met Lincoln and Kenneth, two men that Eric would work closely with for over a year in his efforts to reach young men at risk of lethal violence or criminal justice involvement in the neighborhood. Both men were years older than Eric, but they came to look upon him as a mentor of sorts in their efforts to maintain and "show change," as Eric once described it (see chapter 1).

Kenneth, the most senior of the three, had struggled with addiction since his college days, after his girlfriend's pregnancy put an end to his promising athletic career. Kenneth gives credit to the leader of a local organization for helping him break his addiction. Lately, he says, that leader has become increasingly political. Kenneth says he prefers the grassroots work of BCH to politics. Kenneth attends a local church, he says, in an effort to keep up his strength and to stay clean. The years of addiction appear to have taken a toll on Kenneth. He speaks in a worn, gravelly voice. During meetings, he sometimes nods off before being nudged awake by a nearby friend. Kenneth's son was shot and killed five years ago; shot in the head, he says. "That's done," he tells a small group attending a meeting called by BCH, "but we have a lot of energy that we want to give back and it has to be used in a righteous way. We done been out there on the negative side. Now we want to do this right." This is not the first time that Kenneth and Lincoln have made an effort to do this kind of work. Kenneth says that he first began working with youth at a local community center twenty years ago. Two decades later, the work remains. Kenneth says that he is happy to be brought back into this work. "We the grassroots," he tells a group called together by BCH, a group that does not include any member of the neighborhood's credentialed class. "We the ones who can touch the neighborhood."

Among the men of the group, Lincoln stands out as the most physically imposing: six feet tall, with a baritone voice and close-cropped hair. I first meet Lincoln at a meeting organized by BCH that is held at a popular storefront church in the neighborhood. The small group of attendees includes others involved in grassroots battles in the city that include challenging redevelopment efforts in Hunters Point and a new ballot initiative that would treat adolescents as young as fourteen in the justice system as adults. Eric has also invited a lawyer to the meeting to talk about the gang injunction, which is what drew Lincoln to the meeting as well. One of Lincoln's sons had been arrested along with two other young men who were named on the gang injunction. Lincoln reports that the police are pressuring his son to "admit" to being a gang member, which his son refuses to do: "He's still in jail with $100,000 bail." His son's experience makes him committed to educating "youngsters" in the neighborhood about this "gang list": "All they know is they name got put on there and they ain't trying to get off it or nothin' cause nobody down there to educate them. So that's what I'm trying to do. Brother Eric, Darrius [another BCH member], and Kenneth, that's what we trying to do."

Lincoln is, of course, also worried about his son. There is a lot of confusion surrounding his arrest. He is not sure if his son is charged with a misdemeanor or a felony. After sharing his son's story, Lincoln looks to me for answers, but I defer to the lawyer in the room, who also seems unsure about how best to advise Lincoln. Not only was his son arrested, Lincoln says, but they also mentioned Lincoln in the police report, suggesting that he was the one who gave the drugs to his son. Lincoln shares how some officers "harass" his sons by threatening to "make me [Lincoln] a gang member." Lincoln shares another story of a son who was made a gang member while hospitalized after a shooting in which he was the victim. The group falls silent after Lincoln shares his story. Eric breaks the silence by offering a way that the group might be able to use its limited capital to help Lincoln. The suggestion is a simple one: call the public defender to ask about Lincoln's son. The public defender is generally well respected in the neighborhood. Eric thinks that "everybody calling down to the courts just inquiring about the brother's name is going to raise up some issues."

This form of help rooted in informal interactions is the type of activity that Eric encourages often. The group setting allows for Lincoln to demonstrate vulnerability as a man and as a father, which contrasts with normative expectations of manhood. He comes to the group for help. Eric and his group give what they can, but it is clear that Eric also believes that in order to really help his son, Lincoln will have to do more than seek out information about how to negotiate the bureaucratic ties of the criminal justice system. Lincoln has a large family. Of the dozen-plus children that he claims (eight boys and six girls), he admits that there are a "couple of bad apples" who are connected to the troubles of the street. He tells the group that he has four hardheaded sons. He recently sent one son out of town so that he would not have to spend a year in juvenile hall. Lincoln knows that his reputation on the streets casts a shadow over his efforts to counsel his kids to do the right thing. When he tries to counsel his sons, he tells the group, they bring up all the bad things that he has done. Like Eric and Kenneth, Lincoln's life has been touched by the violence of the street. He has had family members on both sides of the violence. Like Eric once did, Lincoln looks to the group gathered around the table for advice on parenting and how to handle situations as they come up with his sons. Despite the challenges he faces, he is not ready to relinquish his sons to the criminal justice system, as some parents in his situation may do. "I want to save my kids," he tells the group.

This is not the first time that Lincoln has attempted to make a change in his life. Nearly twenty years ago, after his release from a state prison, he took on a leadership role in the Midnight Basketball league that was popular in the city. The leagues were attempts in the late 1980s and early 1990s to organize warring sets of young men in the city. President Bill Clinton made Midnight Basketball leagues a key part of his neighborhood crime prevention plan. His administration invested heavily in these programs. Lincoln first heard of the program when he had about five months left on his sentence. He hoped that the program might lead to a more stable position with the city's Park and Recreation Department, but that never happened. Lincoln also hoped to get paid more than the twelve dollars per hour that the program offered. Eventually, he quit the position altogether, returning to a more reliable way of making money.

The advice that Eric gave to Lincoln—that if he really wanted to help his son, then he would have to recast his identity, change his behaviors, and, ultimately, change his life—is advice he has given to other men. Guys he used to run with as an adolescent now have sons. Men that others see as failures, Eric sees as parents with potential. Eric's advice is also embedded in a belief that change in one man's life can effect change in another's. That is how he did it, and, he believes, it is the type of work that is necessary in order for others to really change their lifestyle. Lincoln had already begun this work before seeking Eric out for information on the gang injunction; his relationship with Eric helps to motivate and maintain that change.

During a conversation at the coffee shop, Lincoln tells me that he gave up everything he was doing on the street about a year and a half ago, after his wife died from an illness. He knew then that he really had to step up for the four kids they were raising together. Lincoln has some money in an account that he has been able to live on while making his transition, and his children collect benefits that flow from their mother's death, but Lincoln does not have a legitimate job. He is eager to volunteer with BCH and to help educate the young men on the gang injunction, or those who are at risk of being placed on the gang injunction in the future. He wants to play a key role in educating "the youngsters" from Haynes: "I want to educate these youngsters on what they name is doing on the list and that's why I'm soaking up everything I can because they don't know. I'm learning something new every day."

Unlike other programs, BCH's work is largely informal and volunteer-based. The work is driven by the appreciation that change occurs gradually over time, not by a need to "get the numbers." In many ways, this is what the group is doing: educating people most affected by the gang injunction. Eric brought Lincoln and Kenneth into this work because they live in the gang injunction zone and Lincoln is already known and respected among youth in the neighborhood. Eric sees this volunteer work and, in particular, placing men like Lincoln and Kenneth in leadership roles within the group as consistent with the organization's mission. He wants to "lift up" the men in the community, he tells the group, the fathers and grandfathers in the neighborhood. He sees his work with Kenneth and Lincoln as the start of getting more men involved in the work of saving the neighborhood: "For me, it's time out for our women. . . . It's time for some of us men to get involved."

Eric's comment illustrates once again how gendered assumptions are reflected in the neighborhood's caretaking efforts. Black women are, it seems, often (though not always) in charge, which can make men like Eric feel as if there is no place for them. Eric and his organization work to create spaces in which they can take on leadership roles and enact forms of manhood that are consistent with traditional conceptions of masculinity. In these spaces their expertise is valued, they can command respect, and they can feel as if they are *allowed* to make a difference.[12] Although Eric believes that women will have to take a "time out" in order for men to "get involved," it is also possible for leadership in the community to be *shared* and not determined by gender categories. A more diverse leadership, by age, gender, and class, would require a fundamental shift in how community residents, both men and women alike, define and respond to the most persistent problems facing the neighborhood, especially violence.[13]

BLACK MEN AS BUFFERS AND BRIDGES

"I learn something new about being a daddy everyday," Lincoln tells me during a conversation at "the office," the coffee shop where the men of BCH often gather to catch up, set agendas, and assign tasks. Since his first appearance at the community meeting, Lincoln has been a diligent volunteer with BCH. It is clear that this work has provided him with an opportunity to rethink what it means to be a good father. During our conversation, he describes how prior to this work he had a rather narrow conception of fatherhood and how this conception has evolved more recently: "I used to think that taking money home, I was the world's greatest Daddy. I wasn't doing it. It's all about time. If you just talk to them for five minutes a day." Lincoln's definition of what it means to be a good father is reflective of Eric's narrative of commitment (discussed in chapter 1) and more recent redefinitions of fatherhood that now circulate in popular culture, including expectations that fathers should encourage strong emotional connections with their children. Lincoln has shared this realization with his sons as well. "You can't do like me," he says he told his son last night. "'But Dad,' they say, 'you ran the streets and gave us money.' That was no Daddy," he says he told them, "I was a 'fill-in.' I wasn't no Daddy. I wasn't there for you. I didn't teach ya'll nothing."

Since taking up with BCH, Lincoln has tried to provide a better model for his children and for other young men in the neighborhood. For these young men, Lincoln has become something of a social father. Social fathers are men who take on some fathering responsibilities for children outside of their homes. For example, recreational basketball coaches often take on some of the responsibilities of social fatherhood for young men.[14] As social fathers, the men of BCH try to instruct the boys on how to behave through discipline, direct instruction, and modeling. In doing so, they hope to encourage young men to think—if not differently then at least more critically—about themselves and their place in the neighborhood. A weekly boys' group, organized by BCH and led by Lincoln, became a regular site for me to observe Lincoln, Eric, and even Kenneth engage in the practice of social fatherhood. Lincoln especially took on a number of different tasks during these meetings, alternating between disciplinarian, motivator, counselor, and mediator. The men used interactional moments during each meeting to instruct boys on a range of issues. This instruction, at times, manifested as a form of gender socialization. For example, when Eric's sister visited the group to discuss entrepreneurial training, Lincoln warned the group to treat her with respect: "She's a lady, watch your mouth. You are supposed to respect ladies, like they are your mom or your sister. Respect her. She's Rev's sister." The men would also instruct the boys about their place in the neighborhood and the city *as young Black men.* These appeals are often terrifying in tone, reminding young Black men that they are always targets of lethal violence at the hands of their peers and the police.

Near the end of one meeting, for example, after watching a documentary about gang-associated youth in Newark, New Jersey, that seems to mirror the lives of the boys and men in the room, Eric becomes especially animated. His voice seems to jump an octave higher than usual whenever this happens, indicating an emotional intensity that he otherwise keeps hidden. The tough-love lecture is intended as motivation but is also tinged with anger and exasperation.

Eric tells the boys that "it's not a game out here," a reference to the gun violence that the boys know well.

"Innocent people get shot now. You can get shot just for tagging along," he yells as he motions to one of the older boys in the room who was recently shot at on his way home. "He and his mama; his mama was holding his baby brother."

The game has changed, Eric tells the group: "It used to be that you didn't shoot at innocent people, but now that's changed. This is serious."

As is often the case, the lecture then morphs into a narrative of personal responsibility. Eric tells the boys they have "an image problem." He recalls a recent experience at City Hall. He was there discussing the City Summer Work Program (CSWP) but was told "the boys from Haynes Homes don't want to work!"

A couple of boys protest, "I signed up for CSWP!"

"You're not listening to me," Eric says. "You got a name, you got a label—these boys from Haynes."

Eric suggests that the young men are wasting potential opportunities that are rarely offered to their adult counterparts: "You raise your right hand now as a young Black man you can get five hundred dollars to be a part of the CSWP. I can't get five hundred dollars as a grown man!" As is illustrated in Eric's outburst, the work of social fatherhood in a neighborhood like the Fillmore does not come without its frustrations.

After the start of one meeting, Lincoln pulls up a chair next to me and whispers an explanation for why some of the regular attendees are not in the room: "The older boys are not here because one of the guys they run with just got out of jail. So they're out there smoking weed now. I went out there to talk to them, but that's why they're not coming." At times, and as one might expect from a group of adolescents, Lincoln and Eric can reach their tolerance levels for the boys' impromptu outbursts, boisterous behavior, and seeming lack of commitment. Occasionally, when they have reached the limits of their patience, they may banish a young man from the group for the night. One night, a boy walks in wearing a hat. Eric asks him to take it off. He does, but then takes to tossing it in the air.

"You know what that hat says?" Lincoln asks. He then quickly answers his own question: "Fuck you."

The boy makes a face. Lincoln responds to the boy's gesture firmly and with a simple direction: "You can leave."

The boy leaves the group for the night. Eric and Lincoln are frustrated, but I expect that the conflict will be resolved; rarely do they refuse to welcome a banished boy back into the group in time for the next meeting.

The work that Lincoln and the men of BCH perform is characterized by both compassion for the social situation of youth who attend the weekly boys' group and the kind of critique illustrated in Eric's monologue. It appears to me, however, that the most meaningful and common set of practices performed by the men is to act as both buffer and bridge for the youth. In doing so, the men are able to exercise attributes commonly associated with manhood—for instance, acting, at times, as protectors—while also expanding conceptions about masculinity through their emotion-based interactions with young men, like helping them to process difficult events in their lives (for example, the discussion about arrests in chapter 3). Sometimes the men of BCH act as buffers between law enforcement and the neighborhood youth, or between neighborhood youth and potential threats of violence, and as bridges between youth and institutional resources and neighborhood organizations, including organizations with an informal policy of avoiding engagement with local youth.[15]

Each week, the earliest stages of bridge work would begin with the simple task of getting the boys in the room. The next step: getting members of the group to return regularly. In the beginning, Lincoln took a hands-on approach to this work. Shortly before the start of the meeting, he would walk around the block, gathering boys up from their regular hang-out spots around the complex. The regular presence of the police in the neighborhood would sometimes intrude on the boys' group meetings, shifting the leaders of the group into buffers. The actions of BCH during a standoff between youth and police in the neighborhood reveal one such effort to buffer the youth from potentially threatening or aggressive encounters with law enforcement.

The scene unfolds during one of the weekly meetings, when police sirens and flashing lights immediately draw the group of youth out of the room and onto the street.

Once outside, we see several cop cars and a police van arranged at different angles in the middle of the street. One of the officers, a task-force officer well known by others in the neighborhood, has a tight hold on a young man dressed in dark jeans and a white T-shirt who he has just pulled to a standing position from the street. He throws the young man into the back of a police car. The crowd of youth, which now includes young men from the meeting and other youth from the neighborhood, yell at the officers as they begin to move, en masse, in the direction of the police car. A loud thud from the direction of the police car ignites the crowd, who register their loud objections to what they perceive to be the rough handling of their peer. The police car screeches off, but the crowd and a small group of officers remain. In an effort to slow the movements of the youth, Lincoln and Eric quickly insert themselves between the crowd and the line of police officers. The men act as mediators, trying to calm both the police and the crowd. They stand their ground between the two groups until both groups appear to reach a calm.

Buffer-and-bridge work is not without its risks. In placing themselves between the youth and the police, the men of BCH risk becoming the targets of aggressive handling or arrest. This sort of risk can discourage others

Figure 6. The men of BCH insert themselves between youth and law enforcement. The men stand their ground until both groups reach a calm. Photo by author.

from working with local youth, because the closer one is to these young men, the closer one is to threats of criminal justice surveillance and, at times, lethal violence. One effort to connect youth to a community center just a couple of short blocks away from their housing complex also reveals the serious challenges associated with bridgework in this setting.

After arriving for a weekly meeting, we notice that the doors to the community room are locked. The group is milling around the locked doors when the executive director of a nearby community center approaches the group. The director asks why Eric and the group don't just walk a couple of blocks over to the center.

"They won't go," Eric replies, loud enough for some of the boys to hear. Over the past several months, Eric had tried to get the boys off the block to attend programs or get services in other neighborhoods. Initially, they were reluctant to do so; instead, they were, as Eric once described it, "locked on the block."

"I'll go," yells one of the boys. "I'll go too," said another.

"Okay," Eric says, somewhat surprised at the boys' announcement. "We're going over to [the community center]."

The director returns to his car as Eric begins to lead the small group of boys to the community center. He leads the boys through a narrow street that passes through a small and rarely used playground. He crosses over two more blocks before arriving at the back end of the recreation center. A palpable wave of anxiety passes over the group. We pass by a woman I recognize from a past tenants' association meeting.

"Where ya'll going?" she asks.

"Over to [the center]," Eric says.

"Oh," she says, "Okay, I'll keep my ears open."

One of the boys jokes that another is scared. Another boy announces that he was in the area recently but got chased all the way back to his housing complex.

"Do you know why they were chasing you?" I ask.

"Because we're not one of them," another boy answers.

The boys engage in a nervous chatter as we approach the center. "I don't care if I have this bag of chips," says the boy who was chased, "if I see them, I'm going to drop it and run."

We walk past the back of the center and begin walking to the front doors. As we do, one of the boys notices another young man dressed in jeans and a black hoodie.

"There go an [enemy set] nigga right there," he says. The youth walks away with a cell phone lifted to his ear.

When we turn the corner, a group of adult men is standing outside near the railing in the parking lot. They stare at us as if we are aberrations. Eric approaches the group and introduces the boys. As he does, a black, four-door sedan drives by slowly. That the black car and its occupants are a potential threat is evidenced in the response of the older men. Someone in the back of the sedan calls out toward the group, but it is difficult to understand what they are saying. It is never said out loud, but it is clear that the entire group is concerned that gun violence could break out as a result of the sighting.

"Take them out of here," orders one of the men. "Take them out the back door."

We heed his warning and start to walk toward the community center. As we do, the car makes a U-turn.

"Take them out the back door," he orders again.

We all walk quickly into the center. "Here, take this," one of the boys says, handing me his bag of chips.

At this point, I am as nervous as the boys are. Eric follows us into the center with his eyes set in a scowl. "This way," he says. "Let's go." The boys walk up ahead of us. They step out the back door and look around, keeping an eye out for the car. I look around too. We walk back toward the complex. As we near their block, the boys go running all the way home. By the time we get back, the boys are nowhere to be found.

This scene provides a vivid illustration of the boundaries that define adolescent boys' social worlds and the challenges facing those who might want to provide services to them. Teenaged boys are essentially walled off from the local institutions that are intended to provide resources to the community. Scaling these invisible walls can make some boys open to the threat of violence. Even in cases like this one, which did not end in violence, the experience of threat—and the flight-or-fight response it triggered in the group of boys—reinforces the imagined boundaries of their social worlds. These types of experiences make the bridge work the men do ever more difficult and ever more important.

In addition to managing the risks associated with buffer-and-bridge work, the men of BCH must also manage "the politics of programs," as I described in chapter 2. For a long time, the boys in the BCH group were discouraged from taking part in activities at the Center, one of the largest youth-serving organizations in the city, which was also just a few steps away from where the boys lived. After organizing the boys' group, Eric and Lincoln partnered with the Center to include young men from their group in the Center's programming. When disturbances involving the youth broke out, workers at the Center often called on Lincoln to mediate the conflicts. After several months of this unpaid intermediary work, Lincoln was named the Center's "Volunteer of the Month," a distinction he held with some pride.

Once the young men began to participate in the Center's activities, it seemed that other program staff began to actively recruit the boys to participate in their weekly group meetings as well. During one meeting that Lincoln led, a boy began to complain about having so many meetings at the Center. According to the men of BCH, this active recruitment by a local violence-prevention program was a thinly disguised effort to get the numbers, not an effort to connect with or invest in the development of the youth the Center once shunned. Lincoln responded to the boy's frustration, telling him that he doesn't "have to go to no meeting that you don't want to go to."

Lincoln then posed a question to the group: "Who do I work for?" he asked. A boy shrugged his shoulders. "Brothers. Changing. The Hood," Lincoln replied firmly. "We volunteer," he said, with an emphasis placed on *volun-teer*. He continued, "We're here because we want to help you."

Lincoln went on to highlight the agency of the boys and young men in the group and the relational bonds that keep the young men coming back: "I know ya'll come here because you respect me and I respect you. Ya'll don't have to go to no meeting that you don't want to go to."

In this moment, Lincoln chose not to operate as a "street broker," taking credit for helping other organizations get the numbers. Instead, he maintained his role as a social father—a man doing this work for the boys in the room, and for himself, as a volunteer, not because he gets paid to do it. Lincoln is aware of how easily other programs, even people who otherwise mean well, can exploit the boys. He is also aware that these same programs might benefit from co-opting his informal work with local youth to get their numbers. Both are outcomes that he hopes to avoid.

Even with the frustrations associated with buffer-and-bridge work, Eric and the group were able to claim some small victories, like gaining the youth access to the Center. Another boy seemingly avoided a more serious penalty for a probation violation because he appeared to be otherwise moving in the right direction: working and going to school. There were setbacks as well, including setbacks that seemed to confirm the fears held by staff at more formal youth-serving organizations. The boys posed a special challenge during a rare and hard-won trip outside of the neighborhood, after Lincoln, Kenneth, and Eric had arranged for the boys to participate in the Center's basketball league. Kenneth took on the role of coaching the team. The boys were required to attend the Monday night groups in order to play, but some did so sporadically. Others, now able to hang out at the Center, which was stocked with video games and computers, found it difficult to draw themselves away from those activities to return to the weekly BCH group. Still, most boys showed up for the games. After one game, a couple of boys jumped off of the team bus, ran into a small convenience store, grabbed handfuls of candy, and ran out before they were caught. Eric was furious. It was clear that Lincoln was reaching his tipping point, too, exhorting that he didn't want to work with the boys at all anymore. Kenneth wanted to continue, but only with the ones who were really serious about change. These exhortations and frustrations typically ebbed and flowed with the behavior of the youth, which seemed at times to be predictable only in its unpredictability.

The buffer-and-bridge work performed by BCH was motivated, in part, by changing the "bad image" of the youth that Eric referred to in his impromptu lecture. The men's commitment to the practices of buffer-and-bridge work was also the expression of both traditional and reimagined understandings of fatherhood. The men did not eschew the role of disciplinarian that is typically associated with fatherhood.[16] They held tight to the role of authority figure and disciplinarian and were upset by demonstrations of disrespect from the youth. They also sought to protect and provide for youth in ways they could, sometimes putting their own bodies on the line. They did not seem at all interested in being a boy's friend, although they did engage in, and perhaps saw equal value in, making relational and emotional investments with the youth. Through these practices, the men were not only remaking or reclaiming fatherhood but also, in some ways, pushing back against otherwise conservative Black gender ideologies. This was true in their work as fathers in private and public settings. As I heard on many occasions from the men of BCH, a man does not just go out, make money, and provide for the family. As Lincoln and other men explained to me, there's more to it than that. Just because you don't have a full-time job doesn't mean that you're not a father or that you can't be a good father. It is through this work that the men come to a shared understanding that fatherhood is not merely a role but a set of practices. It is about what you do, your relationships, and your level of engagement and involvement with children.

Some scholars have argued that embracing the "softer side" of parenting is a form of avoidance that leaves all of the hard work of parenting to the female heads of households.[17] That may be an accurate assumption if it is viewed through an apolitical lens of normative understandings of gender. The same practices viewed through a Black feminist lens can be seen as a necessary push on the boundaries of Black masculinity, which has always been constrained and devalued by understandings and expectations of masculinity that center on White (and wealthy) men. Who does it serve to have parenting or childcare practices be determined by gender? As Collins argues, such expectations have never served Black people well, even when they are embraced by Black women, men, and families.[18] To be sure, some of the buffer-and-bridge work performed by the men of BCH reproduces normative understandings of masculinity, but the seeds of a more progressive and liberating set of Black gender ideologies and practices can also be found in their so-called softer practices. Their investment in the emotional worlds of other men and the youth they work with reflect understandings and evaluations of family formations and responsibilities that are not solely determined by gender categories. As Collins writes, this investment holds the potential to encourage new definitions of Black masculinity: "Definitions of masculinity that would enable Black men to see their worth in more than a steady paycheck would create space for new ideas for Black male strength."[19] To be sure, it is necessary for others to see the worth in these practices as well.

THE FRAGILITY OF FATHERHOOD AND FREEDOM: JARRED'S STORY

For Lincoln, the work of BCH operates as both hook and scaffolding for his efforts to maintain a break from the street. In this work, he both reinforces and reimagines aspects of Black masculinity and fatherhood. His physical and emotional presence in his home and with youth in the neighborhood is just the type of commitment revered by people who believe that, to return to the words of President Obama, "nothing keeps a young man out of trouble like a father who takes an active role in his son's life." Yet what those people may sometimes miss is the degree to which "good fatherhood" is shaped not only by political and economic circumstances but also by ongoing contact with the criminal justice system. Those who essentially have to live with law enforcement have a much different experience of childhood and parenting than those who live free from this ongoing surveillance. Parenting in a neighborhood in which the police facilitate the objectives of parents (e.g., by keeping kids "safe") is much different than parenting in a setting in which your kids are always in the sightlines of law enforcement. The story of Lincoln's efforts to free one of his sons from this web of surveillance and enforcement highlights the fragility of freedom in the neighborhood and the limits of a redeemed Black fatherhood as a salve for the vulnerability of Black youth to entanglement in the justice system.

Over the course of my time in the neighborhood, it became common practice for the men of BCH and me to accompany young men to court hearings. One visit took on a feeling of greater importance because Jarred was one of Lincoln's youngest sons. He had not yet followed fully in Lincoln's path or that of some of his other family members, and we were all hopeful that this hearing would free him from his entanglements with the justice system for good.

On this day, Lincoln, Eric, myself, and Alexis, a graduate student who has been co-facilitating the GED workshop, form Jarred's support group. The five of us manage to squeeze into Eric's tan-colored Mercedes-Benz to make our way to the juvenile justice center. The tan leather seats are softened by wear and slightly cracked in some spots. As I hop into the front seat for the ride to pick up Lincoln and Jarred, the glove compartment opens up. I reach out to put it back in place but Eric stops me: "It's going to stay that way."

On the ride to the juvenile justice center, Lincoln, who is sporting a BCH T-shirt underneath a large green coat and jeans, provides us some background for today's hearing. Jarred's last hearing was about a year ago. His probation was transferred to another county, Lincoln says, but that county refused to accept him. Today's hearing is to request that the county accept and dismiss Jarred's probation. On the ride over, Jarred, dressed sharply in jeans, a brightly colored, sequined graphic T-shirt, and a hooded black cotton jacket, is somewhat quiet, except when prodded by his father, who teases him a bit on the way to the center. Eric jokes that the teasing "helps him be a man."

After we arrive at the center, it becomes clear that this is a familiar setting for Jarred. A White man with long white hair and a white beard greets him with a casual hand slap as he enters the building. He is familiar too, as we all are, with the officers, conveyor belt, and metal detector that greet us after we enter the building. After each member of the group makes it through security, we head to the courtroom. The courtroom usually meets in the basement, an officer tells us, but is meeting upstairs today. Jarred makes his way up the stairs with no particular sense of urgency but with an appearance of knowing how things operate here. Lincoln is the last to make it through the metal detector and instructs us to follow Jarred's lead, which we do.

Jarred walks up the stairs to a waiting room filled with wooden benches and, it seems, mostly people of color. Two middle-aged, medium-complexion Black men stand in the room with clipboards in hand. They ask people their names and the number of the courtroom to which they have been assigned. One of the men approaches our group. "We're with Jarred Jackson," I tell the man. As we wait for our turn, Eric and I look over a board that advertises various youth programs. "Any of these for real?" I ask. Eric points to an organization known for working with young women in the city: "They're doing good work."

Shortly after entering the waiting room, Jarred stops to chat with a young, dark-skinned woman that he seems to already know; he spots another boy from the neighborhood in the waiting room as well. The boy tells him that there had been a laptop sting operation in the neighborhood that morning. In the early morning hours, the police placed a laptop on the seat of a car and then took up surveillance in a vacant housing apartment. The young man says he took the laptop and was easily apprehended by the police. Lincoln joins us in the waiting room and quickly recognizes someone too. A tall, middle-aged man wearing slacks, a dress shirt, and a tie enters the room, approaches Lincoln, and greets him warmly. The men reconnect and reminisce about the Midnight Basketball league that Lincoln once coached in. They call Eric over too, who joins them. I use Eric and Lincoln's absence as an opportunity to strike up a conversation with Jarred. He has never been a talker like some of the other young people I have met through the GED class, but in this moment he seems unusually quiet.

"What's new?" I ask.

"Nothing really," he replies.

He expresses a small bit of enthusiasm after I ask about his brightly colored T-shirt. He opens up his jacket so that I can get a better look at the designer T-shirt. After complimenting his style, I ask how long this court process usually takes.

"Phst," he mutters, forcing a whiff of air through his front teeth, which I interpret as "a long time."

"The lawyer can usually make it go faster," he says. The lawyer has not yet arrived. Until they do, we sit and wait.

When the lawyer arrives a few minutes later, Lincoln gathers first Jarred and then the group for a quick meeting in the hallway. He uses the time to begin to make the case for Jarred's release from probation.

"This is the professor who's been working with Jarred," Lincoln says as he hands the lawyer the letter of support that I have written for Jarred. The lawyer, a short woman with salt-and-pepper, shoulder-length hair that falls on a gray suit jacket, turns to me.

"Nikki," she repeats as if it is taking a moment to place my name and, perhaps, my appearance, with the letter. She looks around, then reads the letter before asking us to return to the waiting room so that we do not get yelled at for crowding the hallway. She reads the letter again. She appears to be a bit confused.

"You are at the University of California, Santa Barbara?" she asks.

"Yes," I say, "but I live in the Western Addition. I volunteer with his organization," I explain, pointing to Eric.

Lincoln repeats that I am a volunteer with BCH and says again that I am a professor, no doubt hoping that my status will reflect positively on Jarred's recent performance. She repeats the introduction aloud, as if she is having trouble interpreting the facts before her.

"Yes," we all say.

"Okay, I've got it now," she says, before asking one more question: "He's not enrolled at UCSB?"

"Not yet," I say with a laugh. "Someday soon."

"He's on his way," she says, seeming to finally make sense of an apparently incongruous association.

"Okay," she says again.

After she steps away from the group for a moment, Jarred and Lincoln laugh at the exchange before Lincoln gathers himself. "Okay," he says, "I shouldn't be joking like that."

Once we are called into the courtroom, just a short time after the lawyer's arrival, things seem to move more quickly. The man with the clipboard that we spoke to earlier announces Jarred's name and then asks each member of our group to introduce ourselves to the judge. Eric goes first, introducing himself as a pastor. Lincoln introduces himself as Jarred's father. Alexis, as a graduate student and volunteer. When it is my turn, I say, with the slight tone of authority I tend to take on when I switch to my "professor voice": "Professor Nikki Jones. I volunteer with Pastor Eric's group in the Western Addition." The judge observes the group and seems pleased with the show of Jarred's support network. "The people" seem less so, waving away Jarred's lawyer's attempt to pass on my letter of support, which a representative of the court has already provided to the judge.

The lawyer explains my relationship to Jarred with none of the confusion she demonstrated just a short while ago. She explains her request to the judge, adding onto the explanation Lincoln provided us in the car hours ago. She explains that Jarred has not had any trouble over the past year and requests that his probation be dismissed. The judge takes in the lawyer's request and asks if the people have any objection.

"None," says the lawyer for the people.

The judge then turns to Jarred. He comments jokingly on Jarred's colorful T-shirt, which encourages a laugh from the otherwise silent Jarred. The judge announces that he will accept the request for dismissal. He explains that barring any fines or restitution payments, Jarred will be released from probation.

"Good luck," the judge says, before adding, "Merry Christmas."

From my seat behind Jarred I can see a broad smile reach the edges of his silhouette. Lincoln turns to the man with the clipboard for confirmation that the judge's decision means that Jarred is off of probation. "Yes," the man says. Lincoln pumps his fist with pleasure and relief. Eric and I share in his glee, but we also remind him that Jarred still has to pay his fines before he is off for good. Stepping out of the courtroom, I notice an almost immediate shift in Jarred's demeanor. His entire body actually seems lighter than I have ever seen, almost buoyant, as he bounces out of the courtroom. He waves to the white-haired man who welcomed him into the building and is now seated in the front row of the waiting area. He bounds down the steps he had trudged up earlier. We all once again follow Jarred's lead, this time with broad smiles on our faces too. Jarred has been on probation since he was fourteen years old, which explains the celebratory air of the moment. It is not just a bureaucratic accomplishment; it is something of a graduation.

As we make our way out of the building, I think to myself: this is what freedom feels like. That it is only a partial freedom is a consideration for another time.

We exit the building, and Jarred points toward the small black windows that line the juvenile justice center's wall. "There's probably kids looking down at me now," he says, as he approaches the gate. Lincoln explains that there is a school inside the center, but otherwise it's like Pelican Bay—the state's SuperMax prison—in there. "The only difference," he says, "is that they don't bring the shower to you like they do in Pelican Bay."

After this reflective moment, Jarred again takes off, skipping like a school kid away from the center. Eric tells him that the car is across the street and up the hill, and Jarred bounds off in that direction, stepping almost directly in front of a city bus.

"He's so happy," Eric jokes, "he's about to get hit by a bus!"

After we pile into the car, Lincoln thanks us all for "showing up for my baby." The moment of levity is interrupted, albeit briefly, by a warning from Eric. He wants Jarred to understand that the stakes are now a lot higher. If Jarred gets into trouble now, he explains, it's "850"—the adult system.

Lincoln warns Jarred that he needs to stay focused even though he's "off paperwork" now. Eric reassures Jarred that he has a good head on his shoulders, but he also doesn't want him to lose focus.

"That's right," I echo, "this is just the beginning." Eric and Alexis nod in agreement as we pull away from the juvenile justice center and make our way back to the neighborhood.

To be sure, Jarred's release was something of a victory for Lincoln, too. His work over the past year had been recognized by the Center, but it also now seemed to be paying off for his children. This affirmed his efforts and seemed to reinforce Eric's earlier advice about the importance of Lincoln redirecting his life if he wanted to have an impact on the lives of his sons. In addition to "stepping up" in the neighborhood, Lincoln also stepped up that day in the courtroom in ways that challenged the kinds of stereotypical notions that others may carry about Black fathers. In addition to standing by his son that day, he also orchestrated the performance of a strong network of social support for Jarred. Other youth in the waiting room that day appeared to have arrived on their own or with parents or guardians, including some in need of the support of translators, which can complicate an already fraught conversation. This show of support, especially a connection to decent and respectable adults, can momentarily disrupt the implicit biases or quick judgments that institutional actors might make about the youth who stand before them. We were willing to stand with Jarred because we witnessed not only his efforts over the past year but Lincoln's efforts as well.

If all it took to keep a young man like Jarred out of the criminal justice system was a "father who takes an active role in his son's life," then Lincoln's efforts ought to have shielded Jarred from system involvement as he entered early adulthood. Yet the fragility of Jarred's freedom, and the degree to which it is shaped by his social setting, was made clear in a phone call I received from Eric just a couple of weeks following the judge's decision to release Jarred from probation.

"We had an incident," Eric tells me, as my partner and I drive along Steiner Street toward the Golden Gate Bridge and Marin.

"What happened?" I ask, bracing myself for what I suspect is bad news.

My stomach sinks when Eric gets to the reason for the call: Lincoln and two of his sons, including Jarred, were arrested. He tells me that Lincoln was also "roughed up" during the arrest and was now at the hospital. I ask where Jarred and his brother are, and Eric tells me that they are at the local police station. Eric is on his way down there now. I tell Eric that I will call him once I return to the neighborhood.

I am shocked and disappointed at the news. I saw Jarred earlier that morning and the day before, when he attended the GED workshop. He told me that he had just seven dollars in restitution to pay and that he planned to pay it off that day. He seemed in good spirits that morning, too. Now, less than *two weeks* from his release from juvenile probation, he is arrested and, as Eric warned, on his way to 850.

A few days later, Eric and I are back at the coffee shop, this time preparing to show up at court for Lincoln *and* Jarred. In the meantime, I had been able to gather some information about the incident. One of Lincoln's sons received a warning from an officer to get off the street.[20] When the officer returned, the young man had not heeded the officer's warning. The officer then got out of the car to address Jarred, which, as expected, drew the attention of a crowd of bystanders. The officer called for backup and, after a second officer entered the scene, the situation quickly escalated, ending with the arrest of Lincoln, who had tried to intervene on behalf of Jarred and two of his other boys.[21] Eric believes that Lincoln and Jarred are being held not because of their involvement in what became a chaotic scene but rather as a means to press for information on other suspected criminal activity in the neighborhood, as had once been the case for Eric. Whether or not that was the true motivation for holding Lincoln's sons, Lincoln and Jarred had a court date and we were ready, once again, to show up to support them both.

The term "850" is the commonly used reference for San Francisco's Hall of Justice; 850 is not the juvenile justice center. This is made clear once you enter and are greeted by multiple metal detectors and a seeming sea of civilians, lawyers, and officers making their way past the detectors and on to the courtrooms or offices where their attendance is required.

I join the mass of routinized movement before taking a seat on one of the hard, wooden, auditorium-style chairs that take up three rows in a medium-sized courtroom. The honey-colored wood that decks the walls stop at a drop ceiling, which helps to muffle the voices that might otherwise bounce off the courtroom's walls. The judge sits on a dais in the front and center of the room. Like others who have also taken up seats in the courtroom, we wait for Lincoln and Jarred's case to be called. I look on as the judge, a white-haired woman with what comes across as an easy but firm demeanor, looks at the papers in front of her and says, "off the record," that this is either going to be nothing or something. She speculates that this incident, which erupted over a seemingly minor violation, might just be a "dog and pony show." As she shakes her head in what may be frustration, disbelief, or a combination of both, I lean over to Eric and whisper my evaluation of the judge's actions.

"That's good," I say. Eric smiles and nods in agreement.

After a few moments, a door opens and Lincoln and Jarred shuffle into the room wearing orange jumpsuits and handcuffs. Other members of Lincoln and Jarred's family have joined us in the courtroom, taking up most of our row. Lincoln looks somewhat sheepishly at the group who has gathered to support him as he is led into the courtroom.

"Hey, Babe," Lincoln mouths to his wife, who is dressed conservatively in a long black leather coat, black boots, and an ankle-length dress with a delicate blue flower print.

Lincoln catches my eye, holds up his handcuffs and shakes his head from side to side. I raise my hands in a "what can you do?" gesture and shake my head too.

"It's alright," I mouth silently.

The public defender assigned to Lincoln and Jarred seems rushed but also somewhat empathetic in his gestures and demeanor. He asks Jarred if he works. Jarred says that he goes to this program and he collects a stipend. I also hear him mention working on his GED.

"There go his teacher right there," says Lincoln, once again hoping that my status provides some protection from a harsher punishment for Jarred. Jarred and the public defender turn to look at me. I wave and smile.

As the public defender gets up to speak on Jarred and Lincoln's background, the judge reviews the papers in front of her. The irritation she demonstrated before Lincoln and Jarred entered the room reemerges. She calls counsel to the bench. Jarred and Lincoln begin to talk to one another but are hushed by the lawyers. The lawyers return to their places in the courtroom, and the judge announces that she will release Lincoln and Jarred on "Project OR," which means that they will have to check in with probation twice a week. They both release a sigh of relief at the judge's announcement, though it is muted in comparison to the joy that followed Jarred's release from juvenile probation. I am left feeling pained that Jarred's newfound freedom, and the sense of well-being and confidence that seemed to accompany his new status, ended so abruptly.

Before the judge brings the proceedings to a close, she warns Lincoln and Jarred to "stay out of trouble." She repeats this warning twice in an effort, it seems, to convey its seriousness. Lincoln looks a bit perturbed by the childish admonishment. Eric and I exit the courtroom and greet the public defender, who uses the introduction as an opportunity to repeat the judge's warning.

"They'll have to stay out of trouble," the public defender warns.

"They have been," I say, also irritated by the paternalistic tone of the suggestion.

The public defender recites a line he says he learned in legal ethics: "First, don't do anything wrong. Second, don't appear to do anything wrong." The simplicity of the warning belies, of course, the degree to which punishment for "trouble" is, as I described in chapter 3, not equally distributed across the population.

Although we are pleased that Lincoln and Jarred have been released, we are also dispirited by the arbitrary nature of the arrest, which takes a toll on Lincoln and Jarred. After his release, Lincoln continues his work with BCH, but he is also wary about spending time in public space.

"I don't even feel right being outside," he tells me during a conversation after his release.

Since the arrest and his release, Lincoln feels like the police are even more focused on his body and behavior than before. Sometimes, he says, they follow him down the street when he is out in public. He shares that Jarred also feels uncomfortable in the neighborhood and wants to go live with a relative in another part of the city. Other family members want that for Jarred, too. Eventually, Lincoln agrees with them, a decision that helps to remove Jarred from the surveillance of local police but also puts an end to his participation in the GED workshop.

When it comes to diagnosing the problem of violence facing residents in distressed urban neighborhoods, the conversation often returns to the structure of the Black family and, more recently, to the moral failures of young Black men and their "absent" fathers. Indeed, the specter of the "bad, Black father" looms large as both symptom and cause of the many challenges facing young people who come of age in neighborhoods like the Western Addition. This belief is one that is shared by policy makers, practitioners, and scholars. It is a belief reflected in President Obama's assertion that "nothing keeps a young man out of trouble like a father who takes an active role in his son's life." It is also a belief that organizes much of Eric's life and his efforts to help other men and boys. It is embedded in the advice he gives to Lincoln. The way to save your son is to change *your* life, to become a better man, to become a better father. Lincoln takes up this challenge, as is reflected in the buffer-and-bridge work that he performs for BCH. Yet, in doing so, he not only reinforces expectations that are associated with traditional understandings of masculinity but also extends understandings of Black masculinity by investing in emotional and relational aspects of caregiving. His efforts demonstrate that strength need not always be coupled with dominance—a revelation that holds the seeds of a radically redefined understanding of Black gender ideologies. Yet, as Lincoln's story shows, there are also limits to what the "redeemed Black father" can provide for youth.

Lincoln's attempts to be a buffer between his son and law enforcement reveals the degree to which what we describe as "good" parenting is socially constructed—produced and reproduced by social institutions like schools, law enforcement, and neighborhoods. His efforts to protect his son from the threat of police violence placed him in the sightlines of law enforcement. However, instead of offering the buffer of protection, as the status of parents in more stable settings may do, Lincoln's attempt to intervene on behalf of his son in that moment made him *and his son* more vulnerable to aggression from the police, from arrest to the use of force. In that moment, instead of being viewed as an advocate for his son, Lincoln was interpreted as a threat and treated as such: he was manhandled, wrestled to the ground, and handcuffed as his son, other family members, and friends, including young men he had worked with over the previous year, looked on. In this moment, the vulnerability of Black fatherhood in this setting was laid bare; its futility in the path of state-sanctioned violence was made obvious once again.

5 "A Rose out of This Cement"

Jay's Story

Two days before President Obama's second presidential inauguration, on the Saturday of the Martin Luther King Jr. holiday weekend, a young man was shot and killed near the intersection of Fillmore Street and Geary Boulevard. His murder would be one of two homicides that holiday weekend and would become one of the forty-eight homicides to take place in the city by the year's end.

The news of this young man's murder reached me in the same way that the news of Corey's murder (described in the opening pages of this book) reached me: by email.

"Jay was mudered [*sic*]," read the brief message from Eric.

I no longer lived in the neighborhood by the time I received this message, but Eric and I still kept in touch. Jay was one of several young men that Eric and his group tried to support shortly after the introduction of the gang injunction in the neighborhood. They had gotten further with him than they had with some others. Eric once brought Jay to a local legal advocacy organization to explore the possibility of his "opting out," as the city describes it, from the gang injunction. Of all the young people I had watched him work with over the years, Jay was, for both of us, among the most hopeful.

Like Eric, Jay had spent most of his adolescence selling drugs. Also like Eric, Jay began to rethink his path as he entered his early twenties. When I first met Jay in 2008, he was, as Eric once described it, "half-and-half": in the early stages of constructing the kind of narrative and life that would lead him away from the street. The materials distributed to a packed church at his funeral highlighted his recent accomplishments. At the time of his murder, he was an "A" student at San Francisco City College, where he was following a dream he had shared with me years before his death: to become a radiology technician. Five years after he first shared this dream with me, I found myself speaking at his funeral.

The story of Jay's life is similar to that of other young men his age who are trying to break free from the street. For some, this period of time—when they are working to break free from the influences and obligations of their former selves—is among the most dangerous moments in their lives. Their efforts to isolate themselves from the places and people they used to associate with may actually make them more vulnerable to violence—those that let their guard down a bit may get "caught slipping," as they say. They may find themselves with less protection from their set or peers, and, though they may have committed themselves to change, others who are holding onto lingering beefs may have little respect for their efforts. This appeared to be the case for Jay, who no longer lived in the neighborhood at the time of his death and had only returned to the area to run an errand with his brother. He was shot as he waited in his car and died within an hour of the shooting. An arrest followed his killing, then a trial and then an acquittal. Three years after his murder, no one has been found guilty of his murder in a court of law.

In chapter 1, I provided an in-depth, ethnographic account of Eric's life story as a way to illustrate common experiences shared by men who begin to reconsider their commitment to the underground economy in their early twenties. Jay's story reflects some of the same experiences. Yet, though Jay and Eric spent much of their youth in the same neighborhood, the settings and historical moments in which they came of age were not identical. Eric was breaking free from the street in the 1990s, early in the shift to targeted policing practices in the city. As a teenager in the early 2000s, Jay came of age under a law enforcement regime far more intrusive than that which Eric experienced. In Jay's story, we see how the expansion and entrenchment of the system in the neighborhood, which was facilitated and legitimized by community members' participation in the crime-fighting community, shaped his understanding of the legitimacy of law enforcement and, in turn, his own actions, especially his involvement in the drug game, and then his efforts to give up on the drug game for good.

Although the two grew up under different circumstances, there are also parallels in their stories. In Jay's story we again see how efforts at change are embedded in relational contexts. We also see the moral struggle that accompanies being "half-and-half" and the interactional work that goes into building up a new reputation in a setting where everyone knows you as who you used to be. Finally, as in the case of Jarred (described in chapter 4), we see how, despite the best efforts of men like Lincoln or Eric to act as buffers and bridges, the setting in which young people work to construct new lives can exacerbate their vulnerability to institutional and interpersonal forms of aggression and violence. Jay's death once again highlights a paradox that young people coming of age in high-surveillance neighborhoods know well but that is often ignored in calls for more aggressive efforts to combat so-called Black-on-Black violence: the police are seemingly already always present, yet the violence that legitimizes that presence persists.

MEETING JAY

I met Jay for the first time at a meeting hosted by Eric and BCH. The group had decided to focus its efforts on raising awareness about the gang injunction. The injunction had made front page news in the city's paper, but most people in the neighborhood did not seem to know what the gang injunction was or how it might affect them or their families. The group designed a plan to enter every public housing complex and deliver a presentation on the gang injunction. Eric also continued to reach out to young men named on the list, and he worked to build relationships in the other public housing complexes affected by the gang injunction. In addition to this work, he continued to help organize a weekly food bank held at the Carter homes. Eric used this work as a way to organize the time and energy of other men, providing a bridge to a daily routine and meaningful work. While there, he met Jay, a young man named in the injunction who was also volunteering at the food bank. Eric invited Jay to the meeting, which was held in the community room of the police station. The police station sits across the street from what some call the "drunk park," a mini-park next to the old Muni substation building where men and some women hang out at all times of the day, sitting on benches, sipping out of brown paper bags, or playing dominoes, gathered around small tables. BCH held a recent "Silence the Violence" event there. Eric likes to hold events there, he says, because these people are members of the community too.

When I arrive, the community room where the meeting will take place is empty except for a middle-aged, dark-skinned Black woman dressed in a fleece and jeans. She lives "over the hill," she says, but attended the recent "Silence the Violence" event, where she received a flyer about tonight's meeting from Eric. We chat a bit about the changes in the neighborhood before the rest of the group trickles in. Within moments, she recites biblical scripture—quickly locating the problems with young men named on the gang injunction with their inability to fully step into the roles of manhood.

She adds that, in order to change the behavior of youth like those on the list, you have to have something "stronger" than what is influencing these young men, and that, she says, only comes from the Bible.

Several more meeting participants arrive after a few minutes, including a representative from a city agency involved with the grant funding, and Eric. Over the years I observed Eric, I noticed how his style of dress became more professional, especially in meetings like this one, where he is dressed in dark slacks and a dress shirt with an open collar. A microphone is set up with the expectation that more people would fill the room, but no one does, despite Eric's efforts to bring people to the table (near the end of the meeting, the district supervisor's assistant shows up, pokes her head into the room, and leaves).

A young man in a baggy blue dress shirt and dark blue jeans walks in, greets Eric, and takes a seat at the table. He has a mahogany complexion, a soft, round face, and a calm demeanor. His hair is braided into neat corn-rows extending from the front of his head and ending in neat curls at the base of his skull. His eyes are slightly downcast.

During introductions, the young man addresses the group: "Hi, I'm Jay and I'm a resident of the Western Addition area. I've been living here for all my life. I'm just here to take notes and see what's going on."

Eric asks Jay to talk about his experience with being named on the gang injunction, which he does. Jay's comments echo a complaint that I heard from other young men in the neighborhood.

"To my knowledge," he says, "the gang injunction is [a way] to keep, is to split up a lot of people that live around each other." From Jay's perspective it is, as another respondent once called it, "a family injunction."[1] "A lot of people [on the injunction] are family, and, um, they like to say that we can't be around our family and um, we can't go outside and just enjoy the weather."

In addition to feeling as if the injunction is overly broad in its reach, Jay feels that the process of placing people, especially himself, on the injunction is heavy-handed, flawed, and unfair. From his perspective, it seems that law enforcement officials are forcing the definition of a gang, including its name, on a particular geographic area; such a wide net entangles those who do not have strong ties with so-called gangs with those engaged in more serious, even violent, actions or behaviors. Jay resists the "gang member" label and tries to explain to his probation officer that he is not the kind of high-risk "criminal" that his probation officer claims to work with regularly: "It's just a few problems I had in my past and it's not really that serious."

Jay does not find the advice that his probation officer gives him—to "stay in the house all the time" as a way to avoid violating the injunction—

particularly useful or realistic. He, along with others in the neighborhood, believes the officer is someone who is out to punish young Black men. Eric validates Jay's reading of the officer with a complaint about the officer's resistance to the most basic of human gestures during visits to the neighborhood. During one such visit, Eric tells the group, he walked up to the officer and extended his hand for a greeting, "as men do," but the probation officer would not even shake his hand. This sort of interactional rejection is significant and meaningful for Eric and others who see themselves as men deserving of some respect but are often not treated as such by institutional actors like this probation officer.

Jay is now trying to "opt out" of the gang injunction, an option introduced by the city attorney after some pressure from the community. Jay hopes that the opt-out process will get his name off the list, which will allow him to avoid potential discrimination in the future. In order to get his name off of the list, Jay is, to borrow from Eric's words, "showing change," trying to prove to his probation officer and others that he is committed to change: "That's basically where I'm at, just trying to explain, explain myself and prove myself."

Eric provides support for Jay's description of the gang injunction as an unfair process with harsh consequences for him and others, but another meeting participant, the middle-aged Black woman I met before the meeting, seems less convinced by Jay's account of his circumstances. Her comments shift the discussion from institutional accountability to personal responsibility:

"You want your liberties back. You want your freedoms back. What are you going to do to get them back?" she asks Jay. Her question illustrates an opinion that is shared by other community members—that is, that these young men "did something" to get on the list and, as such, hold the burden of the responsibility to free themselves from the system's reach. From this perspective, a young man's acceptance of his responsibility for his actions matters less than whether or not the process of placing people on the gang injunction was fair or just.[2]

Jay responds by making his case for his freedom: "I currently have two jobs and I volunteer with Eric, which I was doing before I had any jobs, and I go to a lot of programs. . . . I went to anger management programs and stuff that my probation officer had recommended me."

"And you're making progress?" the woman asks.

"Yeah, I'm making a lot of progress," Jay says, before offering a comment that highlights the role of both individuals *and* institutions in the process of criminalization: "I believe you should look at what people are doing and if they conducting themselves in a humanly manner [then] they shouldn't be labeled as gang members."

Jay knows that even doing everything right will not get his name off of the list. He will have to go through an undoubtedly heavy bureaucratic process of petitioning for the return of his "liberties." This seems like an unfair burden to Jay, which only heightens his sense that the system is unfair.

At the age of twenty-two, Jay is the target of surveillance in a neighborhood that is considered a "hot spot" for violence. Jay's attendance at the community meeting hosted by Eric seems to be a step in a positive direction, one that began earlier with his participation in, and completion of, programs recommended by his probation officer and his volunteering efforts at the local food bank. He hoped that his efforts to show change would indicate to others that he was committed to pursuing a different path. One year after Jay's appearance at the community meeting, he seemed to be firmly on that path. This feeling was reinforced when Jay made a trip with Eric and Lincoln to a symposium on gang injunctions in Santa Barbara. I had invited a couple of other young men from the neighborhood to participate in the day-long symposium at the university. The others had agreed, but by the time the group left San Francisco that morning, Jay was the only young man in the van.

My then-colleague Victor Rios and I, along with a small group of graduate students, organized the symposium as an effort to bring together two groups of young people from very different settings, both of whom had been labeled as gang members. Victor is an expert on gang-associated Latino youth and has written on the importance of building a "youth support complex" for young people who have been labeled as gang members.[3] In addition to increasing youth's awareness of gang injunctions beyond what is passed along on the street or by law enforcement, we also hoped that welcoming the young people to the university setting and treating them as experts deserving of dignity and respect would provide a meaningful and motivating experience for the young people involved.

During the event, Jay shared the story of his recent arrest, incarceration, and release with the group. His arrest stemmed from a drug sale to an undercover officer who, Jay says, was planted in the neighborhood to buy large amounts of drugs. Jay was lured by the potential to make sales that would garner hundreds of dollars. His payoff was, instead, arrest and incarceration: "did my crime, did my time."[4] Jay reiterates his complaints about his probation officer for a new audience, along with the other challenges he has faced since his release.

"It's hard when your probation officer is against you, trying to lock you up," he tells the group. He says that his probation officer comes into his room, finds some of his artwork and poetry, and then uses his poetry as "evidence" that he's in a gang. In addition to his troubled relationship with his probation officer, Jay also tells the group about his experience as a target of police surveillance. He says that he and his family members are frequently stopped and harassed by the police. He shares a story about a recent stop. Two officers, including one Black officer, stopped him, took him out of his car, sat him down, and then proceeded to search his car. The officers asked if he was on probation. "Yes," he answered. They ask for what, he says, but he did not tell them. Instead, he asked the officers to explain the reason for the stop.

"Why did you stop me?" he asked.

Jay recalls one officer's response: "Because you're a Black man driving at night."

In the same way that Jay's stories bears similarities with Eric's transition, his story highlights similarities with the experience of young Latino men in Santa Barbara—distinctions that are often buried in tensions between such communities in California. The young Latino men from Santa Barbara tell similar stories about experiences with the police.[5] They, too, have experienced forceful raids. They describe ten-year-old kids frozen with a shotgun pointed at their face. The stories they tell echo the legal cynicism evidenced by young men in the Fillmore. The police create reasons to arrest them. The evidence is in the charges: assaulting a peace officer, resisting arrest, etc. The sense of alienation and isolation is palpable. One of the young men explains how a sense of unfairness becomes a part of the reason why they call themselves a gang. Here, however, the similarities end. Lincoln shifts into the role of Old Head and social father as he expresses his confusion at one young man's claim to be a gang member:

"You call yourself a gang member?" he asks.

"Yeah," a young man replies.

"You got *tats*?" Lincoln asks.

"None visible."

"Okay," Lincoln says before asking: "Don't you think that is going to make things harder for you?"

Victor interjects to offer a brief explanation of the differences in how Black and Latino communities describe gang association, but the explanation does little to move Lincoln's thinking. Lincoln shares the language that I have become accustomed to over my time in the Fillmore to describe groups of associated youth: "We're not gangs—[we're] sets, turfs, street families, etc." This self-definition and distinction makes the migration of the gang injunction to Black communities like the Fillmore confusing for Lincoln. Yet such self-definitions make little difference to law enforcement, which has the ultimate authority to define behaviors and, as such, the set of sanctions to follow. Jay's response to a student's query about how they can help highlights the futility of individual efforts to push back against the power of this official labeling: "Study the law—let us know how [we] can get off the list without filling out an application."

At the end of the day, Eric, Lincoln, and Jay leave campus with, it seems, a newly found sense of accomplishment, inspiration, and confidence. This positive sentiment and good spirit is on display during one final, unplanned encounter when we bump into a colleague on the way to their van. Mrs. Stokes, a middle-aged Black woman, greets the group warmly.

After explaining Jay's background, I watch as Mrs. Stokes gives Jay a much different lecture than what he was exposed to a year ago. This lecture, part pep talk and part mini-sermon, is full of encouragement for Jay and his effort to pursue another path. Jay listens intently with a respectful and engaged demeanor. The entire group seems to be moved by her inspirational message. After she leaves, the guys tease Jay, saying that he looked as if he was near tears as Mrs. Stokes delivered her sermon. Jay jokes that a bug flew in his face, yet it is clear that the message resonated with him on an emotional level. The message was clear to Jay: his past is his past and he shouldn't let it define his future. Jay wants to believe that, but he's also aware, he says, that he's not the one doing the hiring—his record makes him open to discrimination.

"You just have to keep showing up," I say, as we gather to give our final farewells. I hug them all before they go. I tell Jay that I'm proud of him. As I walk away from the group I hear Eric say, "God works in mysterious ways."

Jay's trip to Santa Barbara provided me with an opportunity to see him interact with others in a different setting, one with which he was not entirely familiar. In that space, I could see Jay's best qualities emerge—qualities that were also on display during the community meeting. During the symposium and in his interaction with others, he was thoughtful, respectful, and engaged. He seemed eager to spend more time on a college campus. His early attempts to construct a life story suitable for sharing at events like the symposium revealed the potential for Jay to become the kind of exemplar of change that so many people want to see: the young man who recognizes his mistakes and redirects himself toward a more respectable path. Such exemplars are imagined as being on an always-upward trajectory—one that takes them far away from the circumstances of their previous life. Thinking back, that is how I also imagined Jay's life at that moment. A few months later I would learn that Jay's trajectory was much more complicated than it appeared.

HALF-AND-HALF

"Jay's out," Eric says. "I saw him drive by."

I am surprised when Eric shares this update with me. A year ago, Jay seemed as if he was ready to step up into becoming an exemplar of change. He handled his speaking commitment at the university with confidence and seemed genuinely moved by Mrs. Stokes's impromptu motivational speech. He was volunteering and holding down legitimate jobs. From all accounts, it appeared that he had already accomplished the change that so many of us wanted for him. But Eric tells me that Jay was arrested and received time served plus six months of probation. We agree to reach out to Jay. It takes some time, but a couple of months later we meet him at Gussie's, a new soul food restaurant that has replaced an old soul food restaurant in the neighborhood. As Eric and I wait, Jay gives a call to let us know that he is on his way. He asks Eric if he should drive or walk. Eric provides an instruction that foreshadows Jay's murder: "That's up to you and your security."

Jay decides to drive. He parks his car, a black Lexus, on the corner. As he enters the restaurant, I notice a change in his style and demeanor. He arrives dressed neatly in a brown-and-tan button-down shirt that hangs to his mid-thigh, jeans, and sneakers, but his face does not shine as brightly as it once did; his cornrows, which always appeared healthy and tight, now seem dull and a bit dry. He also seems more drawn in—a sense of sadness lingering closer to the surface than I remember. Early in our conversation, he shares the shame he has carried since his most recent arrest. He is disappointed in himself, he tells us, and he feels that he has also disappointed others invested in his transformation, especially his mother, but also Eric and me.

Jay was twenty-three years old at the time of our interview, about the same age as Eric was when he began to rethink the trajectory of his life. Like Eric, Jay had also spent nearly a decade selling drugs by the time he entered his early twenties. For the first time, Jay shared with me the story of how he became a drug dealer. His brief retelling is filled with a sense of nostalgia that belies his chronological age. Years after his murder, the ease with which he became "hooked" on what he would go on to describe as a "bad habit" is haunting.

"The first time I ever sold," he says, "I remember it like it was yesterday."

A man in the neighborhood asked him to "watch their stuff [drugs]." If someone came by looking to make a purchase, Jay was told to "sell it to them." Jay was approached by a potential buyer and, with some help from an onlooker, made his first sale.

"So I did that," Jay says. He pauses for a moment as if reflecting on a meaningful accomplishment before finishing his thought, "first twenty dollars."

Jay waited around for a couple of more hours, but eventually grew tired of the playground. He went inside, leaving the package he was supposed to be watching behind. When he came back, it was gone. He suspected that the onlooker who helped him make the sale was the one who took it. He later learned that the package was recovered by the man who originally asked him to hold it. Jay was relieved. When the same man asked if Jay had sold anything, Jay said he hadn't.

"And that was twenty dollars." Over a decade later, Jay speaks with a sense of awe about his first sale.

"Wow," he says as he thinks back on the moment. "Twenty dollars— that was fast money. I am twelve years old. That is my allowance every other week. Do you know what I am saying? I got it in a *day*."

After his first sale, Jay sought out more information on how the business worked. He approached the man who asked him to hold the package with questions: "How do I make money? How do it work?" Jay was especially puzzled by how people who wanted to buy drugs knew whom to approach for a potential sale: "What do you just go ask people? I know you just don't go ask people do you want some drugs? [If you do that] you go to jail, they are going to say no and call the police on you. I really couldn't understand that." His new mentor "told [him] how it worked" including "those key words and everything."

"It got broke down to me, I understood it. . . . Then I understood it and I started doing it."

By the time he entered his early twenties, Jay was still "doing it." Jay's account of his entry and eventual exit from the business of drug dealing highlights important similarities and differences in his and Eric's experiences as young people coming of age in the same neighborhood in different historical moments. For both, the money associated with drug dealing, which may seem like a relatively small amount to people with more means and resources, was a pull into the neighborhood's not-so-underground economy. Unlike Eric, Jay did not see himself as part of a set or crew. Instead, he thought of himself as an "entrepreneurial criminal"—one who happened to be from a particular geographic area but who did not sell drugs for the benefit of a particular set or crew: "I did my crimes for me not for the gang. I'm not trying to raise money to buy guns to, um, have, you know, resource[s] for the gang [or] as a resource for a gang that I want to go use on people. I do it for my own benefit."

For both boys, as their involvement in that "lifestyle," as Eric called it, or "bad habit," as Jay describes it, deepened, they both struggled in other aspects of their lives, especially schooling. Jay failed the seventh grade, an outcome he associates with his other "bad habits" of cutting school and using marijuana. In both cases, their ability to reflect critically on their involvement in the game appeared to improve as they entered early adulthood. Jay's experience also reveals the significance of "half-and-half" as a phase in the process of changing one's life. When I ask Jay if he might use Eric's phrase of "half-and-half" to describe his experience, he agrees: "Yes, exactly. That's a good way to describe it." He explains that he was "all the way out at one point" but was drawn back by both financial and psychological demands.

Yet, in contrast to Eric's description of his half-and-half status, Jay attributes his long-standing commitment to his "bad habit," at least in part, to his "hostility" against "the system," which he believes treated him and people like him unfairly. His comments reveal that, whereas shifts in punishment acted as a push factor in Eric's life—one option he wanted to avoid was "going to the pen"—the persistent, all-encompassing, and seemingly illegitimate intrusions of law enforcement acted to *strengthen* Jay's commitment to the underground economy: "So yeah, before I had a lot of, say, hostility against the system. So, I liked to rebel. I wanted to rebel."

When Jay makes this point during our interview, I ask him to elaborate: "When you say you felt like you were rebelling against the system, did you feel like the system was unfair?"

"Yeah," he says, and goes on to explain the relationship between his perception of the fairness of the system and his actions. "I felt like *it* was unfair so *I* should be unfair."

When I ask for an example of this unfairness, Jay returns to his critique of the gang injunction, which he sees as part of a larger effort by the system to target "young, African American males": "They want to target and eliminate 'em out of where they are by making stipulations of where they can and can't go and who they can and can't be with."

Jay repeats a critique of the injunction that we have heard before. The term "gang" lacks specificity, lumping together "entrepreneurial criminals" like Jay with those who may be more committed to a set or crew, Jay explains. From Jay's perspective, a person is labeled a gang member not for a specific illegal activity but for engaging in illegal activity in a specific geographic area. In this way, the police essentially manufacture the gang members they are then called on to police. Jay goes on to highlight the real consequences associated with this label not only for young men's encounters with the police but also for a young man's sense of himself as a *citizen*.[6]

"It puts a label on me," Jay explains. "The police put that label on you and so now the police see that, 'Okay, he's in a gang. He's in this gang so you shouldn't treat him as a normal citizen.'"

Jay's insight about the ways that the official label of gang member constricts one's sense and experience of citizenship is profound and provocative. It also demonstrates the ways in which citizenship is an interactional accomplishment. In Jay's words, a person who is marked as a gang member is not treated as a "normal citizen." I ask Jay if he feels that happened to him after he was named on the gang injunction: "[Did you feel] like police were paying more attention to you after your name was on it?"

"Yes," he says, and describes the intrusive search he typically receives after a traffic stop as one example of how a criminalized identity places him within another category of personhood, one without the rights and protections given to others. He explains:

"Instead of a [police officer] pulling a regular person over, you know that person might get a thousand warrants but if the police officer sees that it's a gang member he is going to assume that he got something in that car or he's hiding something you know. So they *always* search me. *Always*," he says, with emphasis on "always" each time.

A "regular person," Jay says, might get a warning without a ticket or a ticket without a search, but that is not the case when he comes into contact with the police. Jay's comments suggest that, once the official label is in place, police officers, especially those charged with policing the neighborhood on a daily basis, orient their behavior toward the master status of gang member. In this setting, a known gang member—that is, a young Black man who is officially labeled a gang member—is not typically treated, as Jay suggests, like a "regular person" or a "normal citizen." Jay believes that this official categorization as a gang member increases his vulnerability to intrusive searches—either of his body or of his property—from law enforcement.

"The search always comes with any interaction with the police?" I ask.

"Yeah."

"If you're on the street you get patted down or if you're in your car you get stopped?"

"You get stopped and your car get searched and [you] also get patted down."

I reflect back on Jay's comments on his frustration with the system: "When you were saying that you get frustrated with the system, is that part of it?"

"Yeah."

"[It's] like they're always on you?"

"Yeah," Jay says.

As Jay observes, being marked as a gang member opens young people up to intrusive searches on the street, reinforcing a distinction between categories of persons: normal citizens who are presumed innocent, and young people who are presumed suspicious until proven otherwise. Jay also believes that police use the bodies of gang members to send messages to others associated with the gang, echoing an intention of Ceasefire-inspired efforts: "I think the police view on gang members is that . . . whatever they effect, they have on that person they have that effect on that gang . . . if they intimidate you they're intimidating your gang." In addition to being ineffective, Jay believes that the placement of a person on the gang injunction is dangerous.

"It puts a spotlight on you," Jay says. That spotlight advertises a status or an affiliation that an "entrepreneurial criminal" like Jay is not actually invested in. In this way, being named on the injunction, which is touted as a way to suppress violence, also holds the potential to make young men more vulnerable to violence.

Although Jay is critical of the system's overarching claims to legitimacy, fairness, and justice, he also recognizes that there are "problems" in his neighborhood. It is not that he wants or expects, for example, "to not get pulled over by the police for not obeying the traffic rules," he just does not want to get pulled over *and* harassed by the police.

"So it's not really the ticket, it's just the harassment that comes after the ticket," he explains.

Jay also sees law enforcement efforts to target young Black men as operating in tandem with the city's effort to remove Black people, especially young Black men, from the Fillmore: "I believe that they are targeting young males because as we grow up we're going [to], um, basically still inhabit Fillmore. We're still going to be here, we're going to have our kids here, so they want to get us out of here so that they don't have to deal with our k-, the next generation."

Jay's insights are rooted in observation, instruction, and experience. He is, to be sure, an expert in interactions with law enforcement, especially negative interactions. Whether he has accurately diagnosed the motivation of officers is less important than the perception of his place in society vis-à-vis law enforcement, a perception that he carries with him each day. Jay's insights also reflect the internalization of the warnings that Eric provided to the young men in the boys' group, most of whom are at least five years younger than Jay. Young Black men have a bad image in this city. They are targets for violence from their peers and targets for aggressive encounters with law enforcement. The city wants you gone. To be sure, these are not the same set of messages that youth coming of age in White, middle-class, or wealthy neighborhoods receive on a daily basis. Again, whether or not Jay's perceptions are in fact "true," they were, for Jay, true to him and, in turn, consequential for his actions and behaviors over the course of his adolescence.

AWAKENING MOMENTS

Jay's legal cynicism appears to have influenced his commitment to the underground economy as an adolescent.[7] Yet this cynicism is not absolute or immutable, as our conversation during the course of the interview revealed. Jay tells Eric and me that, since his last arrest, he has slowed down, focusing once again on showing change: "I'm just trying to just be in school. Trying to go to school and just look toward the future . . . for a good career."

"Right now," he says, he's trying to "obey the system" and "complete something significant in my life."

He still carries the anger about his past experiences with law enforcement with him, but it seems that he is able to think more critically about the long-term consequences of his actions. This is revealed in our conversation about his recent experience of incarceration and his commitment to change since his release. During our conversation, I become more convinced that Jay is, this time, indeed committed to a new trajectory. Of course, I had thought that before and, it seemed, was wrong. In hindsight, I realize that earlier on Jay was, like Eric, half-and-half, and I better understand how moving through that stage is, in fact, *part of the process*. Still, it seems to me that, at the time of our interview, there was a difference in Jay. What was it? In looking back and reviewing the transcript, I think that what struck me at the time was Jay's reflection on what I would now describe as two awakening moments that stemmed from his most recent arrest. Like Eric, these moments were deeply rooted in relational contexts. The first of these moments involved his mother.

"What's been the hardest part of the last year for you?" I ask Jay, about an hour into our conversation.

"The hardest part had to be sort of recently it's not that I got into trouble it's the effect that it had on other people."

When I ask whom he means when he says "other people," he replies, "Like my family—my mom specifically."

Prior to his arrest, Jay was living with his mom. Now he has a stay-away order as a condition of his probation. In contrast to the gang injunction, which prohibits legal and illegal behaviors in a defined geographic area, "stay away" orders prohibit people from returning to specific areas or addresses, including the homes of family members. Such orders are often issued as a condition of probation. Since Jay was also named on the lease for his mom's unit, his arrest, along with his placement on the gang injunction, has compromised his mother's living situation. Jay had also planned to live with his mom after his release, which makes him wonder about his own living situation. Ultimately, he was more worried about his mom than his own precarious situation. He knew she could be excluded from any housing authority unit in the city if efforts to evict her were successful. Jay's mom was fighting the eviction but, he says, the fact that he put his mother's living situation in jeopardy "really broke my heart."

During our conversation, Jay shares that his recent arrest and incarceration "really opened his eyes" to how his behavior affects the people around him, including Eric and me. He tells us that he is "really disappointed with how I affected ya'll." His comments reveal an awareness of our efforts to construct him as an exemplar of change and attributes his recent fall not solely to the unfairness of the justice system but to his own personal failures: "I was supposed to be a prime candidate for the movement that's going on right now with the gang injunction [but] with my greed . . . and laziness I let ya'll down. I let ya'll down in the sense that I'm getting the people who support the gang injunction more ammunition against ya'll instead of giving ya'll more ammunition against them." This realization broke his heart, he says: "I think outside of my family I think to ya'll who were also trying to help who I hurt by getting into trouble [that] played a big role in my unhappiness about myself in my actions of what I did."

Much like Eric's earlier experience, Jay's awakening was not prompted by repeated stops and intrusive searches at the hands of the police or even his most recent arrest. As he told us, that intrusive surveillance served to deepen his commitment to what he described as his "bad habit." Instead, what moved him most was the same realization that moved Eric over a decade ago: the emergence of a more critical understanding of how his behavior affected others whom he cared about deeply and who, he knew, cared about him. Also like Eric, working with other men in similar situations helped to move Jay further along the pathway toward change. However, whereas Eric was able to situate his efforts to change in a storefront church, Jay had to rely on what resources were available on the inside to help him along the pathway toward change.

Before he got out, Jay had been incarcerated in the county jail for four months. I asked him what time was like for him when he was inside. He says that the loss of his liberty combined with the unsanitary conditions of a jail setting was "a spirit breaker." Yet he also spoke fondly of a relationship he developed with his "bunkie," who Jay described as an "old guy" and an addict. Jay was initially wary of his bunkie, but his fears and prejudices were disconfirmed shortly after his arrival.[8] Jay soon learned that the man was "very intelligent," "used big words when he talked," and "was very knowledgeable about the Bible." Nearly every night, Jay says, the two spent time reading and discussing the Bible along with another book that Jay had finished shortly before his new bunkie arrived, *When Bad Things Happen to Good People*.[9]

Among the most memorable stories from his nightly study periods was the Book of Job—a tale of a man handling a set of oppressive burdens throughout his life before God rewards him for his faith and perseverance. Jay provides a brief summary of the parable, explaining that Job's faith was "challenged by the Devil." Bad things happened to him "even though he was good." I ask Jay if he carries any lessons from his intensive study period now that he is out of jail. He says he does. He now understands more clearly that there are, as he says, "consequences for your decisions."

As it did for Eric years ago, engaging in discussions about faith helped Jay discover a sense of enlightenment while incarcerated. According to Jay's recollection, the relational context—not merely reading the Bible on his own—was important. These discussions led him to rethink the relationship between his treatment at the hands of the police and his behavior. In the past, Jay's awareness of the arbitrary, aggressive, and, at times, racist practices of the police made him think "since the police don't always protect, I'm thinking that the laws don't always protect." If the police are bad, laws are bad too. So, there is no need to follow them. Jay explains, "When [the police] are being corrupt and confusing the law and defying the law, it makes the overall law seem like it's not right."

Now, Jay says, he is more committed to sticking to a "more straighter line of doing things." He admits that he is "not saying that I'm obeying every rule"—a measure of honesty that departs from the image he portrayed in Santa Barbara. Jay's comments also highlight the importance of time to the process of change, especially for adolescents: "It take time for people . . . to make that transition to obey every rule." In the meantime, he jokes, "I'm not going to list the rules that I'm not obeying."

Eric, Jay, and I talk for nearly two hours. Near the end of our interview, Jay reflects on his years selling and his time spent half-and-half. He knows that it will take time for him to move further across the dividing line of half-and-half. He is also aware of the role that a steady income will play in that process: "The whole thing, that habit, to break it is to have a sufficient income." Like Eric, Jay is also aware of how difficult it can be to make a new life in your old neighborhood. It's important, he says, "to be in an area where it is not in high demand, you know. That does not have demand at all would be best. Where there is not a demand and to have sufficient income." For Eric, it took daily interactional work for him to construct a new identity apart from his old identity as "the weed man." The same holds true for Jay. There is a psychological benefit to being "known," to being somebody with some status in the neighborhood. As long as people recognize you as that person who can satiate their demand, then you receive that benefit: "All them years of doing it, it comes to a point where um as long as they want it I am going to give it to them. You probably be rich and still selling you know what I am saying? Just because of the thrill probably cause of the habit that you got of providing or having it available. So that was my situation."

I ask Jay if the "thrill" of being known and being a provider would be "the hardest thing to give up."

"It is pretty hard," he says. "Especially like I said when it is in demand and when people are demanding it . . . when people are asking you."

Like Eric, Jay has to contend with people who knew him as someone else: "People still ask you because they know that is what you have done for a long time." He continues: "It is a reputation that I have built."

"So you have to build a whole other reputation," I say.

"Yeah."

As Eric and Jay tell it, spreading the word about one's new reputation is as important as finding a new and reliable stream of income. Jay sums it up this way: "So the whole thing about quitting is communication." Yet developing this new reputation comes with a cost. I ask Jay if it is "hard to go from the person that can provide to now being on unsteady ground."

He agrees and adds, "It is. It's just hard."

Jay lists the various anxieties that accompany his effort to construct a new reputation. Among his concerns is an anxiety that young men in his position are often aware of but that is rarely discussed in programmatic settings: making a break away from the street can actually heighten a young man's vulnerability to violence.

"You have to worry about where you are going to go and how you are going to be safe. You don't have nowhere to be safe now. You don't have the resources."

At the end of our conversation, Eric and I provide Jay with a bit of a pep talk. I encourage him to reach out if he needs help finding an apartment or in school. I encourage him not to let the shame and disappointment that he shared with us hold him back. I encourage him to keep moving in the right direction.

"As long as you are willing to do that," I say, "we are willing to help you."

Eric tells Jay that he is heartened by his talk of scripture and encourages him to hold onto faith: "One thing that they say is a saint is nothing but a sinner that got up so the most important thing is when you fall you got to get back up." This is especially important, Eric says, when things are not going your way. At those times, you need to hold on tighter. He also encourages Jay not to get stuck in disappointment: "Don't look at it as disappointment—it is something that moved you forward."[10]

"Jay decided to make a change."

A speaker stands in the center of a circle during a vigil held in Jay's honor. His announcement validates much of what Jay shared with Eric and me during our last conversation. The vigil takes place on the block Jay grew up on, not far from where he made his first twenty dollars and just blocks away from where he was shot and killed. At the center of the circle stands a tall, thin man with a sturdy build. His dark walnut complexion stands out in contrast to the light tan scarf he has tucked into his black leather bomber jacket. His deep voice is laced with emotion, grief, and pain. A small group of friends and family members, mostly women and a couple of men, look on.

The furrows atop the man's brow deepen as he makes appeals to end the violence in the neighborhood. He shares his personal struggle to not meet the violence of Jay's death with retaliation: "Jay wouldn't want that," he says, and the crowd murmurs in agreement. The man, who had spent twenty-five years in the penitentiary, identifies as Jay's "mentor." He testifies that Jay was changed after he left jail.

"He decided to make a change," he says.

"Yes," the crowd whispers in response.

He tells the crowd how excited Jay was each time he received a good grade at City College. He says that he was nearby when the shooting occurred. He heard that a black car was involved and his mind quickly turned to Jay and his beloved black Lexus.

"He was a rose out of this cement," the man says, a reference to Tupac Shakur's book of poetry, *The Rose that Grew from Concrete*.[11] The title of the collection is also the title of a poem that symbolizes the sense of alienation experienced by many young men like Jay as well as the indomitable spirit that is required to change the trajectory of one's life under inhospitable conditions.

A local news report documented Jay's pursuit of "fresh air," as Shakur describes it in his poem—his commitment to do right that he shared during our conversation and over the last year of his life. He was "earning A's and B's in classes such as human anatomy, algebra, and physics, according to his school transcript provided by his family. He spent hours at a hospital volunteering, partly to help him with his coursework. He worked at night parking cars to help pay his bills. He had earned enough to put a down payment on an apartment, his father said. He was trying to make a better life for himself—a kid who had grown up in the Western Addition, a rough part of the city."[12]

The report contained details of the murder that were not communicated in Eric's email. Jay was shot as he waited in his car for his brother, who had stopped at a local cell phone store to pay a bill. Another brother, fourteen years old at the time, was in the car when Jay was shot. Jay tried to drive away but lost control of his car and crashed near the intersection of Fillmore and Geary. He was later pronounced dead at a local hospital.

The report also documents a final, posthumous accomplishment, one that would have made Jay proud. After his murder, San Francisco City College awarded Jay "a certificate in diagnostic medical imaging because his professor told his family that he would have passed the class had he lived." The certificate reads in part that Jay had been an "exceptional student" who exhibited "extreme potential and enthusiasm for learning, helping others and personal growth." To be sure, these are qualities that Eric and I saw in Jay all along.

Jay's story reveals the fragility of freedom in neighborhoods like the Fillmore. This precariousness is produced, in part, by the objectives and orientation of the crime-fighting community.[13] Rather than acting as a deterrent, the ever-expanding and intrusive surveillance of the system, including the minor indignities uttered during face-to-face encounters with the police, served to deepen Jay's commitment to his "bad habit." A so-called entrepreneurial criminal, Jay believed that he was unfairly "made" a gang member by law enforcement and, in turn, treated as such—not as a normal person, as he described it, but as a person who occupied a degraded citizenship status that made him open to routine and invasive searches at the hands of the police. Jay's awakening and his efforts to pursue a legitimate career emerged from a desire to protect and make proud those closest to him, especially his mother. Yet his efforts to break free did not protect him from the same sort of violence that legitimizes and tightens the hold that law enforcement has on the neighborhood and its residents.

Conclusion

Lessons from the Field

I left the Fillmore in December 2009. I returned several times over the subsequent six months to conduct observations and interviews and to catch up with the men from Brothers Changing the Hood. Each time I returned, I noticed the ways that the neighborhood had changed since the first summer I spent there in 2005. The "office" on the ground floor of the Fillmore Center has new floors and a new granite countertop that extends into spaces where tables once sat. The larger service area allows for the café to serve the new clientele more efficiently, including many more White people than I remember just a few years earlier. I stop in at the café after turning in the keys to my apartment a day before New Year's Eve. I expect to see Eric or one of the guys there, but the only faces I recognize are those of the men who work behind the bar. Eric's office has moved to a new location across the street, caddy corner to the café. I walk over to the community center where his office is now located and find him there chatting it up with a friend. After the friend leaves, Eric tells me that his buddy and his buddy's son had a run-in with private security the night before. He says both of the men were thrown to the ground. Eric says that having his office in the community center is like having a window into the community's level of frustration. People come in here frustrated, he says, and want his organization to "do something." Later, as I write up my field notes from this visit, it becomes clear to me that Eric has finally found a new place in his old neighborhood—a real office where people come to him for help, to vent, for guidance, and for comity. Eric is now clearly someone other than "the weed man." He looks pleased, content, motivated, and happy.

What lessons are we to learn from Eric's trajectory, from the experiences of his organization, and of the young men whose stories I have shared here? How can the findings presented in this book help others who want to change their lives, the lives of others, or both? How does understanding the politics of the crime-fighting community described here help us to develop better responses to the persistent problem of violence in urban neighborhoods across the country? In the end, who is most "qualified" to do the work of saving the neighborhood?

Responding to this set of questions is ever more important given current calls to crack down on so-called "Black on Black" violence. The racist rhetoric that ramped up the era of mass incarceration has returned in the "law and order" campaign and now administration of Donald Trump. It is, of course, those communities already under heavy surveillance that are likely to feel the brunt of a doubling-down on the sort of intrusive and aggressive policing that is now endorsed by the president and his attorney general, Jefferson Sessions. To be sure, the findings from my fieldwork push back against the wrong-headed assumption that the heavy hand of law enforcement is the sole solution to the persistent problem of violence in cities across the country. Justice system responses to this violence, especially when the violence involves young people, should reflect an appreciation of how structural circumstances *and* institutional interventions interact in ways that produce and reproduce the behaviors that law enforcement is called on to address. This work also challenges the project of institutionalizing community involvement in the project of *crime fighting;* it would be more effective to organize in a more inclusive way around a more liberating objective, such as building buffers and bridges, instead of more expansive surveillance technologies and jail cells, for youth most vulnerable to violence and contact with the criminal justice system.[1]

The lessons I learned in the Fillmore have both theoretical and practical implications. In this final chapter, I begin by highlighting the theoretical contributions of the findings I report here. My findings contribute to an emerging body of literature that highlights the unique aspects of desistance for young people, especially for youth of color who come of age in inner-city neighborhoods, while also bringing new and much-needed attention to the ways that racial politics and Black gender ideologies shape this process on the ground. I conclude with a brief discussion of three programs that reflect the theoretical and practical lessons I learned from writing this book. For those interested in improving the lives of young people like those I write about here, these lessons should operate as a touchstone, especially in a political climate that threatens once again to place young people of color directly in the sightlines of federal, state, and local law enforcement agencies.

History shapes biography. This simple yet profound sociological observation is widely accepted but often ignored when it comes to discussions of violence experienced or perpetrated by Black youth.[2] Instead, individualistic explanations and solutions often identify Black youth as both symptom and cause of the problem. Such a framing is, of course, not original. Among the most persistent justifications for racially targeted exclusion and punishment, from slavery, to the racial terror of Jim Crow, to present-day policing and punishment practices, has been that there is something about Black people that *requires* their harsh and disparate treatment. This reasoning persists despite its falsity. In order to design effective solutions to the persistent problem of violence in distressed urban neighborhoods across the country, we must begin with a clear understanding of the problem, one that does not focus primarily on the people as *the* problem. It is misguided to place the blame for the problem of violence squarely and solely on a group of individuals, like Black youth or failed Black fathers, rather than on a set of structural circumstances and, more precisely, on the interactions between the two.

This individualistic focus is also common in theoretical and popular discussions on desistance or transformation. In such conversations, change is often framed as an individual's personal journey, but a key takeaway from this study is that successful change is better imagined as a group process that evolves over time, which means that both the individual and their community has a role to play in encouraging change. Although the finding that social interaction matters in the process of change is not new, it rarely serves as a *starting point* for studies of desistance, especially among young Black men in the city. In neighborhoods like the Fillmore, men like Eric confront a distinct set of challenges when they try to change their lives while still living in the neighborhoods they grew up in. Many in the neighborhood know them as the men they used to be: drug dealers, hustlers, or addicts. After breaking free from the street, men like Eric must find a new place in the neighborhood, one that replaces the sense of belonging and sociability that they once found on the block. In order for them to complete the process of changing their lives, others in the neighborhood must, at some level, *validate the new selves these men have constructed.* This group of meaningful others includes not only their friends from the street but also their neighbors, family members, and members of the crime-fighting community. In this way, change is a group process; it requires not only a commitment to personal change but also some participation, namely, *acceptance of that change,* on the part of others. This understanding should guide interpersonal *and* institutional efforts to incorporate people who have made or are making that change into neighborhood and civic life.

Another important takeaway from the stories of the men and youth in this book is that, for many people, change does not happen overnight. As other scholars have noted previously, a changed life is often a gradual accomplishment.[3] For adolescents, trajectories of change are likely to be marked, as they were for Eric and Jay, by a series of setbacks and successes. Eric's discussion of being "half-and-half" is especially significant for those working with youth in late adolescence and early adulthood. To the general public, young people in this stage might appear to be distant, stagnant, or even opposed to change efforts. During this phase of their lives, adolescent boys and young men may in fact straddle the line between the street and legitimate work opportunities. Among this group, such behavior is better viewed as *normative*, not oppositional. They might, as Eric did, hold a job with a local agency while continuing to put in time dealing drugs. To others, these kinds of efforts at change may seem disingenuous, yet they represent a key phase for those who are thinking about changing their lives but are unsure about how to do so. It is during this phase that the resources provided by the community are perhaps most consequential. Had Eric not evaded long-term incarceration, his daughter would have been one of the millions of children with an incarcerated parent. His ability to move *through* this period of his life—a period that is also likely experienced by middle-class youth as they emerge into adulthood—was no doubt aided by his ability to hold down part-time jobs provided by local employment programs for at-risk youth. His part-time jobs, illicit and legit, allowed him to meet the common expectations and obligations of fatherhood, a task that became much harder after he eventually gave up on the game.

This work also highlights the degree to which *relationships*, not just roles, *are transformative*. An individual's pathway to change may begin with an internal awakening, but successful efforts at change are often sustained with and for others. This was made clear to me in the exercise I conducted with Eric, where the moments that mattered most to his transformation were clearly linked to his relationships with family members, especially his daughter. It was also made clear when Jay's fear of his mother's potential eviction more strongly motivated his transformation than any of his interactions with law enforcement. This observation pushes back once more on theories of focused deterrence, which leverage the heavy hand of law enforcement, especially federal law enforcement, to motivate people to change their lives. On the ground, such efforts may, as I observed in the Fillmore, sow confusion, resentment, and fear among those targeted for intervention—feelings that do not provide the best context for decision-making. The stories in this book suggest that it is not fear of what might be done to oneself that necessarily motivates change but, rather, a deep appreciation of how one's actions might complicate the lives of those they love, like their children or parents. Interventions should make such "hooks for change," as they are described in the literature, easier to grasp, not harder.

An additional empirical lesson from the work of Brothers Changing the Hood extends the discussion of hooks for change by highlighting the importance of institutionalizing buffers and bridges for young people who are trying to make a change during the period of early adulthood. Buffers do not prevent people from taking hits, but they do soften the blow and, in doing so, limit the damage done to a young person figuratively and, at times, literally. Bridges provide support as young people cross over from one setting to another. For some, the gap may be small, but for others it may be a chasm—crossing over can induce uncertainty, anxiety, and even terror. It is to be expected that young people will take a few steps back as they make their way; it is the responsibility of the community to ensure that the bridge is maintained over time.

RETHINKING BLACK GENDER IDEOLOGIES

The analysis presented here reveals the role that institutions and institutional actors play in co-constructing the sort of behaviors that they are then called on to suppress. The book also illustrates how the neighborhood operates as a gender-making institution; the Black gender ideologies that are called on and accomplished in everyday interactions and discourse shape men's efforts to break free from the street and their understanding of their proper place in their social and intimate networks. The work of individual change is intertwined with notions of Black respectability and, in turn, both *encourage and constrain* men's efforts to change their lives. Conservative Black gender ideologies rely heavily on a belief in the complementary nature of gender. Such a belief system reinforces assumptions about natural differences between men and women and the proper roles that men and women should play in the private and public spheres. These deeply rooted beliefs about gender complementarity are shared by and about men (and women) in casual conversations, public meetings, and community events. Such beliefs exert pressure on Black men to reclaim—*even if it means claiming for the first time*—their so-called natural place in their families and the neighborhood's social order.

A commitment to conservative Black gender ideologies also encourages a central contradiction that men must reconcile as they work to break free from the criminal justice system and the street. Marginalized Black men are often encouraged to give up on a belief system that is grounded in dominance—in short, the code of the street—while still being called upon by intimates and others to be protectors and providers. For some, the pressure to meet the protector-provider expectation is what encouraged their long-term involvement in illegal hustles. Men who give up on the illicit hustle soon learn not only that the pressure to protect and provide remains but also, as Lincoln learned, that stepping into these new versions of the protector-provider role can make them and their loved ones *more vulnerable* to sanction and punishment.

Policies and programs that seek to encourage what is sometimes described as "responsible fatherhood" among marginalized men should pay equal attention to the gendered expectations that bear on men's performance of parental responsibilities and obligations, and they should work to redefine them in ways that not only fit the circumstances of contemporary Black families, which include lesbian and gay families, but also provide more liberating gender ideologies for men, women, and families. Some have argued that Black men who reclaim fatherhood by investing in the "softer" side of parenting (such as spending quality time and building relationships), as Eric often encouraged men to do, are avoiding responsibilities by ceding the most difficult parts of child-rearing to mothers.[4] Yet, viewed through the lens of Black feminist thought, investing in the "softer side" of parenting is also a radical move for Black men in heterosexual partnerships because it imagines a home in which responsibilities for caring for the family are not divvied out—or evaluated—purely along gendered lines. A shared responsibility for the various economic, social, and emotional resources required in a family that did not rely on traditional gender assumptions would also reflect the degree to which the engagement of Black men and women with the labor or financial markets has much to do with histories of political and economic exploitation that harm *all* Black people. In such an arrangement, as Patricia Collins explains, "economic dependency would be neither glorified for women or demonized for men" and "dependency and vulnerability would not be gender specific": "Those who could, would lead. Those who needed support would get it. Talent and need, not gender, would determine political and economic behavior."[5]

The danger of adhering to programming that aims to redeem Black fathers or help boys to become so-called men is illustrated in Paul Butler's discussion of "Black male exceptionalism." Such exceptionalism, Butler writes, is a "discourse shaped as an appeal for intervention." This particular framing implores policy makers and scholars to "treat Black males as a distinct group, separate and apart from Black women and other men." Black male exceptionalism is, Butler argues, also a form of "currency both ideologically and economically, structuring not only how we frame civil rights interventions but how we fund them." Further, Black male exceptionalism is the foundation of a "million dollar industry."[6] Yet such programs can also obscure and potentially harm Black women, reinforce damaging stereotypes about Black men, and ultimately undermine racial justice by, in part, reinforcing a gender-based hierarchy that is harmful to those across the gender spectrum: "In a patriarchal system, empowering men poses potential dangers" not only to others but to themselves as well.[7] This point is made especially clear in my consideration of how policing and punishment intersect with traditional Black gender ideologies in ways that perpetuate gendered forms of violence.

As I described in chapter 4, each time a young man experiences stop-and-frisk or witnesses such encounters as they are experienced by others, it encourages—either directly or indirectly—the transference of this aggression onto the bodies of Black women and girls or other-gendered outsiders in the neighborhood. An appreciation of the gendered consequences of stop-and-frisk broadens our understanding of the implications of aggressive policing in poor, Black neighborhoods without requiring the silencing of Black women and girls. Theorized in this way, stop-and-frisk becomes an issue for anyone who cares about the young Black men who are the frequent targets of these encounters *and* the women and girls who share time and space with them. This kind of empirical interrogation is informed by an intersectional analysis that highlights, to borrow from Butler, how "systems of oppression overlap to produce detrimental effects on all African Americans."[8] A key takeaway from Butler's discussion of Black male exceptionalism, as well as the findings presented in this book, is that it is important to interrogate the ways that *Black gender ideologies* shape the experiences of Black men in ways that are consequential not only for Black men and boys but for women and girls as well. The solution to the problems facing the Black community is not to turn Black boys into men; what is needed is a framework for understanding how, for example, structural violence and interpersonal violence, police violence, and street harassment are *interconnected*. This observation is not an insult to masculinity or manhood; it is a call to organize around a shared vulnerability to violence. It is a call to organize as allies, not subordinates.

FROM CRIME FIGHTING TO CAPACITY BUILDING

To return to the question first introduced in the beginning of this book: Who is "most qualified" to do the work of saving the neighborhood? The question is, of course, deceiving. The relevant question is not who is most qualified but rather who is most qualified to do what, exactly? The answer to that question has a lot to do with the organizational structure of a community or program. The stories in this book illustrate how the institutionalization of the crime-fighting community relies on a select group of community members to participate and, in turn, legitimatize targeted policing and punishment in high-surveillance neighborhoods. The crime-fighting community that was constructed over the course of the past several decades holds the potential to isolate those most likely to be vulnerable to violence at the hands of law enforcement and at the hands of their peers. These young people are seen as problems by a range of institutions that ought to be intent on serving their needs, even if doing so is challenging. In a "law and order" climate, it is ever more important for institutional actors to stand with, not against, young people; to build their capacity, not facilitate their containment and confinement. An enduring challenge for those who work within the context of traditional programs is to build the capacity of people in ways that can be sustained long after the program or their participation in it ends. Meeting this objective would require a different sort of social organization and a different set of qualifications.

One of the most popular violence-intervention efforts in the country is Operation Ceasefire. Although the program has certainly evolved since its inception, its original objective of "focused deterrence" remains popular in law enforcement. As I described in chapter 2, the program leverages collaboration among various law enforcement agencies and identifies leaders to send a message to (often) young adults most involved in violent activity in neighborhoods across the country: stop shooting. In recent years, the program, which relies heavily on the stop shooting "or else" message, has made more of an effort to provide resources and services to those targeted by law enforcement. One of its early architects, David Kennedy, has also emphasized how important it is for police departments to acknowledge and apologize for racial harms of the past.[9] Still, the intertwining of law enforcement and "the community" continues to exacerbate fault lines in neighborhoods like the Fillmore. Ceasefire (or Ceasefire-inspired programs) is not the only model for violence intervention that has proven to be effective. The three approaches I highlight below rely not on the heavy hand of law enforcement but rather on the key lessons that I outlined above.

Cure Violence

The first program I describe here once shared a name with Operation Ceasefire but operates from within the framework of public health instead of law enforcement.[10] The program, Cure Violence, has received a great deal of national attention, especially after the release of the documentary *The Interrupters*. For Cure Violence, cooperation with law enforcement is a last resort, "a back-up to the back-up" as described by Gary Slutkin, who first brought the program to Chicago in the late 1990s.[11] Cure Violence also frames the problem in a fundamentally different way from traditional Ceasefire programs. From the Cure Violence perspective, people who use violence are viewed not as problems but as potential patients who require a health-based intervention, not punishment. Framed in this way, the solution to the problem of violence is not "focused deterrence" but rather capacity building at both the individual and the community levels. Cure Violence operates from an understanding that social networks and social relationships matter when it comes to influencing the behaviors of those most likely to be involved in violence. Like Ceasefire, the delivery of services relies on a network of community members and street outreach workers, but it is expected that their participation in the program will, through trainings and the taking on of additional responsibilities over time, also build or strengthen the individual capacity of community participants as well as a community's infrastructure, leaving it stronger and more capable of responding to epidemics, like violence, than prior to the program's arrival. In contrast, programs that rely on the external threat of a punitive response from law enforcement run the perpetual risk of weakening a community's infrastructure by legitimizing ever more intrusive and targeted forms of law enforcement and removing individuals from the community via arrest and incarceration.

A recent book that examines the role of women violence interrupters in the Cure Violence program, including the role that the program plays in the personal transformation of the interrupters, reinforces the findings I present here.[12] In *Transforming Justice, Transforming Lives*, April Bernard highlights the importance of relationships and social context to the process of transformation. Her study of women who act as street outreach workers—or violence interrupters, as they are called—reminds us that these relationships are situated in particular contexts:

> Even in communities characterized by high rates of crime, poverty, and unemployment, perhaps the greatest assets that can be found by persons seeking to refrain from reoffending are supportive relationships. Supportive relationships with women, found in churches and community service organizations, were instrumental in helping people commit to desist from crime. The supportive relationships that were instrumental for women's desistance were found in churches and community service organizations.[13]

Bernard's latter point reinforces a finding discovered during the course of my field research: people work to change their lives *with* others. This finding encourages us to think about ways to support already existing efforts on the part of those working to change their lives and to work to provide more places within which people can construct what Bernard describes as "caring communities." By Bernard's account, the Cure Violence program works because it provides people with a sometimes material but always *social* place to do the work of changing their lives. The program provides a place where a person can participate with others in the construction of a new self, and where others can validate a person's new identity. It is a place where people can "show change," as Eric once put it. The Cure Violence model still confronts many of the challenges associated with "saving the neighborhood," including the heavy burden of labor that is taken on by the people who do this work, regardless of their gender identification. The labor that men like Lincoln and the women in Bernard's study are called on to do is hard work. Turnover and burnout are constant threats to the stability of these types of interventions, as are the precarious sources of funding for outreach workers.

Homeboy Industries

The importance of relational and social contexts is also highlighted in one of the most popular gang intervention programs in the country, Homeboy Industries. Like Cure Violence, Homeboy Industries works to break (not reinforce) ties between formerly gang-involved men and women and the criminal justice system. Homeboy Industries is not a community-based intervention, but its efforts to transform the lives of its participants reflect an appreciation of the social nature of personal transformation and redemption. Like Cure Violence, the project focuses on building the capacity of its participants. Here, again, the people are not the problem. The program's orientation to redemption as a process—one that relies on integrating (not extricating) people from the community—is summed up in one of the program's popular sayings: "We don't hire Homies to bake bread, we bake bread to hire Homies."

In contrast to the "focused deterrence" framework, Homeboy Industries' efforts, described by sociologist Edward Flores as "integrative redemption," are shaped by a Catholic theology that emphasizes "recovery by way of reintegration into the mundane world."[14] Homeboy Industries acts as a launching pad of sorts: outfitting men and women with the equipment they need to gain a grasp on a conventional life and then sending these reformed men (or men in the process of reforming) out into the world. Much like the participants described in Bernard's work, Homeboy Industries helps people (men and women) to find a place—one that replaces the sociability and sense of belonging that they got (or, for some, get) from the gang.

Although Cure Violence and Homeboy Industries are organized in different ways, it is clear that they share a set of *practices* that encourage change. Each program appreciates the importance of place, time, and community as well as the power of transformational relationships. The degree to which these practices hold importance across lines of race, ethnicity, or gender further highlights the significance of the social when it comes to the consideration of personal change.

A final program that embraces each of these practices is relatively new in contrast to the programs discussed above, but it is gaining more attention nationally. Some of this attention is generated from the widely circulated description of the program as one that simply "pays criminals not to commit crime." The program itself, of course, does much more than is reflected in these types of headlines.[15]

The Richmond Model

Richmond, California, is a small city in the San Francisco Bay Area. It is a diverse city; the percentage of its Black population is quadruple that of San Francisco. It is also a city that has faced many of the challenges I describe in this book, especially the problem of persistent violence. From 1986 to 2005, seven hundred young men under the age of thirty were lost to gun violence in the city. The Richmond model was created to interrupt this violence. Unlike the traditional Ceasefire model, the Richmond model (inspired, in part, by the Cure Violence model) operates *in parallel* instead of in intimate collaboration with law enforcement. The "focused deterrence" approach and the Richmond model begin with a similar premise: "a small number of very exceptional kids whose names we know [are] doing things we understand pretty damned clearly."[16] The two differ in important ways on what to do next. Ceasefire-style programs demand change now—get caught again and the hammer comes down. Ceasefire leverages the involvement of federal law enforcement agencies—the big stick—whereas the Richmond model operates from an engagement paradigm, one that is informed by an appreciation of the time that relationship-building takes. Instead of a big stick, the Richmond model makes a big investment in the lives of youth most vulnerable to becoming perpetrators or victims of violence. Perhaps the most significant distinction is that, instead of a "focused deterrence" framework, the Richmond model relies on the concept of "the beloved community."[17] It is a program that is based on engagement, encouragement, and, above all things, love.

Another key difference between the Richmond model and many other violence-intervention models is that Richmond-model workers are *city employees*. The founding director of the program, DeVone Boggan, elevated the status of street outreach workers by creating a new classification for city employees that would leverage the mark of an official criminal record for applicants. Preferred qualifications for the outreach positions would include past experience of incarceration *and* a felony gun charge. The "Neighborhood Change Agents," as they are officially categorized, must also be familiar with the neighborhoods in which they intervene. They are unionized. Their jobs come with benefits and, in general, a level of stability that other intervention models lack. Put simply, the jobs they have are good jobs, especially for men and women who may be excluded from other good job opportunities because of how employers typically treat applicants with criminal histories.

Although the program focuses solely on gun violence and interrupting violent retaliations, its approach is holistic in nature. Specifically, it views the young people it works with as something other than "criminals" or "shooters." The approach relies not on the heavy hand of law enforcement to change behavior but on the motivating and transformative nature of mentoring relationships that are centered not just on accountability but also on respect, dignity, love, care, and compassion. The change agents are trained to meet young people where they are, but also to push them to expand their geographical and psychological boundaries. One example of such an effort is requiring participants to travel with young people from warring sets to new settings both domestically and internationally. Instead of "we need you to stop shooting," the participants in the program are told simply: "We need *you*."

It is within this larger programmatic context that the "payment," as media often describes it, is situated. The payment is actually part of a fellowship offered by the Office of Neighborhood Safety (ONS).[18] It is an eighteen-month fellowship that is not mandated by any law enforcement agency. The fellowship has seven components:

1. The development of a life management action plan

2. Access to multiple healthy adults

3. Connection to social services

4. A lifemap milestone allowance that is paid after six months of participation in the program

5. Transformative travel experiences (e.g., to colleges or international travel)

6. Access to an elder circle

7. Job preparation (a component that has been added since the start of the program)

The measures of success are about more than who stops shooting: it is about who is *alive* or uninjured and not a suspect in a new crime. Nearly a decade after the ONS was created, 94 percent of the eighty-two participants in the fellowship's first four cohorts were still alive; 83 percent were not injured by a firearm; and 77 percent were not suspects in a new firearm crime. These efforts are correlated with a 71 percent reduction in gun violence across the city since the creation of the ONS.[19] According to DeVone Boggan, the founding director of the program, its success is rooted not merely in targeting the right people but also in flooding these people with compassion and respect instead of fear.

The programs and practices highlighted above encourage us to invest in capacity building, not simply crime fighting; to invest in people and relationships, not just programs. Programs come and go, but the people, their relationships, and the lessons they take away from their engagement with others remain.[20] An old adage familiar to many is that hurt people hurt people. It is also true that *free people free people.* Once one person breaks free from the street, they want to help others do the same. People will do this whether we are looking or not. Our efforts here should help—not hinder—their efforts to change their lives.

The programs described above also encourage us to think less about crime fighting and more about *freedom.* Scholars, practitioners, and professionals may be interested in crime fighting, gang suppression, or violence prevention, but people are interested in changing their lives: in getting clean, in staying safe, in getting free and staying free. The narrow discourse of crime fighting erases the structural forms of violence that play a part in the construction and manifestation of what we define as "crime." The lives of the men and boys I describe in this book, like the young people who come of age in tough neighborhoods in Chicago, Philadelphia, or Baltimore, are shaped by the history of systematic exclusion and differential punishment that has shaped Black communities since the beginning of the first wave of the Great Migration. In many ways, "the city" has never desisted from the violence it does/has done to Black people either directly or indirectly through the violence of exclusion and disinvestment. Any effort to alter the behaviors of those who use violence that is not grounded in this history essentially lets the city and the system—along with the history and legacy of structural racism and White supremacy—off the hook. We can no longer afford such an approach.

Notes

1. #BlackLivesMatter was created by three self-identified Queer Black women, Alicia Garza, Patrisse Cullors, and Opal Tometi. See Garza (2014) for a herstory of the #BlackLivesMatter movement. Cobb (2016) documents Garza's role in the movement as well as contestation over who should be identified as the movement's original "founder."

2. On Twitter, the #BlackLivesMatter hashtag was used nearly 59,000 times per day in the three weeks following Brown's death. The use of the hashtag would spike to 172,772 on November 25, 2014, the day after a grand jury decided not to indict police officer Darren Wilson for Brown's death, and to 189,210 on December 4, 2014, the day following a grand jury's decision not to indict police officers involved in the death of Eric Garner in New York City, "the most it was ever used in a single day." See Anderson and Hitlin (2016, 15–17).

3. See, e.g., Foreman (2017) and Fortner (2015).

4. Vargas (2016) writes about the ways that political turf wars, especially battles over ward designations, and street turf wars between gangs and the police over the social control of neighborhood blocks are consequential for the persistence of violence and the social organization of violence prevention. Using the case of Little Village, a barrio in Chicago, Vargas writes that to "understand the persistence of violence, we must examine the consequences of competitive relationships among not only gangs, but also politicians, nonprofits and police" (6–7).

INTRODUCTION

1. All names are pseudonyms. In this study, the neighborhood's small size and the public nature of the battles I describe here (some of which can be verified via a determined Internet search) complicate efforts to ensure absolute anonymity. See Lubet (2017) and Jerolmack and Murphy (2017) for a discussion

of the benefits, limitations, and obligations of anonymity in ethnographic projects. See Kasinitz (1992, 362–63) for a comment on the importance of "historical specificity" in ethnographic projects, which is facilitated by identifying the true identity of *places* (e.g., neighborhoods), as I do here. In addition to providing some protection for respondents' true identities, I also use anonymity in an effort to de-personalize battles that are often attributed to individual animosities but, as I argue here, are actually rooted in the social history and social order of the neighborhood. In this way, anonymity allows the reader (perhaps especially those with some familiarity with the neighborhood) to make more general comparisons *across* settings.

2. I use the Fillmore, Western Addition, and Lower Fillmore interchangeably.

3. See Harding (2010) for a discussion of how neighborhoods shape adolescent identity.

4. Ibid. See also Sharkey (2013).

5. This phenomenon has been observed in other settings as well. See, e.g., Harding (2010), Brooks (2009), and Goffman (2014). For a discussion of the challenges faced in constructing official definitions of gangs, see Justice Policy Institute (2007, 9–11).

6. See Vargas (2016).

7. See Miller (2014) for a discussion of the consequential role such demonstrations play in evaluations of success among professionals and para-professionals who work in community-based re-entry services.

8. Maruna (2001). Maruna also reports on the important role that "giving back" plays in the construction of redemptive scripts among desisters.

9. Ibid.

10. Ibid., 155–64. Other scholars have reported on the importance of social interaction in the process of desistance. In the final chapter of *Making Good*, Maruna addresses the importance of "rituals of redemption," which often *require* the participation of "conventional others" (emphasis mine). Fader (2013) also highlights the importance of social relationships among formerly incarcerated young adults in Philadelphia: "Internal, identity oriented change relied heavily on external support from others" (164). In this work, I draw on the importance of interaction to the change process *as a starting point* and consider how such practices unfold in this setting and the degree to which these interactions are shaped by larger social forces. See also Anderson (1999, 293). See Giordano, Cernkovich, and Rudolph (2002) on the importance of factors *external* to the individual in the desistance process.

11. The respondents in this study did not make distinctions based on gender identity or gender expression. I suspect that, if asked, they would identify as cisgender and gender-conforming (i.e., their gender identity/expression aligns with the sex category they were assigned at birth).

12. To say this another way, both men and women rely on "hooks for change" during the *process* of transformation. These hooks may be gendered (e.g., the good mother) but the function of hooks operates similarly across gender distinctions. In this work, I am interested not just in types of hooks men

rely on but also in the ways that Black gender ideologies shape the construction of such hooks; the risks and contradictions that emerge from hanging one's identity on a hook that reflects normative Black gender ideologies; and the ways that men recraft these ideologies as a response to these contradictions.

13. This analytical approach is consistent with the type of intersectional analysis that Fader and Traylor (2015) call for in their review of the literature on desistance. Such an approach *"extends beyond descriptive sex differences and examines how gender—as performed and enacted—can be understood to support or inhibit desistance"* (254; emphasis mine).

14. Collins (2004, 200).

15. Fall 2010 Resources Guide at http://momagic.org/files/2011/01 /guidefall2010.pdf.

16. See Gans (1982, 142–62).

17. Drake and Cayton (1993).

18. See Patillo (2007, 117–21).

19. I am not the first to use the term "credentialed class." Collins (1979) warned of the rise of the "credential society," which has only expanded since the publication of his now classic work. Chenoweth (1998) reports on the rise of the African American credentialed class. In his popular memoir, Coates (2008) also makes reference to "the credentialed class" as he highlights the differences between his father, something of a self-made scholar, and other Black intellectuals. Of his father, he writes, "But he was all brainpower. He dropped out of high school but could think in ways that the credentialed class could not conceive" (86). I use the phrase here to bring attention to the particular set of meaningful status-based distinctions that order social relations as I encountered them in the neighborhood.

20. See, e.g., Bernard (2015) and Vargas (2016).

21. Brothers Changing the Hood is a pseudonym.

22. See www.sfgate.com/bayarea/article/SAN-FRANCISCO-Western-Addition-deadliest-city-2618419.php (last accessed on June 30, 2014).

23. See Braga, Onek, and Lawrence (2008) and San Francisco VPIU (2011, 8).

24. Violent crime rates remain near historic lows. Recent upticks in violent crime are largely attributed to spikes in violence in a small number of cities.

25. See www.cdc.gov/violenceprevention/youthviolence/stats_at-a_glance /ca.html (last accessed on June 30, 2014).

26. See Harris (2012).

27. See, e.g., Blumstein and Wallman (2006) and Zimring (2006).

28. Vargas (2016, 89). Vargas makes a convincing case for why this is so in Chicago. Yet San Francisco politics differs in a number of ways from Chicago (e.g., larger swaths of geographic space are controlled by District Leaders instead of Aldermen, and San Francisco is a smaller city in population and geographic area). And, though Vargas attributes less violence to the presence of more nonprofits, the story I tell here documents the ways that the existence of a large nonprofit infrastructure can actually operate to make some youth more vulnerable to criminal justice surveillance and intervention.

29. Anderson (1999, 10). In a quantitative test of adherence to the code of the street among youth, Stewart and Simons (2009) found: "Consistent with our hypotheses and Anderson's ethnographic description, our multilevel analysis indicates that neighborhood street culture is a significant predictor of violent delinquency" (16).

30. Anderson (1999). See also Jones (2009) and Stewart and Simons (2009). In a forthcoming book, Stuart (2017) writes about how demonstrations of "the code" have migrated to social media among youth in Chicago.

31. Anderson (1999, 10).

32. See Lane (2016) for an in-depth analysis of the role that social media plays in the lives of urban youth, including in relation to crime and violence.

33. Several scholars in this area have drawn our attention to how race, class, and exposure to violence shape the emotional worlds of young men. See, e.g., Harding (2010) and Rich (2009).

34. Collins (2004, 190).

35. Ibid.

36. Middlemass (2017) describes well how this contradiction complicated the "homecoming" of formerly incarcerated men. She writes, "Being a man was very important to the men in Group." Prior to their incarceration, "many of the men took care of all of the financial responsibilities for their immediate family and extended family. Their 'job' may have consisted of selling drugs, robbing people, banks, or cash centers, or committing burglaries, but their criminal behavior was acceptable because the end result was being a good provider who took care of his family and financial responsibilities" (77). After incarceration, when many of the men were financially dependent on others, especially women, "many male participants experienced a sense of hopelessness and uselessness that pervaded their psyche and made them question their sense of self and what it meant to be a man" (77). Fader (2013) finds that the formerly incarcerated young men in her study responded to this contradiction by seeking other ways to demonstrate their "mastery of masculinity" in other settings, including a return to criminalized activities like drug-dealing.

37. Collins (2004, 299–300).

38. In other work (Jones 2009), I describe the existence of a parallel narrative that seeks to explain the problems of young Black women. This narrative is tied to the failures of single Black mothers or so-called ghetto chicks who are believed to be inadequately equipped to raise Black girls to be respectable Black women.

39. Obama (2014). See also Butler (2013) on the limitations of what he describes as the "Black Male Exceptionalism" framework.

40. Collins (2004, 189–90).

41. These visits took place in January 2004, July–September 2005, and June 18–24, 2006.

42. Parts of this section are revised from Jones and Jackson (2012, 86–92).

43. See Small (2008) and Broussard (1993).

44. See Daniels (1980) and Jones and Jackson (2012).

45. Johnson (1944).

46. Ibid., 3.

47. See Jackson and Jones (2012).

48. See Pepin and Watts (2006).

49. Broussard (1993, 142).

50. Ibid.

51. Johnson (1944, 29).

52. See Anderson (2015) for a discussion of how historic patterns of residential segregation influenced the construction of "White space" and "Black space" and the consequences of these boundaries for contemporary race relations.

53. In an ethnography of Hunters Point, Hippler (1974) writes: "[T]he presence of thousands of semiskilled and unskilled Black shipyard workers who had been laid off immediately after the war and who stayed on in San Francisco represented what city officials considered a civic problem" (14).

54. Broussard (1993, 231).

55. As was the case in other cities across the country, the presence of Black residents was one of the official criteria used to categorize the neighborhood as a slum.

56. Hartman (2002); Bellush and Hausknecht (1967); Lai (2012).

57. Hartman (2002).

58. Beveridge (2008, 361).

59. Wilson (1980, 1987, 1996); Anderson (1999); Massey and Denton (1993).

60. See, e.g., Van Derbeken (2006).

61. Jones and Jackson (2012).

62. American Community Survey (2010), 5-year estimates of population under 18 living in poverty. The racial category is listed as "Black or African American alone."

63. In an adjacent census tract (153), about 15 percent of the residents are Black or African American.

64. Beveridge (2008, 364).

65. A number of scholars attribute these shifts to the rise of neoliberalism and its enmeshment with carceral politics, including Garland (2002), Simon (2009), and Wacquant (2009), among others.

66. The voices in this book are most often the voices of men. This is an empirical reflection of the degree to which I was embedded in the social networks of BCH. Outside of community meetings, I was often the only woman working closely with Eric and BCH, which had both benefits and drawbacks as a researcher. The composition of the group allowed me to observe how Black gender ideologies were constructed among men in semi-private settings as well as how others read the men of the group and masculinity in public space. During the course of field research, I was only aware of being excluded from a group meeting once, when Lincoln gathered together a group of men to talk about their experiences as fathers. I used this exclusion as an object of analysis that revealed the sensitivity and vulnerability that can accompany the topic of

fatherhood among men with criminal histories. In chapter 3, I provide another example of how being a woman among men and boys allowed for a way of knowing that might have eluded me. See Leverentz (2010) for an in-depth examination of the re-entry and desistance experiences of women.

67. Emerson, Fretz, and Shaw (2014, 172).

68. Such a break from the street is described as "knifing off" among desistance scholars and is often considered to be key to achieving desistance. Maruna and Roy (2007) identify the limitations of "knifing off" and make recommendations for refinement and clarification of the concept.

69. Agee (2014).

CHAPTER ONE. ERIC'S AWAKENING

1. Johnson (1944).

2. National Research Council (2014); Alexander (2012).

3. Matza (1964).

4. See Fader and Traylor (2015), which calls for an intersectional approach to studying desistance. Their review also highlights ways that structural circumstances influence patterns of offending and desistance among African American men from urban areas. Such an approach would help to explain, for example, why the onset of desistance occurs later for those who must contend with multiple and intersecting forms of oppression.

5. See also Harding (2010) for a discussion of cross-generational relationships in urban neighborhoods.

6. See Brooks (2009, 125–26) for a discussion of the importance of not "looking poor" among inner-city youth.

7. See Bersani and Chapple (2007) for a discussion of how late grade retention and school failure operate as negative turning points in the lives of adolescents. See also Kirk and Sampson (2013).

8. See also Hippler (1974) for a discussion of clubs and "bopping gangs" in Bayview-Hunters Point.

9. The description of youth from this area has changed over generations. I observed this change during my time in the neighborhood. This fact was also revealed to me by older residents who, when a new name for the set came up during conversation, often said something like, "Oh, that's what they're calling it now?"

10. See also Contreras (2012).

11. Western (2006).

12. Wilson (1980, 1987, 1996). Patillo (2007) pushes back against Wilson's argument for "Black flight." Patillo argues that if, in fact, the Black middle class fled, they did not get very far. She makes the point that the Black middle class lives in close proximity to the urban poor, a characteristic that makes the lived experience of White middle-class and Black middle-class neighborhoods qualitatively different. The presence of the Black middle class in gentrifying areas is evidenced by the experiences of Black "middlemen."

13. In 1994, California voters approved Proposition 184, a "three strikes" law that mandated increased prison time for "repeat offenders." A third strike would trigger a life sentence with parole considered only after twenty-five years.

14. National Research Council (2014); Alexander (2012); Provine (2007).

15. Anderson (1999). See also Hippler (1974) for a discussion of policing practices in the 1970s and Agee (2014) for a discussion of the evolution of policing practices in San Francisco from 1950 to 1972.

16. I describe this program in greater detail in chapter 2.

17. Natapoff (2011).

18. Braga, Onek, and Lawrence (2008).

19. Marshall (1996).

20. See Schiraldi, Western, and Bradner (2015) and Schiraldi and Western (2015).

21. In an in-depth review of the desistance literature, Paternoster and Bushway (2009) write that Sampson and Laub (1993) appear to have "abandoned the metaphor of a good marriage as a 'turning point'" (1150). In summarizing Sampson and Laub's more recent writings on how marriage and conscription "influence desistance from crime," the authors write that, according to Sampson and Laub, these institutional interventions influence desistance in one of four ways: "(1) they 'knife off' the past from the present; (2) they provide greater supervision and monitoring of the person and provide new sources of social control and 'growth'; (3) they change and structure routine activities; and (4) they provide for identity transformation" (1150). See also Laub and Sampson (2003), Maruna (2001), Bushway et al. (2001).

22. Giordano, Cernkovich, and Rudolph (2002, 1053). See also Rumgay (2004) and Fader and Traylor (2015).

23. Paternoster and Bushway (2009, 1124).

24. This finding is consistent with Fader (2013), who found that "youth moved back and forth across the relatively fluid boundary between the legal and underground economies. 'Part-time hustlers' spent the vast majority of their time engaged in law-abiding behavior, but needed to maintain their connections to the underground economy in order to tap them at a moment's notice" (220). This type of straddling is consistently reported in desistance studies. Yet youth are often exposed to harsh consequences when they are caught on the illegal side of half-and-half, from exclusion from programs to secure detention. Eric's description and Fader (2013) also highlight the ways that *economic circumstances* influence this type of movement among youth.

25. Lofland and Skonovd (1981, 378). Fader (2013) also documents how young, formerly incarcerated men in her study use pro-social ties to construct a new pro-social identity. Fader found that pro-social ties were used as an audience for young men to try out performances of a new self. As I illustrate in greater detail in chapter 2, the interactional work performed in these settings is not only about performance and having that performance reflected back to you (though that is important) but also about having a secure place in a new social order.

26. Lofland and Skonovd (1981, 378).

27. In their discussion of desistance and the "feared self," Paternoster and Bushway (2009) highlight the importance of identity change in the process of desistance. Identity change did not appear to be a primary motivating force in Eric's case, though it was important. As a youth, he had a place as "the weed man," which is certainly tied to identity (in some ways, a professional or occupational identity less than a criminal identity). His eventual new role as a pastor and director of a nonprofit would also provide a new identity. Yet these new identities were the outcome of a change in actions motivated by a separate set of material concerns: the threat of getting killed; the potential to have to kill; and the possibility of incarceration. Although it was clear that he had fears for his future self, those fears were about the kinds of actions he would be drawn into, actions that were more serious than the sort of actions he was currently involved in and that could, in turn, bring more serious forms of punishment. Put simply, he did not describe his fears as fears of who he would become (e.g., a shooter, a prisoner, a dead man) but of what would be done to him or what he would *have to do* (e.g., kill, get killed, or go to the pen). Furthermore, for Eric, selling drugs was not entirely *inconsistent* with being a "good father," since doing so helped him to provide for his family. As I show in subsequent chapters, it would take time for a change in his daily interactions to produce a new identity *that would be recognized by others*, which again highlights the degree to which identity change is a *group process*.

28. Fader (2013).

29. Lofland and Skonovd (1981, 374).

30. See Flores (2013) for a discussion of the different ways that faith encourages identity transformation among Latino men with criminal histories.

31. Fader (2013) also documents the performative aspect of change among youth transitioning from incarceration.

32. See also Leverentz (2010) for a discussion of how neighborhood context influences desistance. Although the respondents there are women, some overlap exists in the ways that Leverentz's respondents frame their old neighborhoods.

CHAPTER TWO. THE CRIME-FIGHTING COMMUNITY

1. My observation of this initial skepticism and of its change over time helped to illuminate the place of Eric and his peers in the neighborhood's social hierarchy. Over the course of fieldwork in the neighborhood, I would often attend meetings with Eric and caretakers with higher status positions in the community. As time went on, it seemed to me that after my status as a professor became known, patterns of talk and interaction would shift during these encounters. People would treat me as if I was the one in charge, even though I was not. I got into the practice of avoiding or deflecting questions or comments back toward Eric during these meetings and, at times, avoiding eye gaze altogether by looking toward Eric or down at my notes. Outside of these networks, my status as a professor, once shared, was often greeted with enthusiasm and

even pride among strangers I encountered in the neighborhood—an indication of the value that is placed on education (and, to some degree, credentials) among working- and lower-class Black people.

2. Maruna (2001). As noted previously, Maruna uses the phrase "making good" to describe the differences between how men who give up on criminal activity and those who persist talk about their lives. Maruna found that the narratives of those who give up on criminal activity are typically characterized by tales of finding "reason and purpose in the bleakest of life circumstances" (2). Men who framed their circumstances in this way appeared to be most committed to developing a new sense of self—one that reflected who they are now, not who they once were. Making sense of their lives in this way, Maruna explains, helped the men to resist the pull to engage in the types of activities that made them targets of punishment from the criminal justice system in the past.

3. Fortner (2015).

4. Agee (2014).

5. Gans (1982).

6. Ibid., 142–43.

7. Ibid., 159–60.

8. Chatelain (2015).

9. Drake and Cayton (1993, 392).

10. See also Foreman (2017).

11. Anderson (1972, 20).

12. Ibid., 21.

13. Ibid., 25–26.

14. Ibid., 20.

15. Patillo (2007, 117).

16. Hippler (1974, 206).

17. Ibid., 205–6.

18. Ibid., 192.

19. Agee (2014, 167–69). These early peacekeeping efforts also allowed space for the critique of police abuses. At the time, policing of the Black community was characterized by a contradiction. In general, the police abdicated responsibility for protecting residents but "when compelled to respond . . . they unleashed disproportionate levels of force" (152).

20. Ibid., 161–67.

21. Ibid., 162. Agee cites one such intermediary in particular, Orville Luster, "a six-foot, 230 pound, . . . young black social worker" with a commanding masculine presence who went on to play a central role in the organization of peacekeeping efforts in San Francisco in the 1960s. Luster took on this role as a "massive infusion of outside money" from the Ford Foundation and then funding streams from the War on Poverty expanded the street outreach program at the heart of peacekeeping efforts in Hunters Point.

22. Ibid., 149.

23. Ibid., 170–73.

24. Ibid.

25. Sharkey (2013).

26. Beckett and Herbert (2011). Organizations can vary in the ways and degrees to which they collaborate with law enforcement. At a minimum, such organizations often participate in information sharing with local police.

27. Meares and Kahan (1999). That the community called for such an ordinance is a point of particular importance for Meares and Kahan: "The ordinance was [originally] passed by an overwhelming margin in the Chicago City Council, with key support from aldermen representing the city's most impoverished, crime-ridden districts, whose residents are predominantly members of racial and ethnic minorities" (16).

28. Ibid., 16. Meares and Kahan argue that African Americans are "no longer excluded from the nation's democratic life" and that African Americans hold far more political power than in previous eras. They also argue that the relationship between African Americans and law enforcement has changed dramatically and is no longer so deeply antagonistic. Recently uncovered cases of overly aggressive policing and police abuses, including a history of police torture in Chicago, as well as the rise of the Black Lives Matter movement, contradict this assessment of both the state of Black politics and the relationship between Black people and the police.

29. Fortner (2015) describes in detail the ways in which the Black community contributed to calls for more aggressive policing and sanctions in New York City and, in doing so, helped to usher in the era of mass incarceration. Rios (2011) and Richardson, Van Brakle, and St. Vil (2014) also discuss the ways that family members rely on the criminal justice system to control seemingly out-of-control youth.

30. Kennedy (2011). See also www.newyorker.com/magazine/2009/06/22/dont-shoot-2.

31. Ibid., 16–20.

32. Ibid., 64–65.

33. Kennedy's initial effort has evolved into one of many supported by the National Network for Safe Communities. The network still aims to involve the community in its efforts, including through participation in forums and as service providers. The network also encourages the strategic use of enforcement: "When arrest, prosecution, and incarceration are necessary, law enforcement should use them as sparingly and tactically as possible. Profligate enforcement can have terrible collateral consequences, alienate communities, and undermine legitimacy. Law enforcement should apply the minimum that is compatible with ensuring public safety." See https://nnscommunities.org/who-we-are/mission#empower-communities-to-prevent-violence (last accessed June 23, 2017). See also Stuart (2016, 20) for an in-depth description of how such approaches encourage "therapeutic policing," which, though couched in a framework of helping, "can cause more problems than it cures."

34. Such approaches would run parallel with the embrace of "Broken Windows" and proactive policing in cities across the country. I describe this shift in greater detail in chapter 3.

35. See McGarrell et al. (2010) for an evaluation of Project Safe Neighborhoods, which incorporates the focused deterrence approach into its objectives.

36. Western (2006, 28–30). Western's conceptualization of mass imprisonment builds on David Garland's definition, which, as Western writes, has two defining features: 1) a rate of imprisonment above a historical or comparative norm, and 2) a demographic concentration of imprisonment that results in the "systematic imprisonment of whole groups of the population." Western adds that mass imprisonment also results from "a high level of incarceration, unequally distributed." This unequal distribution of incarceration among Black people "converts young black men with little schooling into a social group." This group is often referred to as the mass imprisonment or mass incarceration generation.

37. Stuart (2016).

38. The crime-fighting community is also shaped by the lingering history of urban renewal. As Mollenkopf (1983) writes, battles over who would represent the community during early redevelopment efforts led to "a new layer of government, the neighborhood level, non-profit alternative as provider" (197). The rise and subsequent *institutionalization* of neighborhood programs "converted political leaders into processors of clients . . . and reduced their accountability to neighborhood residents" (211).

39. As Vargas (2016, 26–27) argues, relationships among "residents, nonprofits, and public officials" are consequential for violence prevention in a neighborhood. This typology of the crime-fighting community focuses on the divisions among residents that are, at times, exacerbated by nonprofits and other institutional actors in the community (or, to borrow from Vargas, in a "neighorhood's field").

40. In contrast to the middlemen of Patillo's Chicago, members of the credentialed class do not always act as intermediaries between the community and the city, although some do.

41. See Collins (1979). The explosion of the credential society in the latter half of the twentieth century, combined with successful efforts at the incorporation of African Americans in the area of higher education over this time, has encouraged the growth of the credentialed class. For those without advanced degrees, a business card with a professional title served as a sort of credential that demonstrated their qualifications to do the legitimate work of the crime-fighting community.

42. As I describe later in this chapter, it is possible for other intermediaries to operate as street brokers. Indeed, the ability to code-switch can demonstrate a degree of authenticity that is of particular value to the crime-fighting community. Yet, on a day-to-day basis, the social organization of the crime-fighting community relies heavily on street outreach workers.

43. Gans (1982, 156). These outreach workers, community organizers, and violence-prevention specialists are expected to take on a role similar to the intermediaries described by Gans over forty years ago: earning the teenagers' respect while placing limits on their "hostility and destructiveness."

44. Of the three groups, Eric fits most neatly among the activists. During my time in the field, the bulk of his efforts seemed to be oriented around the work described here. See also Rios (2011) for a discussion of the relationships between hypercriminalization and social activism.

45. Hegranas (2005).

46. George did not work as a street outreach worker, yet his ability to bring the youth to the table, which is often a struggle for members of the credentialed class, positioned him as a street broker at this meeting.

47. The "call-in" described here is a Ceasefire-inspired initiative. This discussion illustrates the *normalization* of the credentialed class's participation in the management of public safety and the leverage and legitimacy given to law enforcement in this work.

48. Gans (1982, 157).

49. There are other often-overlooked consequences of funding patterns in the neighborhood. Funding patterns encourage a sporadic feel to the life of programs in the neighborhood. A program or initiative may be funded from eight weeks to three years—and at the end of this time it is almost always required that they provide some evaluation of their efforts. Future funding may rely on their ability to demonstrate positive outcomes. Yet this work is also rife with challenges that make it difficult to do so (I describe some of these challenges in greater detail in later chapters).

50. See also Collins (1979).

51. The paid outreach worker that Mrs. Cook refers to here was not of the community. In many ways, he appeared to be a member of the credentialed class in-the-making (in style of dress and educational status).

52. Anderson (2003, 209).

CHAPTER THREE. TARGETS

1. Bulwa (2007); Doyle (2007).

2. Gordon (2005).

3. See Lee (2015) for reporting on trends in Bay Area homicides from 2001 to 2015.

4. Braga, Onek, and Lawrence (2008).

5. Ibid.

6. Beckett and Herbert (2011, 95).

7. Doyle (2007).

8. See Jones (2009, 42) for a discussion of a similar sentiment shared among young women and girls in Philadelphia.

9. Bulwa (2007).

10. See Maxson, Hennigan, and Sloane (2005) and Grogger (2002) for a history of gang injunctions in California and its effects on crime. Both report limited short-term effects on crime in gang injunction zones, but no long-term effect on crime reduction.

11. Beckett and Herbert (2011). The following quote, from the city attorney of nearby Richmond, California, which was considering a gang injunction in 2009, is a rare candid illustration of how policing petty crimes can work as a tool to remove citizens identified as a "nuisance" from the neighborhood: "'We are prosecuting these guys for municipal code violations,' Aljoe said, such as urinating in public and gambling in public housing projects. The terms of probation, which last as long as three years, can then limit movement and association with stay-away orders. . . . This is stuff that is done very quietly or it doesn't get done." http://richmondconfidential.org/2009/10/15/richmond-considers-gang-injunction (accessed April 27, 2015).

12. Bulwa (2009). During a packed community meeting in 2007, the new district captain introduced the approach to policing that he intended to bring to the district, which included officers' initiating more contact with residents. He told the crowd that he wanted his officers to get to know people in the community and to get out of the car and talk to people.

13. I draw on data from multiple sources in this chapter. Some encounters I observed directly; some information I gathered either by listening to stories of encounters as they were shared among neighborhood residents or learned through formal and informal interviews with locals; some observations are from a collection of video records acquired from a local resident during the course of my field research in the neighborhood. Here, I use transcriptions of selected videos from this archive to illustrate key concepts.

14. Rosenbaum (2006, 253–54) and National Research Council (2004) document disparities in police contact. Members of minority groups consistently experience higher rates of contact with the police *and yet* police legitimacy is lower among minority groups.

15. Anderson (1999).

16. Maher (2010).

17. I use the term "high surveillance" to draw attention to how the penetration and expansion of the system is experienced by residents, rather than rely on the official institutional definition of these areas as hot spots, which privileges the perspective of law enforcement.

18. Rios (2011) reports a similar set of findings in ethnographic studies grounded in Philadelphia and Oakland, respectively. Whereas they both focus on the centrality of the justice system, I focus in particular on the intersection between law enforcement and the *gender socialization* of youth in high-surveillance neighborhood settings.

19. Collins (2004, 231).

20. See Freire (1970). This relationship bears similarities to what is commonly described as "horizontal violence." I would argue that the institutional role in encouraging violence in this way is also not adequately contained in this frequently used term, which *quite literally* places the violence among those who are marginalized at the center of the analysis. The ethnographic findings presented here bring to the fore a compelling illustration of how, as Freire originally

noted, violence is *initiated* by those who hold the power and, as is the case for police officers, the power to reinforce their authority with force. The excerpts in this chapter also reveal how masculinity can tie men with varying degrees of power and status (for example, police officers and Black men in high-surveillance neighborhoods) *together* through acts that demonstrate their dominance over women. In these ways, "horizontal violence" fails to capture the dynamic and shifting ways that aggression operates on the ground.

21. Becker (1971, 4–5).

22. Ibid., 15. Becker and Horowitz write, "In San Francisco, as everywhere, the forces of decency and respectability draw the line somewhere and can be every bit as forceful and ruthless on the other side of that line as the forces of decency and respectability anywhere else" (Becker 1971, 13). This was perhaps especially true for the city's African American population who, since their arrival in the city, had been seen as a civic problem: "[M]embers of Black communities may be no worse off than ever, but they are considerably worse off than whites and know it" (15).

23. Hippler (1974, 174). Agee (2014, 150) describes similarly structured groups as "jacket clubs."

24. Hippler (1974, 175).

25. Hippler (1974) reports that the area "with its few small stores and combination nightclub-bars, became a completely isolated, self-contained, totally black world" (174). The aggressiveness of the quarantine approach also shaped residents' perceptions of law enforcement: "The existence of fighting gangs and other 'gang trouble' provoked the police to adopt an even more aggressive 'quarantine' procedure (of exceedingly doubtful legality), which in turn further enraged the inhabitants of the area against the 'legitimate law and order' of the city" (174). See also Agee (2014, 152), which documents the ways that the quarantine approach was coupled with exploitation of the poorest members of the city.

26. Agee (2014, 146).

27. Ibid. Agee writes: "The tactical stance mirrored the disproportionate neglect that urban police had practiced in predominantly Black neighborhoods. The 1968 National Advisory Commission on Civil Disorders found that in the nation's impoverished urban Black enclaves, the 'strength of . . . feelings about hostile police conduct' was 'exceeded by the conviction' that residents of color were 'not given adequate police protection'" (146).

28. It is now well documented that the FBI infiltrated the Black freedom movements of the Civil Rights and Black Power era. Here, I am referring to the increase in overt and proactive law enforcement, in contrast to otherwise covert and subversive efforts.

29. Chronicle Washington Bureau (1988). By 1988, the DEA was also reporting that the popularity of crack was waning: "About the only good news in the study is evidence that the crack fad is cooling off in some cities. In San Diego, for example, where crack made an early appearance in 1981, its availability lately has been 'diminishing at a significant rate,' the DEA reported."

30. Lempinen (1988b).

31. Chronicle Washington Bureau (1988).

32. Ibid.

33. John Dilulio, who popularized the "Super-predator" argument in a *Weekly Standard* article published in 1995, would later recant his argument in an *amicus brief* submitted to the U.S. Supreme Court.

34. Fitzgerald (2013) reported on this study for the *Philadelphia Inquirer.*

35. Provine (2007, 18).

36. Stone and Taylor (1988). In 1988, annual cocaine sales in the United States were estimated to be a twenty billion dollar industry that relied on a vast network of producers and distributors that originated outside of the United States. Twenty percent of those sales were believed to be generated in California, "where cocaine flows in by air, land and sea."

37. Lempinen (1988a).

38. See Desmond and Valdez (2013) for a discussion of the rise of "third-party policing" and its consequences for poor women.

39. Farrell (1988).

40. Ibid.

41. Ibid.

42. Kelling and Wilson (1982). In their foundational article, published in *The Atlantic* magazine, Kelling and Wilson write: "Many citizens, of course, are primarily frightened by crime, especially crime involving a sudden, violent attack by a stranger. This risk is very real. . . . But we tend to overlook another source of fear—*the fear of being bothered* by disorderly people. Not violent people, nor, necessarily, criminals, but disreputable *or obstreperous or unpredictable people:* panhandlers, drunks, addicts, *rowdy teenagers,* prostitutes, loiterers, the mentally disturbed" (emphasis mine).

43. Braga, Onek, and Lawrence (2008); San Francisco VPIU (2011, 8).

44. See Stevens, Morash, and Lind (2011) for a discussion of the net-widening effects among young women and girls.

45. Rosenbaum (2006, 247) and Rosenbaum (2007). Some research suggests that "focused police interventions," which include "direct patrols, proactive arrests," and other forms of what is typically described as problem-oriented or proactive policing can effectively reduce crime rates in "hot spot" areas; Rosenbaum highlights the consequences and contradictions of such approaches in minority neighborhoods.

46. Geller et al. (2014) document the psychological harms done to young men aged eighteen to twenty-six in New York City as a consequence of aggressive policing. The findings from the population-based telephone survey suggest a need for less invasive tactics to be used among this population and for greater attention to be given to the consequences of aggressive policing for mental and community health.

47. Rosenbaum (2006, 253). See also Brunson and Miller (2005, 613–18), Rosenbaum (2007, 30–31), and Rios (2011).

48. Rosenbaum (2006, 255–56); Stewart (2007); Brunson and Miller (2005); Brunson and Weitzer (2009).

49. Rosenbaum (2006, 253–54); Tyler (2006).

50. National Research Council (2004).

51. Ibid.; Brunson and Weitzer (2009).

52. Brunson and Miller (2005, 615–18). In a report to the U.S. District Court in 2010, Jeffrey Fagan concluded that the New York City police department's stop-and-frisk activity was concentrated in precincts with high concentrations of Black and Latino residents and that "NYPD stops were significantly more frequent for black and Latino citizens than for white citizens." He also found that arrests occur in less than 6 percent of these cases. See also Rosenbaum (2007, 21).

53. Zimring (2012, 211), cited in Laub (2014).

54. Larson and Richards (1989, 502).

55. This recording is one in a larger collection of video recordings acquired from a local resident who has recorded daily life in the neighborhood since the late 1990s. The collection includes recordings of football games, fashion shows, and funerals, among other events that are meaningful to local residents. His collection also includes almost 200 encounters involving law enforcement in the neighborhood. See also Jones and Raymond (2012) for a more detailed explanation of how these recordings can be used as illustration or evidence in ethnographic projects.

56. For a recent example, see the New York police department's implementation of "Omnipresence" in the wake of a legal challenge to their stop-and-frisk program. Portions of the analysis presented here were published in Jones (2014).

57. Goffman (1961, 23).

58. See Matthews (2015) for an analysis of bystander participation in police encounters with residents in a high-surveillance neighborhood.

59. Garfinkel (1956, 420).

60. Jones (2009).

61. The power of police discretion is widely acknowledged in the policing literature. See Moskos (2009, 111–57) for a discussion of the use of discretion in arrests in inner-city Baltimore's drug zones. See also Terrill and Paoline (2007).

62. I observed this phenomenon firsthand in a separate research project in which I conducted ride-alongs with police officers. During one ride-along in a high-surveillance area, I found myself "jumping out" of the van with the officers (I was video recording their encounters with the public) as they stopped, searched, and then quickly arrested a young man. I was surprised by how quickly the encounter began and ended. I asked the officers if jumping out on people was a standard practice, and they said yes. They went on to explain that doing so reduces time spent in a vulnerable position, since arrests can quickly attract bystanders and then escalate. The jumping out I observed during my field research in the Fillmore did not end in arrest. Instead, it appeared that the officers ended the encounter abruptly, once it was clear that the encounter was being observed by others. The seemingly capricious nature of the encounter, coupled with the forms of intimidation also shared by young men, like the

drawing of a gun, gave the impression that jumping out on young people was, at least for some officers, something other than a preventative police procedure.

63. See also Tyler, Jackson, and Mentovich (2015); Geller et al. (2014); Sewell and Jefferson (2016); Sewell, Jefferson, and Lee (2016).

64. Fagan (2010).

65. *Terry v. Ohio* 392 U.S. 1 (1968).

66. Fagan et al. (2009); Fagan (2010).

67. See *Hiibel v. Sixth Judicial District Court of Nevada,* 542 U.S. 177 (2004) for the U.S. Supreme Court's opinion on "reasonable suspicion."

68. Beckett and Herbert (2011).

69. Goffman (1961).

70. The difference between a stop-and-search and a social contact is that a social or voluntary contact does not require reasonable suspicion. In such cases, an officer may initiate an encounter with a question like "How are you doing?" or "Can I talk to you for a second?" If there is no probable cause to detain a person, the civilian can lawfully decline to engage with the officer. This is not the case if a citizen is lawfully detained, which requires, at a minimum, reasonable suspicion.

71. In some settings, there is an assembly-line feel to these encounters. In such cases, groups of young men "assume the position" with little prompting from police officers who have arrived on the scene. See also Brunson and Miller (2005).

72. Mercer Sullivan, personal correspondence, n.d.

73. Goffman (1961, 41).

74. Brunson (2007).

75. Goffman (1961, 33).

76. Collins (2004) writes, "[I]f African-American men need women to bring their Black masculinity into being, then women who seemingly challenge that masculinity become targets for Black male violence" (233). Here, the "challenge" to masculinity was not direct, yet it triggered a similar effort to use a female body to repair an injury to one's manhood.

77. These two cases are not intended to provide an exhaustive analysis of the experiences of gender-specific violence experienced by Black women and girls in public space. Rather, I present these two cases as real-time illustrations of how structural violence moves through the bodies and minds of young Black men and onto the bodies of women and girls.

78. Goffman (1961).

79. The enmeshment of the criminal justice system and popular culture is revealed in a popular (at least at the time) clothing brand: State Property.

80. The strip search might also be described as a body search or a cavity search.

81. See Collins (2004, 233–42).

82. Ibid., 233.

83. Goffman (1961, 16).

84. Collins (2004, 233).

85. Lee (2012, 254).

86. U.S. Department of Justice, Civil Rights Division (2015).

87. U.S. Department of Justice, Community Oriented Policing Services (2016). In the wake of several high-profile shootings in the city and a scandal involving the sharing of racist text messages among officers, the Department of Justice's COPS division conducted an assessment of SFPD policies and practices. The assessment found evidence of institutional bias against African Americans and other minority groups in the city and provided 272 recommendations for improving department procedures and practices.

88. I expect that this shift also has consequences for other gendered outsiders, including LGBT and gender-nonconforming youth. During my time in the neighborhood, there were discussions of a rash of violence against gender-non-conforming or gay youth in the neighborhood, but I did not directly observe organized efforts to address this issue.

CHAPTER FOUR. BUFFERS AND BRIDGES

1. Gordon (2005). This is how the *San Francisco Chronicle* described the neighborhood in 2005, the year I began conducting field research there.

2. Wilson (1980, 1987, 1996). See also Anderson (1999).

3. Tach and Edin (2011); Young (2011); Wilson (1980, 1987, 1996); Roy et al. (2010); Edin, Kefalas, and Reed (2004); Nurse (2004).

4. See also Jeffries (2013).

5. Obama (2014).

6. Collins (2004, 189–90).

7. Fader (2013) reports a similar finding among young men returning from incarceration to neighborhoods in inner-city Philadelphia.

8. This effort to reclaim or redefine manhood has been observed by scholars conducting research in other settings. To be sure, the narratives, if not the practices, of fatherhood have changed substantially over the past several decades. In a study of inner-city fatherhood, Edin and Nelson (2013) describe this distinction as an effort to embrace the "softer side" of fatherhood.

9. See Fader (2013); Edin and Nelson (2013).

10. Recent (and seemingly outsized) attention given to the rise of "stay-at-home dads" illustrates the degree to which normative fatherhood is still associated with men working outside the home.

11. See Bernard (2015).

12. Fader (2013) articulates the importance of a sense of "mastery" in her discussion of young men's efforts to demonstrate mastery in their lives, which often leads them back to the kinds of activities that once led them to incarceration.

13. Collins (2004, 201–6).

14. See Brooks (2009).

15. This informal policy was shared with me on at least two occasions by a relative of Eric's who once worked with one of the largest youth-serving

organizations in the neighborhood. In her words, the "Haynes kids were off limits."

16. Edin and Nelson (2013).

17. Ibid.

18. Collins (2004).

19. Ibid., 204.

20. He was riding a small motorized vehicle at the time.

21. In a group conversation with a police lieutenant following the incident (organized by BCH), the lieutenant explained that the officer, relatively new to patrolling the neighborhood, mistakenly made an officer-in-distress call, which contributed to the strong and seemingly disproportionate response from other officers.

CHAPTER FIVE. "A ROSE OUT OF THIS CEMENT"

1. See Jones (2014).

2. See Foreman (2017).

3. See Rios (2011).

4. According to local reports, Jay's first arrest may have actually been a state indictment. I did not confirm this with Jay prior to his death.

5. See Rios (2017).

6. Jay's observation of his liminal citizenship status resonates with Miller and Alexander's (2016) discussion on carceral citizenship: "Attending to the legal and extralegal sanctions imposed on the criminalized poor, their families, and the communities to which they return; the host of actors administering such sanctions; and the outcomes produced through legal exclusion and stigma, we find that carceral expansion has in part produced a new form of citizenship for the Black and Brown poor—what we refer to as carceral citizenship" (294).

7. More recently, Bell (2017) has brought attention to the distinctions between legal cynicism and legal estrangement.

8. The relationship with a cellmate requires a forced intimacy of sorts, and Jay had a number of categories of people that he wanted to avoid having as a cellmate, including "young people," "gay people," "old people" who "probably stink," and "addicts." Jay explains that "everybody want a cell mate that you're comfortable with."

9. Kushner (1981). After searching on this title, it seemed that this was likely the book that Jay read while incarcerated.

10. In this moment, Eric and I are *participating* in Jay's construction of a "redemptive script," which once again highlights the interactional dimensions of individual change.

11. Shakur (2009).

12. In an effort to protect Jay's anonymity, I have not included the citation to the news article described here. The original article is on file with the author.

13. See also Duck (2015).

CONCLUSION

1. Rios (2011) calls for an investment in a "youth support complex" instead of a "youth control complex" that criminalizes Black and Brown youth. See also Fader (2013) and Schiraldi and Western (2015), among others, for alternative justice system responses to young adults.

2. Mills (1959).

3. See, e.g., Giordano, Cernkovich, and Rudolph (2002).

4. See Edin and Nelson (2013).

5. Collins (2004, 206).

6. Butler (2013, 486).

7. Ibid.

8. Ibid.

9. Kennedy (2011).

10. Ceasefire is still used in some cities to describe what is actually a Cure Violence model. Cure Violence is in the process of relabeling all of its programs to eliminate confusion between the two approaches. (Personal correspondence with Gary Slutkin, Dec. 13, 2017.)

11. Personal communication, Dec. 13, 2017.

12. See also Fader (2013) for a consideration of the types of programs and practices that are likely to be most beneficial for young people returning to their communities after a period of incarceration.

13. Bernard (2015, 51).

14. Flores (2013) contrasts this type of redemption process with the process of "segregated redemption," in which programs create a relatively closed community that satisfies the varying needs of its members as they work to change their lives.

15. For an exception to this type of popular coverage, see Gilligan (2014).

16. Kennedy (2011, 41).

17. See "The King Philosophy" of the King Center: www.thekingcenter.org /king-philosophy#sub4 (last accessed Sept. 15, 2017). See also Collins (2004, 299–301) for a discussion of the "the prominent place" of love—the foundation of any beloved community—in African American intellectual and social justice traditions. Collins cautions against viewing Black youth as problems: "Black youth who have come of age during the four decades following the civil rights movement not only have not seen its promise of a beloved community come to fruition, they have been deemed the problem of America (not its hope for the future)" (301).

18. The ONS was created in 2007. The fellowship was first implemented in 2010.

19. Personal correspondence, DeVone Boggan, Dec. 27, 2017.

20. See also Vargas (2016) for a discussion of the important role of relationships in preventing street violence in Chicago.

References

Agee, Christopher Lowen. 2014. *The Streets of San Francisco: Policing and the Creation of a Cosmopolitan Liberal Politics, 1950–1972.* Chicago: University of Chicago Press.

Alexander, Michelle. 2012. *The New Jim Crow.* New York: New Press.

American Community Survey. 2010. "Black Concentration in San Francisco, 2010." Prepared by Social Explorer (based on data from U.S. Census Bureau), www.socialexplorer.com (accessed June 20, 2017).

Anderson, Elijah. 1972. "Black Shadow Politics in Midwestville: The Insiders, the Outsiders, and the Militant Young." *Sociological Inquiry* (Wiley) 42, no. 1 (Jan.): 19–27.

———. 1999. *Code of the Street: Decency, Violence, and the Moral Order of the Inner City.* Chicago: University of Chicago Press.

———. 2003. *A Place on the Corner.* 2d ed. Chicago: University of Chicago Press.

———. 2015. "The White Space." *Sociology of Race and Ethnicity* 1, no. 1: 10–21.

Anderson, Monica, and Paul Hitlin. 2016. *Social Media Conversations About Race: How Social Media Users See, Share and Discuss Race and the Rise of Hashtags Like #BlackLivesMatter.* Washington, D.C.: Pew Research Center.

Becker, Howard Saul, ed. 1971. *Culture and Civility in San Francisco.* Piscataway, N.J.: Transaction.

Beckett, Katherine, and Steve Herbert. 2011. *Banished: The New Social Control in Urban America.* Oxford, Engl.: Oxford University Press.

Bell, Monica C. 2017. "Police Reform and the Dismantling of Legal Estrangement." *The Yale Law Journal* 126, n. 7: 2054–2150.

Bellush, Jewel, and Murray Hausknecht, eds. 1967. *Urban Renewal: People, Politics, and Planning.* New York: Anchor Books/Doubleday.

Bernard, April. 2015. *Transforming Justice, Transforming Lives: Women's Pathways to Desistance from Crime.* Lanham, Md.: Lexington Books.

Bersani, Bianca E., and Constance L. Chapple. 2007. "School Failure as an Adolescent Turning Point." *Sociological Focus* 40: 370–91.

Beveridge, Andrew A. 2008. "A Century of Harlem in New York City: Some Notes on Migration, Consolidation, Segregation, and Recent Developments." *City & Community* 7, no. 4: 358–65.

Blumstein, Alfred, and Joel Wallman. 2006. *The Crime Drop in America.* Cambridge, Engl.: Cambridge University Press.

Braga, Anthony A., David Onek, and Sarah Lawrence. 2008. "Police Enforcement Strategies to Prevent Crime in Hot Spot Areas." Crime Prevention Research Review No. 2, Department of Justice Office, Community Oriented Policing Services. Washington, D.C.: DOJ.

Brooks, Scott. 2009. *Black Men Can't Shoot.* Chicago: University of Chicago Press.

Broussard, Albert S. 1993. *Black San Francisco: The Struggle for Racial Equality in the West.* Lawrence: University Press of Kansas.

Brunson, Rod K. 2007. "'Police Don't Like Black People': African-American Young Men's Accumulated Police Experiences." *Criminology & Public Policy* 6, no. 1: 71–101.

Brunson, Rod K., and Jody Miller. 2005. "Young Black Men and Urban Policing in the United States." *British Journal of Criminology* 46: 613–40.

Brunson, Rod. K, and Ronald Weitzer. 2009. "Police Relations with Black and White Youths in Different Urban Neighborhoods." *Urban Affairs Review* 44: 858.

Bulwa, Demian. 2007. "7 injured as feud rages in the Western Addition/Housing complex's residents terrifed—2 attacks in 12 hours." *San Francisco Chronicle*, June 15.

———. 2009. "S.F. struggles to stop, solve killings." *San Francisco Chronicle*, Jan. 2.

Bushway, Shawn, Alex Piquero, Lisa Broidy, Elizabeth Cauffman, and Paul Mazerolle. 2001. "An Empirical Framework for Studying Desistance as a Process." *Criminology* 39, no. 2: 491–516.

Butler, Paul D. 2013. "Black Male Exceptionalism? The Problems and Potential of Black Male-Focused Interventions." *Georgetown Law Faculty Publications and Other Works:* 485–511.

Chatelain, Marcia. 2015. *South Side Girls: Growing up in the Great Migration.* Durham, N.C.: Duke University Press.

Chenoweth, Karin. 1998. "Growth among the credentialed class." *Black Issues in Higher Education*, July 23.

Chronicle Washington Bureau. 1988. "SF crack dealers tell their story: Shocking epidemic of crack use has spread outside the cities." *San Francisco Chronicle*, April 7, A12.

Coates, Ta-Nehisi. 2008. *The Beautiful Struggle: A Father, Two Sons and an Unlikely Road to Manhood.* New York: Spiegel & Grau.

Cobb, Jelani. 2016. "The Matter of Black Lives: A New Kind of Movement Found Its Moment. What Will Its Future Be?" *New Yorker*, Mar. 14.

Collins, Patricia Hill. 2000. *Black Feminist Thought.* New York: Routledge.

———. 2004. *Black Sexual Politics: African Americans, Gender, and the New Racism*. New York: Routledge.

Collins, Randall. 1979. *The Credential Society: An Historical Sociology of Education and Stratification*. San Diego, Calif.: Academic Press.

Contreras, Randol. 2012. *The Stickup Kids: Race, Violence, and the American Dream*. Berkeley: University of California Press.

Daniels, Douglass. 1980. *Pioneer Urbanites: A Social and Cultural History of Black San Francisco*. Berkeley: University of California Press.

Day, Noel A., and Zenophon A. Abraham. 1993. *The Unfinished Agenda: The Economic Status of African Americans in San Francisco, 1964–1990*. San Francisco: Polaris Research and Development.

Desmond, Matthew, and Nicol Valdez. 2013. "Unpolicing the Urban Poor: Consequences of Third-Party Policing for Inner-City Women." *American Sociological Review* 78, no. 1: 117–41.

Doyle, Jim. 2007. "Living in the cross fire/Western Addition: After 7 shot this week, apartment complex has a ghostly feel." *San Francisco Chronicle*, June 16.

Drake, St. Clair, and Horace R. Cayton. 1993. *Black Metropolis: A Study of Negro Life in a Northern City*. Rev. and enl. ed. Chicago: University of Chicago Press.

Duck, Waverly. 2015. *No Way Out: Precarious Living in the Shadow of Poverty*. Chicago: University of Chicago Press.

Edin, Kathryn, Maria J. Kefalas, and Joanna M. Reed. 2004. "A Peek Inside the Black Box: What Marriage Means for Poor Unmarried Parents." *Journal of Marriage and Family* 66, no. 4 (Nov.): 1007–1014.

Edin, Kathryn, and Timothy J. Nelson. 2013. *Doing the Best I Can: Fatherhood in the Inner City*. Berkeley: University of California Press.

Emerson, Robert M., Rachel I. Fretz, and Linda L. Shaw. 2014. *Writing Ethnographic Fieldnotes*. Chicago: University of Chicago Press.

Fader, Jamie. 2013. *Falling Back: Incarceration and Transitions to Adulthood among Urban Youth*. New Brunswick, N.J.: Rutgers University Press.

Fader, Jamie, and LaTosha L. Traylor. 2015. "Dealing with Difference in Desistance Theory: The Promise of Intersectionality for New Avenues of Inquiry." *Sociology Compass*: 247–60.

Fagan, Jeffrey. 2010. "Report of Jeffrey Fagan, Ph.D. to United States District Court Southern District of New York, David Floyd et al. (plaintiffs), against City of New York et al. (defendants)." https://ccrjustice.org/sites/default/files/assets/files/FaganSecondSupplementalReport.pdf.

Fagan, Jeffrey, Amanda Geller, G. Davies, and V. West. 2009. "Street Stops and Broken Windows Revisited: The Demography and Logic of Proactive Policing in a Safe and Changing City." In *Race, Ethnicity, and Policing: New and Essential Readings*, edited by Stephen K. Rice and Michael D. White, 309–48. New York: NYU Press.

Farrell, Dave. 1988. "New war on drugs in S.F. housing." *San Francisco Chronicle*, Dec. 17, A6.

Fitzgerald, Susan. 2013. "'Crack baby' study ends with unexpected but clear result." *Philadelphia Inquirer*, July 21.

Flores, Edward. 2013. *God's Gangs: Barrio Ministry, Masculinity, and Gang Recovery.* New York: NYU Press.

Foreman, James, Jr. 2017. *Locking Up Our Own: Crime and Punishment in Black America.* New York: Farrar, Straus and Giroux.

Fortner, Michael Javen. 2015. *Black Silent Majority: The Rockefeller Drug Laws and the Politics of Punishment.* Cambridge, Mass.: Harvard University Press.

Freire, Paulo. 1970. *Pedagogy of the Oppressed.* New York: Bloomsbury Academic.

Gans, Herbert. 1982. *Urban Villagers: Group and Class in the Life of Italian-Americans.* New York: Free Press.

Garfinkel, Harold. 1956. "Conditions of Successful Degradation Ceremonies." *American Journal of Sociology* 61, no. 5: 420–24.

Garland, David. 2001. "Introduction: The Meaning of Mass Imprisonment." In *Mass Imprisonment: Social Causes and Consequences*, edited by David Garland. London: Sage Publications.

Garza, Alicia. 2014. "The feminist wire." *TFW, LLC.* Oct. 7. www.thefeministwire .com/2014/10/blacklivesmatter-2 (accessed Sept. 18, 2017).

Geller, Amanda, Jeffrey Fagan, Tom Tyler, and Bruce Link. 2014. "Aggressive Policing and the Mental Health of Young Urban Men." *American Journal of Public Health* 104, no. 12: 2321–27.

Gilligan, Heather Tirado. 2017. "How One California City Began Bringing Its Murder Rate Down—Without Cops." *The Nation* (online), Nov. 12, 2017. www.thenation.com/article/how-one-california-city-began-bringing-its-murder-rate-down-without-cops (accessed Dec. 22, 2017).

Giordano, Peggy C., Stephen A. Cernkovich, and Jennifer L. Rudolph. 2002. "Gender, Crime, and Desistance: Toward a Theory of Cognitive Transformation." *American Journal of Sociology* 107, no. 4 (Jan.): 990–1064.

Goffman, Alice. 2014. *On the Run: Fugitive Life in an American City.* Chicago: University of Chicago Press.

Goffman, Erving. 1961. *Asylums: Essays on the Social Situation of Mental Patients and Other Inmates.* New York: Anchor Books/Doubleday.

Gordon, Rachel. 2005. "Western Addition deadliest city area/3rd slaying in 8 days prompts response from police, mayor." *San Francisco Chronicle*, Aug. 5.

Grogger, Jeffrey. 2002. "The Effects of Civil Gang Injunctions on Reported Violent Crime: Evidence from Los Angeles County." *Journal of Law and Economics* 45, no. 1 (Apr.): 69–90.

Harding, David J. 2010. *Living the Drama: Community, Conflict, and Culture among Inner-City Boys.* Chicago: University of Chicago Press.

Harris, Kamala. 2012. *Homicide in California 2011.* Sacramento: California Department of Justice.

Hartman, Chester. 2002. *City for Sale: The Transformation of San Francisco.* Berkeley: University of California Press.

Hegranes, Cristi. 2005. "What's really wrong with the Lower Fillmore? Could it be the activists who claim they're trying to rebuild it?" *SF Weekly,* Sept. 21.

Hippler, Arthur. 1974. *Hunter's Point: A Black Ghetto.* New York: Basic Books.

Jackson, Christina, and Nikki Jones. 2012. "'Remember the Fillmore': The Lingering History of Urban Renewal in Black San Francisco." In *Black California Dreamin': Social Vison and the Crisis of California's African American Communities,* edited by Ingrid Banks, Gaye Johnson, George Lipsitz, and Ula Taylor, 57–73. Santa Barbara, Calif.: UCSB Center for Black Studies Research.

Jeffries, Michael. 2013. *Paint the White House Black: Obama and the Meaning of Race in America.* Stanford: Stanford University Press.

Jerolmack, Colin, and Alexandra K. Murphy. 2017. "The Ethical Dilemmas and Social Scientific Trade-offs of Masking in Ethnography." *Sociological Methods and Research* (online), Mar. 30, pp. 1–27.

Johnson, Charles S. 1944. *The Negro War Worker in San Francisco: A Local Self-Survey.* San Francisco: Race Relations Programs of the American Missionary Association.

Jones, Nikki. 2009. *Between Good and Ghetto: African American Girls and Inner City Violence.* New Brunswick, N.J.: Rutgers University Press.

———. 2014. "'The Regular Routine': Proactive Policing and Adolescent Development among Young, Poor Black Men." *New Directions in Child and Adolescent Development* (Mar.): 33–54.

———. 2016. "The Gender of Police Violence." *Tikkun Magazine* 31, no. 1: 25–28.

Jones, Nikki, and Christina Jackson. 2012. "'Just don't go down there': Learning to Avoid the Ghetto in San Francisco." In *The Ghetto,* edited by Ray Hutchison and Bruce Haynes, 83–109. Boulder, Colo.: Westview Press.

Jones, Nikki, and Geoffrey Raymond. 2012. "'The Camera Rolls': Using Third-Party Video in Field Research." *Annals of the American Academy of Political and Social Science* (July): 109–23.

Justice Policy Institute. 2007. *Gang Wars: The Failure of Enforcement Tactics and the Need for Effective Public Policy.* Washington, D.C.: JPI.

Kasinitz, Phillip. 1992. "Bringing the Neighborhood Back in: The New Urban Ethnography" (review). *Sociological Forum* 7, no. 2 (June): 355–63.

Kelling, George L., and James Q. Wilson. 1982. "Broken Windows: The Police and Neighborhood Safety." *The Atlantic,* Mar. www.theatlantic.com/magazine /archive/1982/03/broken-windows/304465.

Kennedy, David. 2011. *Don't Shoot: One Man, a Street Fellowship and the End of Violence in Inner-City America.* New York: Bloomsbury USA.

Kirk, David S., and Robert J. Sampson. 2013. "Juvenile Arrest and Collateral Educational Damage in the Transition to Adulthood." *Sociology of Education* 86: 36–62.

Kushner, Harold S. 1981. *When Bad Things Happen to Good People.* New York: Schocken Books.

Lai, Clement. 2012. "The Racial Triangulation of Space: The Case of Urban Renewal in San Francisco's Fillmore District." *Annals of the Association of American Geographers:* 151–70.

Lane, Jeffrey. 2016. "The Digital Street: An Ethnographic Study of Networked Street Life in Harlem." *American Behavioral Scientist* 60, no. 1: 43–58.

Larson, Reed, and Maryse H. Richards. 1989. "Introduction: The Changing Life Space of Early Adolescence." *Journal of Youth and Adolescence* 18, no. 6: 501–9.

Laub, John. 2014. *Understanding Inequality and the Justice System Response: Charting a New Way Forward.* New York: William T. Grant Foundation.

Laub, John H., and Robert Sampson. 2003. *Shared Beginnings, Divergent Lives: Delinquent Boys to Age 70.* Cambridge, Mass.: Harvard University Press.

Lee, Henry K. 2015. "Bay Area cities' homicide rates show striking drop." *San Francisco Chronicle,* Jan. 18.

Lee, Jooyoung. 2012. "Wounded: Life after the Shooting." *Annals of the American Academy of Political and Social Science* 642, no. 1 (July): 244–57.

Lempinen, Edward W. 1988a. "Detention, drug tests for the crack addicts." *San Francisco Chronicle,* Apr. 7, A12.

———. 1988b. "A ruthless new breed." *San Francisco Chronicle,* Apr. 7, A12.

Leverentz, Andrea. 2010. "People, Places, and Things: How Female Ex-Prisoners Negotiate Their Neighborhood Contexts." *Journal of Contemporary Ethnography* 39, no. 6: 646–81.

Lofland, John, and Norman Skonovd. 1981. "Conversion Motifs." *Journal for the Scientific Study of Religion* 20, no. 4 (Dec.): 373–85.

Lubet, Steven. 2017. *Interrogating Ethnography: Why Evidence Matters.* Oxford, Engl.: Oxford University Press.

Maher, Sean. 2010. "Target in fatal North Oakland shooting had been named in gang injunction." *Mercury News,* Dec. 8.

Marshall, Joseph. 1996. *Street Soldier: One Man's Struggle to Save a Generation, One Life at a Time.* San Francisco: Delacorte Press.

Maruna, Shadd. 2001. *Making Good: How Ex-convicts Reform and Rebuild Their Lives.* Washington, D.C.: American Psychological Association.

Maruna, Shadd, and Kevin Roy. 2007. "Amputation or Reconstruction? Notes on the Concept of 'Knifing Off' and Desistance from Crime." *Journal of Contemporary Criminal Justice* 23, no. 1: 104–24.

Massey, Douglass, and Nancy A. Denton. 1993. *American Apartheid: Segregation and the Making of the Underclass.* Cambridge, Mass.: Harvard University Press.

Matthews, Katherine. 2015. "Ask Him If You're Being Detained: Bystander Resistance in Street Police Encounters." Master's thesis, Department of Sociology, University of California, Santa Barbara.

Matza, David. 1964. *Delinquency and Drift.* New York: Wiley.

Maxson, Cheryl L., Karen M. Hennigan, and David C. Sloane. 2005. "'It's Getting Crazy Out There': Can a Civil Gang Injunction Change a Community?" *Criminology & Public Policy* 4, no. 3 (Aug.): 577–605.

McGarrell, Edmund F., Nicholas Corsaro, Natalie Kroovand Hipple, and Timorth Bynum. 2010. "Project Safe Neighborhoods and Violent Crime in US Cities: Assessing Violent Crime Impact." *Journal of Quantitative Criminology* 26, no. 2: 165–90.

Meares, Tracey L., and Dan M. Kahan. 1999. "When Rights Are Wrong: The Paradox of Unwanted Rights." In *Urgent Times: Policing and Rights in Inner-City Communities,* edited by Joshua Cohen and Joel Rogers, 3–30. Boston: Beacon Press.

Middlemass, Keesha. 2017. *Convicted and Condemned: The Politics and Policies of Prisoner Reentry.* New York: NYU Press.

Miller, Reuben Jonathan. 2014. "Devolving the Carceral State: Race, Prisoner Reentry, and the Micro-Politics of Urban Poverty Management." *Punishment & Society* 16, no. 3: 305–35.

Miller, Reuben, and Amanda Alexander. 2016. "The Price of Carceral Citizenship: Punishment, Surveillance, and Social Welfare Policy in the Age of Carceral Expansion." *Michigan Journal of Race and Law:* 291–314.

Mills, C. Wright. 1959. *The Sociological Imagination.* Oxford, Engl.: Oxford University Press.

Mollenkopf, John Hull. 1983. *The Contested City.* Princeton, N.J.: Princeton University Press.

Moskos, Peter. 2009. *Cop in the Hood: My Year Policing Baltimore's Eastern District.* Princeton, N.J.: Princeton University Press.

Natapoff, Alexandra. 2011. *Snitching: Criminal Informants and the Erosion of American Justice.* New York: NYU Press.

National Research Council. 2004. *Fairness and Effectiveness in Policing: The Evidence.* Washington, D.C.: National Academies Press.

———. 2014. *The Growth of Incarceration in the United States: Exploring Causes and Consequences.* Washington, D.C.: National Academies Press.

Nurse, Anne. 2004. "Returning to Strangers: Newly Paroled Young Fathers and Their Children." In *Imprisoning America: The Social Effects of Mass Incarceration,* edited by Mary E. Patillo, David F. Weiman, and Bruce Western, 76–96. New York: Russell Sage Foundation.

Obama, Barack. 2014. "Remarks by the President on 'My Brother's Keeper Initiative.'" https://obamawhitehouse.archives.gov/the-press-office/2014/02/27/remarks-president-my-brothers-keeper-initiative.

Paternoster, Ray, and Shaw Bushway. 2009. "Desistance and the 'Feared Self': Toward an Identity Theory of Criminal Desistance." *Criminology* 99, no. 4: 1103–56.

Patillo, Mary. 2007. *Black on the Block: The Politics of Race and Class in the City.* Chicago: University of Chicago Press.

Pepin, Elizabeth, and Lewis Watts. 2006. *Harlem of the West: The San Francisco Fillmore Jazz Era.* San Francisco: Chronicle Books.

Provine, Doris Marie. 2007. *Unequal Under Law: Race in the War on Drugs.* Chicago: University of Chicago Press.

Rich, John. 2009. *Wrong Place, Wrong Time.* Baltimore, Md.: Johns Hopkins University Press.

Richardson, Joseph, Mischelle Van Brakle, and Christopher St. Vil. 2014. "Taking Boys Out of the Hood: Exile as a Parenting Strategy for African American Male Youth." In *Pathways to Adulthood for Disconnected Young Men in Low-Income Communities,* edited by Kevin Roy and Nikki Jones. Special issue of *New Directions for Child and Adolescent Development* 2014, no. 143: 11–31.

Rios, Victor. 2011. *Punished: Policing the Lives of Black and Latino Boys.* New York: NYU Press.

———. 2017. *Human Targets: Schools, Police, and the Criminalization of Latino Youth.* Chicago: University of Chicago Press.

Rosenbaum, Dennis. 2006. "The Limits of Hot Spots Policing." In *Policing Innovation: Contrasting Perspectives,* edited by David Weisburd and Anthony Braga, 245–66. Cambridge, Engl.: Cambridge University Press.

———. 2007. "Police Innovation Post-1980: Assessing Effectiveness and Equity Concerns in the Information Technology Era." *Revue de l'IPC Review* 1 (Mar.): 11–44.

Roy, Kevin, Colleen Vesely, Megan Fitzgerald, and Nicolle Buckmiller Jones. 2010. "Young Fathers at Work: The Influence on Parental Closeness and Contact on Employment." *Research in Human Development* 7, no. 2: 123–39.

Rumgay, J. 2004. "Scripts for Safer Survival: Pathways out of Female Crime." *Howard Journal of Criminal Justice* 43: 405–19.

Sampson, Robert J., and John H. Laub. 1993. *Crime in the Making: Pathways and Turning Points through Life.* Cambridge, Mass.: Harvard University Press.

San Francisco Violence Prevention and Intervention Unit. 2011. "Street Violence Reduction Initiative: San Francisco Plan." www.dcyf.org/modules /showdocument.aspx?documentid=231.

Schiraldi, Vincent, and Bruce Western. 2015. "Time to Rethink the Age of Adult Court Jurisdiction." *Translational Criminology* (Fall): 9–11.

Schiraldi, Vincent, Bruce Western, and Kendra Bradner. 2015. "Community-Based Responses to Justice-Involved Young Adults." Harvard Kennedy School Program in Criminal Justice Policy and Management, National Institute of Justice. www.hks.harvard.edu/sites/default/files/centers /wiener/programs/pcj/files/ESCC-CommunityBasedResponsesJusticeInvol vedYA.pdf.

Sewell, Abigail A., and Kevin A. Jefferson. 2016. "Collateral Damage: The Health Effects of Invasive Police Encounters in New York City." *Journal of Urban Health* 93, Supp. 1 (Apr.): 42–67.

Sewell, Abigail A., Kevin A. Jefferson, and Hedwig Lee. 2016. "Living Under Surveillance: Gender, Psychological Distress, and Stop-Question-and-Frisk Policing in New York City." *Social Science & Medicine* 159 (June): 1–12.

Shakur, Tupac. 2009. *The Rose that Grew from Concrete.* New York: MTV Books.

Sharkey, Patrick. 2013. *Stuck in Place: Urban Neighborhoods and the End of Progress Toward Racial Equality.* Chicago: University of Chicago Press.

Small, Mario Luis. 2008. "Four Reasons to Abandon the Idea of 'the Ghetto.'" *City and Community* 7, no. 4: 389–98.

Stevens, Tia, Merry Morash, and Meda Chesney Lind. 2011. "Are Girls Getting Tougher, or Are We Getting Tougher on Girls? Probability of Arrest and Juvenile Court Oversight in 1980 and 2000." *Justice Quarterly* 28, no. 5: 719–44.

Stewart, Eric A. 2007. "Either They Don't Know or They Don't Care: Black Males and Negative Police Experiences." *Criminology & Public Policy* 6, no. 1: 123–30.

Stewart, Eric, and Ronald L. Simons. 2009. *The Code of the Street and African-American Adolescent Violence.* Washington, D.C.: U.S. Dept. of Justice, National Institute of Justice.

Stone, Allyn, and Michael Taylor. 1988. "Crack Network Is One of the Biggest Businesses in the U.S." *San Francisco Chronicle,* Apr. 7: A13.

Stuart, Forrest. 2016. *Down, Out, and Under Arrest: Policing and Everyday Life in Skid Row.* Chicago: University of Chicago Press.

———. 2017. *Gang Violence in the Digital Age.* Newark, N.J.: Racial Democracy, Crime, and Justice Network Annual Meeting.

Tach, Laura, and Kathryn Edin. 2011. "The Relationship Contexts of Young Disadvantaged Men." *Annals of the American Academy of Political and Social Science* 635, no. 1 (May): 76–94.

Terrill, William, and Eugene Paoline. 2007. "Nonarrest Decision Making in Police-Citizen Encounters." *Police Quarterly* (Sept.): 308–31.

Tyler, Tom. 2006. *Why People Obey the Law.* Princeton, N.J.: Princeton University Press.

Tyler, Tom R., Jonathan Jackson, and Avital Mentovich. 2015. "The Consequences of Being an Object of Suspicion: Potential Pitfalls of Proactive Police Contact." *Journal of Empirical Legal Studies* 12, no. 4 (Dec.): 602–36.

U.S. Department of Justice, Civil Rights Division. 2015. *Investigation of Ferguson Police Department.* Washington, D.C.: DOJ.

U.S. Department of Justice, Community Oriented Policing Services. 2016. *Collaborative Reform Initiative: An Assessment of the San Francisco Police Department.* Washington, D.C.: DOJ.

Van Derbeken, Jaxon. 2006. "Western Addition shootings jolt City Hall/More police patrols, another spy camera are being pushed." *San Francisco Chronicle,* Aug. 17.

Vargas, Robert. 2016. *Wounded City: Violent Turf Wars in a Chicago Barrio.* Chicago: University of Chicago Press.

Western, Bruce. 2006. *Punishment and Inequality in America.* New York: Russell Sage Foundation.

Wilson, William Julius. 1980. *The Declining Significance of Race: Blacks and Changing American Institutions.* Chicago: University of Chicago Press.

———. 1987. *The Truly Disadvantaged: The Inner City, the Underclass, and Public Policy.* Chicago: University of Chicago Press.

———. 1996. *When Work Disappears: The World of the New Urban Poor.* New York: Vintage Books.

Young Jr., Alford A. 2011. "Comment: Reactions from the Perspective of Culture and Low-Income Fatherhood." *Annals of the American Academy of Political and Social Science* 635 (May): 117–22.

Zimring, Franklin E. 2006. *The Great American Crime Decline.* New York: Oxford University Press.

———. 2012. *The City That Became Safe: New York's Lessons for Urban Crime and Its Control.* New York: Oxford University Press.

Index

community, calls for, 61, 67–68,
186n27; definition of, 9; funding
agencies, accountability to, 61, 70, 71,
81, 85, 114; limits of, 78, 160; police
abuse and violence as underestimated
or ignored by, 68, 186n28; privileging
rights of some community members
over others, 67–68, 70; as pushing
youth out of civic life, 74, 114. *See
also* bureaucratic work ("numbers
game," "paper game"); desistance—
as group process; gang injunctions;
high-surveillance neighborhoods;
surveillance
—SOCIAL ORGANIZATION OF: overview,
27, 70–71, 187n39; activist subgroup,
72–74, 78, 188n44; alienation and
exclusion of desisting men from, 10,
61; as ceding responsibility for
discipline and control to law
enforcement, 9, 27, 60–61, 74, 80,
85–86; credentialed class status as
elevated by, 9, 27, 60; ethnographic
narrative of meeting, 74–80,
188nn46–47; spokesperson
subgroup, 71, 75, 78, 79; street
broker/intermediary subgroup, 72,
75, 78, 187n42, 188n46; turf wars
within, as mimicking and
contributing to street turf wars, xiii–
xiv, 4, 12, 163, 177n4, 179n28. *See
also* alternative justice system
response; credentialed class, Black;
informal/internal caretakers; street
outreach workers
criminal justice system: overview,
27–28; adolescent brain development
as consideration in, 45; crack
epidemic and changes to, 96; 850 as
term for, 138; hearing in,
ethnographic narrative of, 138–40;
popular culture enmeshment with,
193n79; reform of, xii, 112–13,
194n87. *See also* alternative justice
system response; crime-fighting
community; juvenile justice system;
law enforcement

"crystallization of discontent," 46–47.
See also awakening moments
Cullors, Patrisse, 177n1
Cure Violence model, 169–71, 172,
196n10
curfews for youth, 67

delinquency: influences and events
operating in, 33; as normative
adolescent behavior, 33, 165; salience
of, vs. "superpredator" theory, 33
desistance: as alternative to "kill, be
killed, or go to the penitentiary,"
31–32, 44; cognitive shifts, 46;
exemplars for change and "always-
upward trajectory" of, 149–50;
intersectional analysis and, 182n4;
lessons necessary for success in,
29–30, 163–66; reason and purpose
as important for, 4–5, 185n2; as slow,
gradual process, 48, 123, 157–58,
164–65, 183n24; total break from
street ("knifing off"), 26, 182n68,
183n21; turning points, 45–46,
183n21. *See also* alternative justice
system response; awakening
moments; transitional stage ("half-
and-half")
—AS GROUP PROCESS: overview, 32, 55;
alternative justice system response
and awareness of, 164, 170–71, 172–
74; awakening moments and, 55;
convincing others of sincere change
(showing change), 4, 5, 13–14,
57–58, 60, 155, 171; convincing
others of sincere change, and opt-
out process for removal of name
from gang injunction, 146, 147;
definition of, 5, 178n10; faith/church
as relational context, 56–57, 157,
159, 170; fatherhood as relational
context, 55–56, 123; and integrative
redemption, 171–72; and love and
compassion as programmatic, 172–
74, 196n17; and redemptive script,
construction of, 195n10; and
segregated redemption, 196n14;